A WALL OF OUR OWN

OUR OWN

AN AMERICAN HISTORY OF THE BERLIN WALL

Paul M. Farber

The University of North Carolina Press *Chapel Hill*

© 2020 The University of North Carolina Press
All rights reserved
Designed by Rebecca Evans
Set in Arno Pro, Calluna Sans, and Seria Sans
by Tseng Information Systems, Inc.
Manufactured in the United States of America
The University of North Carolina Press has been a member
of the Green Press Initiative since 2003.

Portions of chapter 3 are adapted from Paul M. Farber, "On Exile:
Tajiri's America," in *Shinkichi Tajiri: Universal Paradoxes*, edited by Helen
Westgeest (Leiden, The Netherlands: Leiden University Press, 2015).

Portions of chapter 4 are adapted from Paul M. Farber, "'I Cross Her
Borders at Midnight': Audre Lorde's Berlin Revisions," in *Audre Lorde's
Transnational Legacies*, edited by Stella Bolaki and Sabine Broeck
(Amherst: University of Massachusetts Press, 2015).

Cover photo of an unnamed soldier by Leonard Freed, Berlin, 1961
(Estate of Leonard Freed/Magnum Photos)

Library of Congress Cataloging-in-Publication Data
Names: Farber, Paul M., 1982– author.
Title: A Wall of Our Own : An American History of the Berlin Wall / by Paul M. Farber.
Other titles: Studies in United States culture.
Description: Chapel Hill : The University of North Carolina Press, [2020] | Series:
Studies in United States culture | Includes bibliographical references and index.
Identifiers: LCCN 2019032061 | ISBN 9781469655079 (cloth) |
ISBN 9781469655086 (paperback) | ISBN 9781469655093 (ebook)
Subjects: LCSH: Berlin Wall, Berlin, Germany, 1961–1989 — In popular culture. | Berlin
Wall, Berlin, Germany, 1961–1989, in art. | Berlin Wall, Berlin, Germany, 1961–1989, in
literature. | Politics and culture — United States — History — 20th century. | American
literature — 20th century. | Arts, American — 20th century. | Cold War — Social aspects.
Classification: LCC NX650.B47 F37 2020 | DDC 700.973/0904 — dc23
LC record available at https://lccn.loc.gov/2019032061

FOR RUTH AND BARRY,
the professor and the poet

FOR AARON,
my heart

It can happen that the personal drama of an artist reflects within half a century the crisis of an entire civilization.

—JOHN BERGER

CONTENTS

ACKNOWLEDGMENTS

The journey of this book began in Berlin. There, from my first visit in 2004 to a summer graduate residency in 2008 and nearly annual trips forward, I was drawn in by the city and its residents to explore, reflect, engage, and write. Over time, I found significant material for consideration in archives, museums, galleries, and academic conferences. I was also led to some of my most inspired and grounded thoughts while walking or biking through the city; outside in streets, parks, and waterways; around the footprint of memorials and monuments; and following the path of the former Wall and its myriad unlikely intersections and points of perspectives. Along the way, I encountered stories of American visitors and expatriates and sought out artworks and texts in which they traced their Berlin projects. In turn, I was also led to narratives of German Jewish émigrés, transnational scholars and artists of color, immigrant and refugee communities, queer and feminist collectives, and many others who lived in the city, together, at one point or another. Berlin spoke to me as a space of haunt and of home, of existential angst and profound understanding, as it has for so many others seeking critical distance over the course of multiple generations. I found a city that beckons a sense of balance, even with its hard edges and the heaviest of burdens that dwell in its history and culture.

In and out of Berlin, the work of completing this book has been nourished by a sweeping group of loved ones, thoughtful mentors, and generous interlocutors. The task of sustaining the writing of the book toward completion is the responsibility of the singular author, but the project's ultimate pursuit is one of co-creation. My editor at the University of North Carolina Press, Mark Simpson-Vos, offered his early belief in this project and has followed through with immense support. He challenged and encouraged me to envision, revise, and build toward publication. I am so grateful for his wisdom and care. Thank you also to the entire team at UNC Press, especially Lucas Church, Jessica Newman, and the two anonymous peer reviewers for sharing invaluable insights that served the final revisions and refinements of this book.

I am extremely grateful to my doctoral committee, who guided and encouraged me in my graduate studies at the University of Michigan. I thank Penny Von Eschen, a phenomenal advisor and advocate. Penny's practice of lifelong mentorship, critical engagement, and compassionate care inspire me to be a better writer and teacher. Her multiple close readings of each chapter, our time spent on transatlantic phone calls, and our trips to archives and public sites of memory in Berlin and Los Angeles have all prepared me for a path of scholarship and engagement. Michael Awkward's encouragement from my first days of graduate school enabled me to have courage to go out on a limb with ideas, and his questions continue to prompt some of my most fruitful critical travels. Sara Blair showed me how to construct aspirational bibliographies and animate close readings of texts, images, and archives and invited me into new ways of seeing and sensing. Amy Sara Carroll was a sage teacher and an architect of transformative thoughts who had time and time again renewed my sense of purpose. Martin Klimke was an invaluable interlocutor who actively created pathways for me to follow. Major thanks to others who impacted my experience at Michigan, including faculty and staff members Paul Anderson, Matthew Briones, Matthew Countryman, Angela Dillard, Kevin Gaines, Kristin Hass, June Howard, Elizabeth James, David Halperin, Lawrence La Fountain-Stokes, Marlene Moore, Nadine Naber, Damani Partridge, Chaquita Willis, Magdalena Zaborowska, and many others.

At Michigan, I was quite fortunate to have been a part of a supportive graduate community. I thank the members of my writing group—Matthew Blanton, Tayana Hardin, and Grace Sanders Johnson—for being so visionary, loving, consistent, fierce, and always of superhero caliber. Outside this writing group, I am so grateful for a treasured group of friends made in Ann Arbor, including Annah MacKenzie, Robert LeVertis Bell, Saida Grundy, Jen Guerra, Jina Kim, Katherine Lennard, Afia Ofori-Mensa, Rachel Afi Quinn, Claire Rice, Wendy Sung, Urmila Venkatesh, Kiara Vigil, and Colleen Woods. While in Berlin, I benefited from gracious and wise friends who invited me to navigate the city on their terms, including Bill Van Parys, Oliver "Dr. Pong" Miller, Magnus Rosengarten, and Silke Hackenesch.

My graduate studies at the University of Michigan were generously supported by the Rackham Graduate School, the Department of American Culture, and the Department of Afroamerican and African Studies. This project also greatly benefited from additional fellowship support that allowed me to pursue research sites and sources in Germany. While in Ann Arbor, I was a two-year graduate resident at the U-M Center for World Performance Studies (CWPS), which afforded me the opportunity to take significant early research trips to Berlin. I thank the late Glenda Dickerson for her service to CWPS and Cheryl Israel for opening opportunities for students to travel and research abroad.

I am grateful to the German Historical Institute (GHI) in Washington, D.C., for granting me a doctoral fellowship in the History of African Americans and Germans/Germany in 2010–11. Much of my research and the writing of my opening chapters occurred during this fellowship, which is a credit to the supportive intellectual environment at the GHI. Martin Klimke was my advisor and the steward of this fellowship program and the co-curator of my first exhibition (Leonard Freed's *An American in Deutschland*). I am grateful to my D.C. community of friends and collaborators, including Kate Damon, James Huckenpahler, Nilay Lawson, and Don Russell for their influence on my writing and curatorial work. While in Washington, D.C., I also benefited from collaborations and conversations with colleagues at the D.C. Jewish Community Center, the German Embassy, the Library of Congress, the Provisions Library, and the Smithsonian National Museum of African American History and Culture. Special thanks to Wilfried Eckstein and Sylvia Blume of the Goethe-Institut, who generously commissioned and supported the first iteration of my *Wall in Our Heads: American Artists and the Berlin Wall* exhibition.

After graduate school, my time as a postdoctoral fellow at Haverford College was incredibly productive and meaningful, thanks to a circle of thoughtful colleagues. Thank you Andrew Friedman (a brilliant scholar, generous mentor, and overall mensch), as well as Jim Krippner, Kristin Lindgren, Janice Lion, Lindsay Reckson, Debora Sherman, Gus Stadler, Terry Snyder, Theresa Tensuan, Sharon Ullman, James Weissinger, and many others. Extreme gratitude to students in my "Divided Cities," "Memory, Monuments, and Urban Spaces," "Philadelphia Freedoms," and "Queer Geopolitics" courses, including research assistants Zach Alden, Alliyah Allen, Freda Coren, Sarah Green, Evan Hamilton, Will Herzog, Amanda Robiolio, and Esme Trontz. Matthew Callinan, a dear friend and astute art mind, was a crucial collaborator for the *Wall in Our Heads* exhibition at Haverford's Cantor Fitzgerald Gallery. To my dear colleagues at the University of Pennsylvania and the Monument Lab team, including Laurie Allen, Meghna Chandra, Clare Fisher, Stephanie Garcia, Justin Geller, Kristen Giannantonio, William Hodgson, Matt Neff, Sebastianna Skalisky, Yannick Trapman-O'Brien, and Victoria Karkov, I am extremely fortunate for the work we do together in Philadelphia and beyond. Thank you to Dinah Berland and Gretchen Dykstra for your expert eyes on these pages.

Throughout this process, I have also been greatly uplifted, empowered, and challenged by mentors. Salamishah Tillet is a guiding light and dear soul. Through your indispensable critical work and stellar advice, you offer a profound form of love that inspires me to keep pushing. Thank you for taking me under your wing. Ken Lum is a kindred spirit who opens doors for me and many others. Our shared passion for public art and history has spawned some of my wildest dreams as a curator and organizer. Alan Light is a steadfast and generous interlocutor. He is an encyclopedic source and supremely kind. Howard Winant and Deborah Rogow, you are beyond bighearted and wise. Your long-standing support means so much to me. Michael Eric Dyson and Marcia L. Dyson, thank you for all your wisdom and love and for keeping me on my toes with your kibitzing and critical thought. Others to whom I owe much and express great appreciation include Jeremy Braddock, Anthony De-Curtis, Jonathan Flatley, Anne Gerbner, Jane Golden, Richard Grusin, Hope Harrison, Paul Hendrickson, Marc Lamont Hill, Maria Höhn, Hua Hsu, Michael Kimmelman, Axel Klausmeier, Andy Lamas, André Robert Lee, Heather Love, Carl Nightingale, Imani Perry, James Braxton Peterson, Meg Rabinowitz, Kirk Savage, Jamel Shabazz, Aishah Shahidah Simmons, Elaine Simon, and Nathan Smith. Rest in power, Byron Davis, Oni Faida Lampley, and Eric Schneider.

To complete this project, I visited a constellation of archives, libraries, and galleries. I greatly benefited from individuals at these sites who helpfully and generously guided my research process. This group includes Matthew Murphy and Michael Shulman at Magnum Photos; Bruce Silverstein and his staff at Bruce Silverstein Gallery; staff at the Beinecke Rare Book and Manuscript Library at Yale University; Kathy Alberts at the Kennedys Museum in Berlin; the Hoover Institution at Stanford University; Julie Herrada at the Labadie Collection at the University of Michigan; Joellen ElBashir at the Moorland-Spingarn Research Center at Howard University; Marvin Taylor at the Fales Library and the staff at the Tamiment Library at New York University; the Schomburg Center for Research in Black Culture and Billy Rose Theatre Division at the New York Public Library; Taronda Spencer and Holly Smith at the Spelman College Archives; Lisbet Tellefsen; Getty Research Institute in Los Angeles; Archives of the Freie University in Berlin; the Mauer Documentation Center in Berlin; Elen Woods at the Keith Haring Foundation; Justinan Jampol and the staff at the Wende Museum in Los Angeles; AnnaLee

Pauls at the Rare Books and Special Collections, Firestone Library, Princeton University; and the Columbia University Rare Book & Manuscript Library.

Elements from the research related to *A Wall of Our Own* have been previously published in books on Leonard Freed (*This Is the Day: The March on Washington* [Getty Publications] and a new critical edition of *Made in Germany* [Steidl Verlag]); Shinkichi Tajiri (*Universal Paradoxes* [University of Leiden/University of Chicago Press]); and Audre Lorde (*Audre Lorde's Transnational Legacies* [University of Massachusetts Press]). Thank you to editors, including Greg Brittion, Stella Bolaki, Sabine Broeck, and Helen Westgeest, for including me in these projects. I also thank fellow panelists and audiences at conferences for the American Studies Association; the American Historical Association; the American Literature Association; the College Art Association; the Experience Music Project; the Association for Slavic, East European, and Eurasian Studies; the Northeast Modern Language Association; and the Texas Institute for Literary and Textual Studies for sharing dialogue about early versions of my chapters.

Several standout individuals are worthy of much admiration and greatly inspired the research portions of this project. Brigitte Freed, I am so profoundly grateful for our visits full of shared wisdom and nourishment. Thank you for generously exchanging ideas and teaching me so much about time and motion. Same to Elke Susannah Freed for making me smile and reflect every time I'm in Garrison. Giotta and Ryu Tajiri, I treasure the time we spent in Amsterdam and Baarlo and thank you for your care of your family's collection. Dagmar Schultz, I am touched by your opening of your personal archive, sharing of your stories, and previewing glimpses of your wonderful film, *Audre Lorde: The Berlin Years*, with me before its release. Stew and Heidi Rodewald, thank you for continually exploding my mind with your spectacular gifts of creativity and music that was a soundtrack to my research.

I extend my deepest gratitude to friends who have shown me the most wonderful forms of love and belief in my life's work. Much appreciation to my dear friend Anna Morin, the first person to encourage me to write a book and believe I could actually do that. Thank you to many great friends, including Anna Aagenes, Titilola Bakare, Ryan Barrett, Ellery Biddle, Josh Buono, Gillian Cassell-Stiga, Erica Chapman, Liz Chernett, Anne Cooper, Elizabeth Cooper, Natalie Fabe Ubias, Jessica Garz, Cassidy Hartmann, Zack Hill, Claire Laver, Matt Leiker, Elizabeth Spector Louden, Beth Millstein, Stephan Nicoleau, Dan Rainer, Sara Schwartz, Tiffany Tavarez, Carmen Winant, Zach Zinn, and many others for sharing this journey with me and continually raising me up.

Much appreciation to my dear extended family—including the Brodys, Gilmores, Libous, Shanks, and Rosenbaums. I treasure all of you, and your support means so much to me. I am privileged to have more family in Melanie and Victor Skypski and their amazing kids and grandkids. To my late grandmother Claire Farber, cousin Joel Rosenbaum, and aunt Libby Rosenbaum, each of whom passed away during the writing of this book, I hope I honor your legacy with work inspired by your memory.

Finally, I am so grateful for my brother Ivan Farber and his wife, Wendy Farber, who so generously share their kind spirit and joyful outlook with me and inspire me to be a better person. To their son, my nephew Sam Farber, you are a special thinker with super smarts and a giant heart. I hope all of your dreams come true. To my parents, Ruth and Barry Farber, you are sublime and the greatest people I know. Thank you for my education, on all levels, and for being so kind and true. And to Aaron, my husband (and our dog Ziggy), you inspire me every day. You make me so happy, grateful, and full. This is for you.

A WALL OF OUR OWN

INTRODUCTION | ROADMAP
American Berliners

On June 26, 1963, President John F. Kennedy proclaimed, "Ich Bin ein Berliner," from the steps of West Berlin's City Hall. A year before, his brother Attorney General Robert F. Kennedy had offered a different sort of declaration in West Berlin. On February 22, 1962, Robert F. Kennedy arrived on an official state visit. He traveled through the city in an open motorcade, with over 100,000 West Berliners greeting him in the streets and later joining him for a speech outside on the plaza at City Hall in Schöneberg. On this trip, as he wove through the city's western side, his itinerary called for stops at observation decks and border areas to assess East Berlin by looking at and over a six-month-old wall separating the two halves of a divided city. The attorney general's visit occurred months after socialist East Germany began enclosing the allied sectors of West Berlin with an increasingly militarized barrier that reestablished the city as a front line of the Cold War. The border system, which soon became known as the Berlin Wall, emerged as a sprawling, interconnected structure merging physical division with symbolic control, marking the larger division of two geopolitical superpowers.[1]

At the end of the daylong visit, Attorney General Kennedy addressed another crowd, this time at the Free University, an institution founded after World War II, in 1948, with American support. He delivered his remarks on the stage of a packed auditorium, standing behind a podium carrying the logo of the U.S. Department of Justice. Kennedy was on a mission to affirm the administration's promise that the United States would protect and, if necessary, fight for "the full freedom of the inhabitants of West Berlin," adding, "and we have not forgotten the men and women of East Berlin and East Germany." He continued, "Berlin will not merely exist. It will grow and prosper. We stand behind all these positions with the full strength of American power," conjuring an undivided city. Throughout his speech, Robert Kennedy outlined his vision for how Berlin, both East and West, configured into an aspirational landscape of American democracy. He joined his vision for freedom in Cold War Berlin with similar goals for the domestic home front of the United States, presented together in a shared "New Frontier" of progress.[2]

Robert Kennedy also shared his observations of the Wall as a site and a symbol of repression. "This surely is the meaning of the Berlin Wall," he proclaimed, "that ugly mass of concrete brick and barbed wire which lies across the heart of your city, like a medieval instrument of torture." He added, "They wall their people in. We set our people free." Toward the close of his speech, Kennedy shared a moment of reflexivity, identifying with the Berlin Wall by recognizing his own nation's racial divides and legacies of repression: "For a hundred years, despite our protestations of equality, we had, as you know, a wall of our own — a wall of segregation erected against Negroes. That wall is coming down."[3]

In his remarks, Robert Kennedy located Cold War Berlin as both an outpost and extension of the divided landscapes of American culture. He acknowledged the Berlin Wall in reference to hostile and entrenched racial divides within the United States, a form of division that both preceded and remained upheld by his own administration. He relayed the shared characteristics of division; by placing the wall of segregation both in the past ("we *had*") and the present ("That wall *is* coming down"), he demonstrated the uneven lag of social change. His speech at the Free University stands out not only for the delivery of "Cold Warrior" rhetoric in a divided Berlin, but also for his confirmation of the contradictions of Cold War culture and the limits of U.S. freedom principles set against the backdrop of the Berlin Wall. In this speech, Kennedy drew on the interplay between physical and social lines of division, and the past and the present. He laid bare the fact that his nation was fighting for global freedom abroad while practicing an incomplete form of democracy at home.[4]

Despite the *New York Times* quoting "a wall of our own" in its coverage of Robert Kennedy's trip, his phrase lacked both the immediate resonance and monumental afterlife of his brother's later "Ich Bin ein Berliner," which dramatically asserted the president's symbolic citizenship of the divided German city.[5] In the early years of the Berlin Wall, both Kennedys asserted their direct identifications with the people of divided Berlin, simultaneous to the civil rights movement and domestic questions of racial equity, access, and citizenship. Democracy promoted abroad, in the shadow of the Wall, ran counter to the embedded practices of discrimination inscribed into U.S. institutions and social structures. The walls of American racial repression, intricate and elusive by design, built over centuries, maintained through quotidian actions, and upheld through his own administration's policies, as Robert Kennedy suggested, shared an uncanny quality with the Berlin Wall's concrete and barbed-wire Cold War border zones. Kennedy, in a passing revelation, demonstrated how imagined forms of citizenship and the injustices of racial segregation functioned as twin by-products of U.S. policy and history. The lack of attention paid to Robert Kennedy's acknowledgment of U.S.-built-and-maintained segregation in relation to the Berlin Wall highlights a political habit of downplaying racial and ethnic division, partition, and separation as fundamental practices of white-dominated American freedom.

A call to identify "our" own walls alongside Berlin's was not an isolated gesture by Kennedy of American connection with the German divided city. Berlin, on both sides of the nascent wall, was a site of pilgrimage to approach or meet the "entanglements and shared destinies" of American and German culture, as Maria Höhn and Martin Klimke suggest, after World War II and throughout the Cold War, especially through frameworks of race as well as gender, sexuality, class, nationality, and other modes of intersectional identity and belonging.[6] In this book, I extend that line of inquiry to argue that division was a central paradigm and paradox of the American Cold War democratic project, linking the geographies of home and abroad by way of the Berlin Wall. The stories of American travelers to Berlin, encountering the Wall and sprawling conditions of division, provoked an awakening and reckoning with structures of physical and social partition back home.

Robert Kennedy may have been one of the first politicians to step into a newly walled Berlin and refer to America's own global footprint and internal divides, especially around racial injustice. But his candid statement can be read as part of a much larger cultural dialogue that had quickly started to unfold in August 1961, within days of the first physical barricades bisecting the city. Almost immediately, American artists, writers, and activists, including those who sought the city as a place of engagement, began drawing attention to linkages between the Berlin Wall and barriers in U.S. democracy. Those barriers included racial segregation and later engaged the expansion of U.S. prison culture, the legacies of Japanese internment, and barriers reinforced through Cold War proxy battles. The cultural figures who were compelled or summoned to Cold War Berlin made observations in and around the American sector of West Berlin and in cultural and political venues in East Berlin. They more broadly reflected on transnational American presence and power while seeking to learn from East and West Germans in adaptive and unforeseen ways. Kennedy joined them, briefly and unwittingly, by referring to the

Wall as a point of reflection for domestic divisions. His utterance of "a wall of our own" is a forgotten rhetorical landmark on a larger geopolitical map of the United States.

Among these early observers who recognized the intersection of multiple dividing lines by the Berlin Wall was Jewish and white American photojournalist Leonard Freed, who attempted to make sense of the Wall while capturing overlapping points of German history in late August 1961, days after the city was divided. Freed was first drawn to Berlin by his own Jewish heritage, as he documented the return of Jewish communities and public memory in post-Holocaust Germany. However, his chance encounter with an unnamed African American soldier guarding the newly erected Berlin Wall inspired another ambitious project: mapping lines and lineages of racial segregation back home.

As Freed would observe across multiple trips to Cold War Berlin, the Wall was never a solitary structure that cut through the built environment with a simple line. Instead, the border included a patchwork of widespread fortifications consisting of alarmed fencing, hinterland walls, guard dogs, searchlights, watchtowers, countersurveillance, and a no-man's-land at the point of no return, known as the "death strip." Freed accounted for the Wall's transnational character and charge, informed not simply by its formidable physical imprint, but also by the social implications of convergence in a city that hosted two newly separated nations of Germans, Western allied military forces, Eastern bloc authorities, and the city's wave of other Cold War Berliners from Turkey, Vietnam, Cuba, and additional sites of connected conflict. In other words, the Wall's force reached well beyond the immediate scope of the border itself. Freed, too, witnessed antiblack segregation in the United States operating in analogous terms. When in the United States, as a traveling white photographer, he sought scenes of racial injustice and meaning-making. Freed viewed divided Berlin and the United States as focal points for his companion photobooks *Black in White America* (1967/68) and *Made in Germany* (1970), each of which critically reflects on German division as well as America's role as the self-appointed guarantor of global democracy during the years following World War II and the civil rights movement. Freed's work in each respective country's border zones produced images of mutual recognition.

Later other artists, writers, and activists similarly routed their own travels and cultural productions through the geopolitical crossroads of divided Berlin, pivoting their work between the United States and the two Germanys. In 1966 African American activist Angela Davis crossed the boundary of the

Wall into East Berlin as a philosophy graduate student in West Germany on a trip with classmates. She opted to spend most of her time in East Berlin, to see family friends and experience the socialist workers' holiday May Day. The Wall was a well-established and embedded structure at that time. Davis later channeled her experiences on both sides of the border toward becoming a leading voice contesting the walls of the U.S. prison system. Her own best-selling 1974 autobiography features scenes that take place on both sides of Germany's divide, for her purpose of critically engaging Western practices of repression and state violence while downplaying and reinterpreting the stereotypical cultural intrigue of crossing through the Wall.

During the late 1960s through the mid-1980s, Japanese American sculptor Shinkichi Tajiri taught as an expatriate college art professor in West Berlin and extensively documented the Wall during its process of systematic structural revamping and aesthetic makeover. As Tajiri stalked the edges of the American sector and allied sectors of walled-in West Berlin, his resulting photographic survey brought him closer to his family's history of internment during World War II and his experience as a U.S. Army veteran confronting anti-Japanese racial hostilities. His extended project, *The Wall Die Mauer Le Mur* (1971), was made to represent the Wall as an architectural symbol of a divided world and the partitions suggestive of the history of the United States.

In 1984, poet Audre Lorde came to West Berlin with questions about U.S. geopolitics in an era of reaccelerated Cold War tensions and antagonisms as well as growing frustration with U.S. military incursions abroad and social divides at home. Lorde, who identified as a "black lesbian feminist warrior poet," among other intersectional distinctions, established divided Berlin as a place of habitual return, as she began building on previously uncharted diasporic solidarities and creating enduring forms of poetry and prose that transcended borders between women writers, especially those engaged with the emerging Afro-German movement. Her book *Our Dead Behind Us* (1986), as well as a series of published and unpublished poetic fragments, journal entries, and prose essays, marked her first of multiple attempts to render the divided city as a space of critical connection, ripe for intervention.

Such individuals were not content to merely apprehend the spectacle of the Wall itself and leave; rather, they habitually revisited the relationships upholding American Cold War politics and ruminated on this line of division, over many years and multiple visits to divided Berlin. The Wall was not the sole structure on their minds in divided Berlin. They envisioned other walls of division that shadowed the practices and symbols of American freedom. Divided Berlin offered the feelings of home and haunting, a dialectic that sparked profound modes of expression and connection, as well as tensions and challenges. In each case, these figures and many others produced books and other artworks and critical discourse directed at American political divides and found ways to represent and weave in their experiences of Cold War Berlin. Thus, such treks to the Berlin Wall offered visitors a parallel site, a complex architectural doppelgänger, to weigh instances and legacies of U.S.-sponsored segregation and marginalization.

This book, *A Wall of Our Own*, traces the Berlin Wall as a site of pilgrimage for critical American cultural producers — artists, writers, and activists — who confronted the contradictions of U.S. Cold War policy and practice while in Berlin. By the Wall, these creative individuals and activists weighed the possibilities and limits of American democracy. They were sparked by their first encounters with the Wall, incorporated their reflections in books and artworks directed toward the geopolitics of division in the United States, and continued to consider divided Germany as a site of intersection of aesthetics and activism over the respective courses of their careers. Alongside historical relationships forged through military and political interactions, the American artists and writers who visited Berlin also treated the city as a place of critical and creative passage. These individuals embodied, challenged, and transformed a broader postwar occupation and cultural preoccupation with the Berlin Wall and its relationship to ingrained and emergent practices of division in the United States.

While an array of Americans sought postwar Paris for their own self-imposed exile in Europe or mined the contradictions of domestic culture traveling the interstate highway system on the American open road, this book reveals that the divided city of Berlin was another option for Americans seeking a critical distance. To identify or be adopted as an "American Berliner" was to conjure the symbolic links between American and German division, in a way, akin to President Kennedy's assertion of symbolic Berlin citizenship, but inclusive of his brother's acknowledgment of the walls of segregation while in the city. The American Berliners at the center of this book are culture producers whose shared focus on divided Berlin informed their sustained, critical engagement with American and German historical ideas, places, problems, and modes of power and belonging. Along with other cities occupied by the Cold War cultural imagination and American military forces alike, Berlin brought into sharp relief the crises of democracy in the United States and beyond. The cohort of critically engaged artists, writers, and activists at the center of this book experienced divided Berlin and approached their time in the city to also better understand the contours and dividing lines of American culture. They were drawn to make sense of Berlin's traumatized past, its militarized present, and its experiments in rebuilding democracy after the chaos of fascism and war.

As self-appointed agents to explore the dynamics of cultural division, American Berliners were prompted or fueled by their experiences by the Wall to produce enduring artworks, publications, and projects about division in American culture through their participation in and perpetuation of what I suggest as Berlin's "circuits of alternative cultural diplomacies." They, too, considered the "walls of their own," to repurpose and reprioritize thinking on division in context with the Berlin Wall. They helped complicate Berlin's place in the cultural imaginary of the United States, and vice versa, in nuanced and meaningful ways. Together, these artists, writers, and activists, and the many others who similarly dwell within this larger history, exemplify a tradition of engaged American travel and critical thinking within footsteps of the Berlin Wall, in a city epitomized by its cycles of freedom and repression. They took no solace in the Wall's existence and the militarized reality that surrounded it. They did, however, approach the Wall physically and conceptually to transform the division as a means to hasten its dismantling and to draw scrutiny to other social and physical barriers in the United States and beyond.

By tracing the movements of these particular figures in and out of divided Berlin here, I seek a history of the Berlin Wall that encompasses a reckoning with U.S. power and presence in this divided city. I refer to "circuits of alternative cultural diplomacy" as an interconnected system of overlapping networks and practices of American culture in divided Berlin, which prompted ongoing visits from hundreds of artists, writers, thinkers, and activists and initiated a shadow roadmap full of detours and improvisations. Such circuits included mechanisms for state-sponsored activities and outcomes, as well as the rise of countercultural communities and expressive spaces beyond governmental oversight. In each case the subjects of this book navigated the spaces between two German diplomacies and critically negotiated their relationships to U.S. power by exploring geopolitical territory with a variety of creative tools. Some of these cultural circuits incorporated sites underwritten by U.S. diplomatic imperatives and sanctioned cultural visitors: the U.S.-backed Free University in West Berlin; state-sponsored programs of cultural exchange, including the German Academic Exchange Service (DAAD) and the Goethe Institute; and notable affiliated cultural venues, such as the Amerika Haus and Congress Hall.

In addition, this framework incorporates practices by those who deliberately worked on the margins of U.S. institutional support: Americans in

Berlin who went to observe the close-up effects and social repercussions of ongoing military operations, those who built relationships of solidarity with radical communities and antiwar activists, and those who took part in cultural rites on the "other side of the Wall" as special invited guests of East Germany. This incorporative cultural framework is seldom used to group historical itineraries of visiting Americans to one or both sides of Berlin, enabling those who followed, strayed, detoured, or deliberately defied U.S. state-sponsored diplomatic projects to be considered together. The protagonists of this book not only circulated through such networks but also authored broader possibilities for engagement within the divided city and U.S. culture, thus shaping alternative diplomacies more broadly for West and East Berliners, as well as for Americans across multiple global sites. In this sense I also draw out the connections between prolonged military occupation and cultural preoccupations to examine legacies of militarized American influence in divided Berlin. This militarization complicates the long-standing U.S. cultural investment in and identification with the city, which continues to this day.

A Wall of Our Own considers works by the cohort of Freed, Davis, Tajiri, and Lorde to build an intergenerational and intersectional counternarrative of Cold War history. These figures are not merely outliers but also represent a collective struggle to explore the possibilities and limits of U.S. democracy, especially from the viewpoints of individuals marginalized by race, ethnicity, gender, sexuality, class, and nationality. The result is a Berlin-fueled cultural imaginary of both freedom and repression. Freed, Davis, Tajiri, Lorde, and others within this tradition did not coordinate their travels and cultural output among one another, but they did move through the divided city with an inadvertent yet collective choreography: each individual would visit a divided Berlin and encounter the Wall or other facets of a divided Germany, create a piece or an entire body of work there, and set that work in the city or elsewhere. The protagonists of this study are standard-bearers of a larger American cultural ritual of locating one's critical reflection in Berlin. In so doing, these figures captured and explored their experiences within productions that intentionally confronted the contradictions of Cold War American culture.

This book moves in and out of divided Berlin along with these cultural actors to make sense of their complex relationships to and renderings of the Wall, the strategies and tactics they used in regard to approaching the border system, and the critical paths of inquiry they followed after encountering it. For example, a brief mention by Davis in her autobiography of her memory crossing the inner border of Berlin as a graduate student leads to a longer, in-depth critical exploration of the U.S. prison system. Lorde worked sites and symbols of Berlin's historical divides into her poetry collections about transnational identity. These examples conjure Edward Said's notion of "traveling theory," a mapping of "the movement of ideas and theories from one place to another [as] both a fact of life and a usefully enabling condition of intellectual activity," involving "processes of representation and institutionalization different for those at the point of origin."[7] In other words, ideas not only transcend national borders and boundaries; they reconstitute a stable sense of place and identity through geopolitical movement.

Together, the protagonists of this book model the sort of critical footwork necessary to interrogate the entangled symbolic and physical life of barriers that continue to haunt the American experience. They draw close to repressive borders as a means to undermine them, compare them across cultures, observe their porous nature, and unpack the ways people seek to coexist despite their imposed separation. When we read the combined histories of such individuals within and outside the immediate contested zones of divided Berlin, their accounts elucidate features of the enduring military presence and diplomatic strategies of American power in this frontline city while also tracing the impact of such creative nonstate actors on the political knowledge of the Cold War period elsewhere. Through a litany of parallel Berlin-focused texts, works of art, and political acts, their works highlight practices and sites of division back home, set against a larger backdrop of postwar recovery and remediation in the German capital. While this book focuses on American narratives, it also channels and reflects on a large body of literature, social programs, monuments and memorials, and other platforms that reckon with the legacies of division and reunification in German culture. It is also an attempt to build on the scholarship of transnational scholars who have explored how U.S. power impacted, intertwined, and/or intentionally interfered with civic practices on both sides of divided Berlin.[8] By taking these scholarly texts together, animating them with archival materials and interviews with collaborators, and exploring related sites of memory in Berlin as well as in the United States, this book proposes to channel what Svetlana Boym deems "a dual archeology of memory and place." My goal is to elucidate the city through artworks and publications that resonate with one another yet have never before been examined collectively in depth with an exploration of the city's cultural memory as viewed from its own layered terrain.[9]

The journeys of this book's American Berliners can also be understood against a deeper historical context of American engagement with Germany after World War II, and eventually engagement directly with the Wall. Since 1945, in the wake of the allied defeat of Nazi Germany, the United States confirmed the fundamental importance of its relationship with post–World War II Germany. Following the halt of Hitler's imperial and genocidal conquests, Germany, along with its capital, Berlin, was divided into four zones of allied influence — governed by the United States, France, Great Britain, and the Soviet Union (USSR), respectively — designed to both punish the country and guard its peaceful reconstruction. As tensions increased between the Western NATO allies and the Warsaw Pact countries of the Eastern bloc nations, with the United States and the USSR as its central players, the Western powers consolidated their occupied sectors as the western Federal Republic of Germany, while the Russians shaped the eastern German Democratic Republic (GDR) within the Soviet bloc. The country split into two hostile, internecine, neighboring nations. The division of the formerly unified city of Berlin, geographically situated 110 miles from the West German border and otherwise surrounded by East Germany, rendered West Berlin an island and outpost of the West. The terms of American occupation and involvement with West Germany's governance and East Germany's status as an adversarial state demanded a complicated understanding of America's geopolitical stance during this period. From the Berlin airlift of 1948–49, when the U.S. Air Force and allies delivered rations and supplies to West Berlin for a year in response to a Soviet blockade of all ground routes to the city, to the Berlin Crisis of 1958–61, when tempers flared between the superpowers around control and access to the city, American politicians and citizens demonstrated a deep investment in the ongoing fate of Berlin. As Andreas Daum notes, a month before the Berlin border was closed, 85 percent of U.S. citizens wanted troops to stay in West Berlin; a month after the border wall materialized, 70 percent would have supported going to war to secure access to the city.[10]

Both sides of Cold War Berlin were pivotal venues for assessing the U.S. attempt to claim status as guarantor of global democracy and freedom against the Soviet Union. Daum suggests that the shift from the popular notion of "Hitler's Berlin" to "America's Berlin" — the "political and symbolic place" both in and out of the United States "that incorporated Berlin into the history of the United States and linked the often dramatic events in the German capital . . . to America's own cultural memory" — occurred in the years after 1961, as the divided city was experiencing both a remilitarization and cultural reinvention.[11] The Berlin Wall's presence marked no simple way to affirm or disprove this transition to "America's Berlin." Instead the many cultural expressions representing the Wall's construction and maintenance demonstrated the flurry of ideological, historical, and transnational perspectives evident in this complex and evolving blockade. The Berlin Wall signified both a fortified border and a geopolitical crossroad, a space where the past protruded into the present and brought to light the mechanics of geopolitical division.

From its beginning, the physical presence of the Berlin Wall amplified its symbolic power. Frederick Taylor and Brian Ladd, among others, powerfully remind us that the name "Berlin Wall" never referred to a single wall but, rather, to a broader system of border fortifications limiting access to the formerly free city of Berlin that was later heavily policed and regulated. The Wall always operated on both physical and symbolic terms and, as Ladd notes, "came to signify all the consequences of the division of Berlin and all of Europe."[12] The structure was a tangible barrier in a conflict of Cold War ideologies in a city that evoked deep American identifications and attachments.

Cold War Berlin was a major focal point of political confrontation, military occupation, and cultural connection. The American public's fascination with the city's walled border was connected to Berlin's defense and to the spectacle of the Berlin Wall. The United States did not build the Wall. But the construction of a fortified border in divided Berlin by East Germany not only bisected the city but also ran within footsteps of its occupied American sector and (symbolically, if not politically) U.S. soil. The expansion of popular American media and consumer spheres of the 1960s coincided with the dramatic images and footage of Berlin's emergent wall, including the option to view the border crisis on network television, as well as on other cultural platforms, including film, popular music, print media, and art venues. This was the case in August 1961, when NBC's *Jack Paar Show* filmed an on-site episode at the Wall days after its initial construction, prompting Senate Democratic majority leader Mike Mansfield to share his view on the floor of Congress: "One would hope that the Berlin Wall, where so much is at stake for this Nation, does not now become the new Mecca for the jaded of the entertainment world."[13] His discouragement was not enough, however, to deter such critical energies and breakdowns of official order at the border. For example, as Penny Von Eschen details, when Louis "Satchmo" Armstrong played a 1965 concert in East Berlin's Friedrichstadt Plaza, he managed to cross the border to West Berlin at Checkpoint Charlie without proper credentials, after East German and American border guards alike recognized and embraced him as "Ambassador Satch" on both sides of the wall.[14]

Not only did Berlin serve as a Cold War hot spot, but perspectives at or on the border related to the recent traumas of German history and lived on the layered cultural landscapes of the divided city. As a central site of Jewish trauma, the city, as a whole, emerged as a potential space for collective remembrance following the Holocaust. The center of a decimated Jewish Berlin, however, was located in the East. The division of Germany and its respective ruling powers thus informed processes of national reparation and memorialization that fit with their own ideological imperatives. For American Cold Warriors and their allies, the western side of the city embodied the transformations necessary to move the nation from fascism to democracy. Further, echoing the popular U.S. claim that equated Soviet totalitarianism with Nazi fascism, the Wall was both characteristic of Soviet desperation and reminiscent of Nazi-era repression.

The GDR, the border's eastern architects, however, neither saw nor spoke of the Berlin Wall in everyday parlance but instead referred to it only in official nomenclature as "an antifascist protective rampart." The Wall was kept purposefully out of proximate sight and reach, with grave consequences for encroachment.[15] The GDR's nefariously expansive regimes of "border control" not only kept its citizens from fleeing in droves, as they had failed to do through the period of nonenforced division of the city, but intended to ostensibly shield those kept there from a Western value system of "supercapitalism" and profit-driven economics that the GDR viewed as responsible for the rise of Nazism in the first place. By the 1970s, as the two Germanys settled into stabilized diplomatic relations, the border area remained volatile. In the fall of 1989, when a sweeping, peaceful revolution emerged led by German peace activists responding to loosening Soviet reforms across the Eastern bloc, they sang the borrowed African American civil rights hymn "We Shall Overcome" to call for dramatic political change but not necessarily the full dismantling of either the state or the Berlin Wall.[16] Such a cultural reverberation serves as a reminder that the simmering conflict at the Berlin Wall throughout its entire existence was tied to competing claims about the previous Nazi era of German history, as well as America's role as a catalyst and foil of freedom in Cold War Berlin.

The story of America's relationship and identification with the Berlin Wall has previously been told through decades of public history, popular culture, and political discourse celebrating the so-called fall of the Wall. A large and still-growing body of historical literature and cultural works references the Berlin Wall in an attempt to make sense of America's role in the Cold War, from its early years through its demise to its afterlife today.

Such narratives of the Berlin Wall within sites of public interpretation and expression often work through the landmarks of presidential visits and military operations, treating cultural expressions as necessary only for background soundtracks and illustrations or as endearing oddities to animate a teleological story from rise to fall. President Kennedy's refrains of symbolic citizenship in 1963 ("Ich Bin ein Berliner" and "Let them come to Berlin") and President Reagan's bold plea in 1987 ("Mr. Gorbachev, tear down this wall") reverberate as dramatic moments of American rhetoric at two opposing ends of this timeline, without much attention to what narratives they obscure and in what ways they are extensively mythologized, parodied, critiqued, and remixed. In other words, they obscure how the lessons from the dismantled Berlin Wall inform and haunt American public discourse on our own walls.

The American fascination with the Wall did not fade after the initial shock of construction in 1961 or during the decades of simmering coexistence or with the dismantling of the Wall in 1989. In fact, over time, the Berlin Wall has become even more embedded within the landscape and discourses of U.S. geopolitics. Hundreds of cultural references express intrigue in Berlin's divided status. Rarer are works that consider the way the story of the Wall has been incorporated into our U.S. national narrative and for what purposes. For example, a broken piece of the former Berlin Wall from the collection of the Smithsonian Institution in Washington, D.C., was included in *The Smithsonian's History of America in 101 Objects* with an annotation qualifying it only by its existence as a fragment ("This one has special meaning precisely because it is broken!"), rather than as an outlier in this quintessential collection of "Americana."[17] Much of our public history related to the Berlin Wall often recounts America's relationship to the Wall in similar fashion, across dozens of prominent sites, supplemented by fields of documentary film and television, museum and library exhibitions, commercials and advertisements, online wikis and memes, and other references to the Wall across cultural formats, often portraying the Wall as a self-apparent symbol of progress without room for critical analysis of its inclusion, let alone comparing our own border controls and networks of divided power.

In addition, video montages and interpretations of historical time lines — especially those used in television commercials for Pepsi and Johnnie Walker, among others; aired during key sporting events, such as the Super Bowl or the World Cup; or placed in museums such as the Smithsonian Institution in Washington, D.C., or the Constitution Center in Philadelphia—often include footage of the Berlin Wall's dismantling to illustrate one sequence in a flow of events that embody a milestone or endpoint to celebrate the progress of U.S. "history." In such productions, the taking down of the Wall slips into the narrative alongside critical markers in American history. Such representations seem to be stuck in a feedback loop that favors the experience of elation rather than historical reflection, a fantasy of freedom that smooths out complication. As Joshua Clover notes, "It is impossible to ignore the extent to which the Berlin Wall's deconstruction, as captured in photos, broadcasts, videos, news reports, and the rest, provides a concrete image of unification as an achieved condition, of the overcoming of contradiction and discontinuity."[18] In mainstream venues, the Berlin Wall slips in and out of perception and in and out of an Americanized, imagined geography.

Beyond the hundreds of references to the Wall in popular and political culture while it was standing, again, one can look to the dozens of pieces of the former Wall that have been placed in dozens of monumental contexts and public spaces across the United States since reunification as proof of this long-standing incorporation. Such remnants—whether they are installed in the galleries of the Smithsonian Institution in Washington, D.C.; along Wilshire Boulevard in Los Angeles; across numerous presidential libraries and college campuses; on a public plaza adjacent to Ground Zero in lower Manhattan; or at the National Underground Railroad Freedom Center along the Ohio River, which once represented the demarcation line between free and enslaving states—speak to America's deep bonds with Berlin. In some instances, the Wall fragments celebrate state-sponsored diplomatic relationships between the United States and reunified Germany; in others, they are self-evident "pieces of history" to reflect narratives of U.S. power and progress; and finally, in rarer cases, their placement refers to the layers and legacies of domestic division as inscribed into our public spaces during this same period.[19] To gain a fuller understanding of the American history of the Wall, one must explore and read across the scores of cultural identifications the Wall's interconnected narratives of liberty and restraint. Such an exploration places cultural production in relation to politics not as an oddity or an afterthought but instead as forms of expressive diplomacy, resistance, and contestation of state narratives. Taking this approach permits a deeper consideration of the complexity of U.S. geopolitics and the imposed limits of freedom. Our walls—past and present, as well as under construction and in contention—directly challenge the notion of a historically indivisible nation.

Americans' ongoing attachment to the story of the Berlin Wall as a site of triumph connected to American democracy, or as a litmus test for how divisive our internal and external borders can be, is fueled by more than a generation of creative agents who reflected on the Wall and other dividing lines as persistent structures in the American culture.

This book attempts to move beyond the tendency of American–Berlin Wall discourse that relies on strict binaries to understand the divided city: *here* and *there*, *East* and *West*, *capitalist* and *socialist*, *truth* and *propaganda*, *us* and *them*, and the simplistic formulation of a *good* and a *bad* side, without room for nuance and complexity, let alone tracing connections to our own domestic crises of division in democracy.

Between 1961 and 1989, American cultural figures drawn to Berlin demonstrated an enhanced clarity about American culture by turning to face this ideological border forged in concrete. Since 1989, with the dismantled Wall in ruins, they continued this focus within a city characterized by its visible scars, redemptive aims, and networks of American affiliation. These artists and writers navigated the intricate and ever-shifting border system between East and West Berlin, which offered interactions with a range of individuals and groups that included American GIs, East German border guards, state officials and grassroots activists (from both sides), dissident artists and writers, and fellow Americans in exile. As they explored the divided city, they encountered a new generation of memorials and monuments that made competing claims about the true trajectory of free and totalitarian regimes.

The products of their artistic labor eventually manifested in an impressive range of published works of cultural regard and political weight that have come to occupy central features, texts, and tenets of art making and activism. This book hones in on a particular cohort of artists and writers who comprise archetypal, critical American Berliners who seek knowledge in relationship to broader questions of their own transnational identities and relationship to freedom. After a first visit to Berlin, these artists, writers, and activists generally returned to divided Germany many times, as a matter of ritual, while the Wall was still up and—without foreseeable anticipation of such a moment— after its dismantling. Their travels often shaped career-long projects and significant modes of inquiry in Germany that probed profound questions about American identity, belonging, and democracy. The Berlin Wall served as a point of entry to access the liminal spaces and fault lines of each nation and thereby to theorize about matters of identity. These American Berliners saw their own country with greater depth after visiting Berlin, worked through their own aesthetic and intellectual issues in the city, and modeled engaged forms of cultural diplomacy. The American Berliners at the center of this book—Leonard Freed, Angela Davis, Shinkichi Tajiri, and Audre Lorde—present a complex rendering of divided Berlin from the periods they spent in the city during the Cold War, their itineraries after visiting Berlin, and their return journeys after the Wall was dismantled. This book treats their stories as a means of approaching divided Berlin as a site to explore intersectional identities, to survey U.S. power through cultural tools, and to summon strategies for coexistence, including those birthed along the fault lines of the city. Their travels and critical thinking correspond to those of others who fit into this larger shared history of encounter in Berlin, including Louis Armstrong, Paul Beatty, Jonathan Borofsky, David Bowie, Christo and Jeanne-Claude, Frank Hallam Day, Jeffrey Eugenides, Allen Frame, Jonathan Franzen, Nan Goldin, John Gossage, Andrew Sean Greer, Langston Hughes, Keith Haring, Oliver Harrington, Michael Jackson, Allan Kaprow, Martin Luther King Jr., Gordon Matta Clark, Joyce Carol Oates, John Cameron Mitchell, Darryl Pinckney, Adrian Piper, Iggy Pop, Paul Robeson, Stew, Stephanie Syjuco, Bill Van Parys, Lawrence Weiner, Billy Wilder, and countless other traveling practitioners.[20] Such individuals produced works that treated the Berlin Wall as a site of gravity as well as a place to pivot, channeling their experiences near the Wall into narratives that jointly troubled Cold War politics at home and abroad. Similarly, as Claudia Mesch notes of West and East German artists during the Cold War, American cultural producers channeled aesthetic questions and practices through "international cultural exchange and the flow of culture across the [inner-German] border."[21] Further, these Americans also fundamentally grappled with social justice and creative expression, and they expanded understanding of social and political issues ranging from racial segregation and mass incarceration to U.S. militarism, immigration, gender and sexual discrimination, urban theory and social order, and historical consciousness, among other matters while in Berlin.

Artists, writers, historians, and scholars linked to Berlin have simultaneously wrestled with the complex histories of the city and Germany as a whole, especially the history and memory of fascism as it pertains to U.S. culture. In addition to exploring the Wall, they have pursued projects in Berlin that led them to engage with post-Holocaust Jewish trauma, the German student movement and other radical political collectivities, Afro-German identity, global sites of apartheid, and, eventually, German reunification in the face of a new-world, post-Soviet, order. They have also written, documented, and produced, in the creative tradition of American self-styled exile narratives, the experience of a type of curious stranger who inhabits the German

American boundaries of Berlin. Gloria Anzaldúa's notion of "borderlands" is instructive here in making sense of this Cold War site within which U.S. zones of geopolitical affiliation and contact, shadowed by legacies of violence and furthered with moments of newfound solidarity, "[merge] to form a third country—a border culture."[22] U.S. dissidents, expatriates, and critical voices are drawn to contested border spaces to view the far-reaching implications of physical and social divides. Berlin's layered history has thus created a context for reflection that has functioned as a precarious and productive cultural and intellectual meeting place.

Cultural exchanges among American artists, writers, and activists who traveled to Berlin during the years of the Wall's existence yielded a wide variety of artworks, performances, texts, and new perspectives on social justice and solidarity. Collectively, the experiences of these American Berliners and their pantheon of cultural works highlight a broader cultural trope of incorporating the Wall into homegrown narratives of American freedom and repression. Across historical eras, artists and writers have continued to pursue a version of exile or exploration in Berlin as a matter of productivity and refuge. As Stuart Braun has argued, "Berlin is Berlin because of its strangers, its wanderers, its many displaced people who have come to build a kind of safe haven."[23]

As noted, the city functions as both home and haunt for many, but for Americans, the resonances abound due to Cold War governance and culture: one still encounters a city with buildings, institutions, and streets bearing prominent American names in the former West, such as President John F. Kennedy, Henry Ford, John Foster Dulles, Lucius D. Clay, and Martin Luther King Jr., as figures of western freedom; on the former East side, names found in official and unofficial sites of inscription such as Paul Robeson, W. E. B. Du Bois, and Angela Davis ring out with a different resonance, to call attention to racial injustice within the United States and beyond.

In addition to these connections, an architectural topography that now includes trails and traces of the wall system runs throughout the reunified city. To this day, there are buildings still riddled with leftover bullet holes, rubble contained just beneath the surface, and in-situ burial grounds from World War II firefights. Beyond the divide between East and West, Berlin signifies as a twin city across historical eras: as a haunted, layered necropolis on one hand and a city of renewal and rebirth on the other. Communities of immigrants and refugees, including those resettled in the shuttered Tempelhof Airport, the site of the former Nazi air operations and later the U.S. airlift, add layers of intrigue to Germany's own rebuilding projects. In Berlin, one can still seek any number of questions about the nature of post–Cold War democracy, including those that deal with or strategically turn away from the iconic wall. This borderland geography of Berlin encompasses and expands well beyond the Wall's former footprint.

———

A Wall of Our Own proposes a renewed call to collectively explore the work of American artists, writers, and activists in Berlin during the Cold War—in part, to make sense of the continued practice of identification with the Wall and other geopolitical discourses that remain vitally connected to Berlin. While an American presence in divided Berlin was originally personified through extensive military deployment and prominent political appearances along this volatile zone, American artists and writers mapped, read, and expanded significant aspects of Daum's notion of "America's Berlin," as a place of democratic longing and experimentation. Berlin continues to be a place where we reckon not only with German history but with American practices of democracy and repression, too. Each chapter of this book explores American cultural productions that were routed historically and conceptually through a divided Berlin. The chapters detail representations of the Berlin Wall and catalog the creative processes that led toward the production of a particular book about U.S. cultures of division and solidarity. Considerations of published works are interanimated with reflections gleaned from archives, encompassing materials from library collections, national holdings, oral histories, and private papers. The various Berlin Wall books exist in distinct genre forms—the photobook, the political autobiography, the conceptual art book, and the poetry collection—but overlap in their methods of production and patterns of critical discovery, whether produced inside or outside Berlin. While disciplinary readings in fields of cultural history, literary studies, or art history allow particular claims to be made within a given chapter, my project aims to "form an archive," as Andrew Friedman puts it in another context, "that arises from a landscape rather than a discipline."[24] Out of the archive of American Berliners' engagement with the border zones and occupied sectors surrounding the Wall, the cultural productions examined in these pages constitute a critical constellation of work made by Americans whose encounters in a walled Berlin led to projects directed at other sites of division.

By focusing on the individuals within networks of artistic and political engagement, this book demonstrates that the Berlin Wall reflected significant histories of social division beyond scripts of state authority and military strategy. U.S. artists, writers, and activists working in and through Berlin

approached boundaries of freedom through a practice that Salamishah Tillet terms "critical patriotism" engaging sites of freedom and repression in a
manner that "neither encourages idolatry to the nation's past nor blind loy-
alty to the state" but through "dissidence and dissent . . . re-engages the meta-
discourse of American democracy."[25]

The American Berliners at the center of this book are intriguing not only
for what they explored and created while the Wall stood; each returned to
Berlin after its dismantling in 1989. Through their returns, they spark and extend historical questions through practices of cultural memory while back
in then-reunified Berlin. Their work on the Berlin Wall builds on previous
themes but remains an incomplete task; as they find productive points of reflection, they strategically avoid closure on matters of history and democracy.

Together, through historical engagement with the period of the Berlin
Wall and excursions through its monumental afterlife, the on-site explorations of the divided city and the Berlin Wall by Freed, Davis, Tajiri, and Lorde
prompted reflections then, as they do now, on the complexities and fault lines
of America's democratic project. Such reflections grappled with Cold War
policies and practices and, when read today, continue to spark engagement
with American global politics and the shared physical and symbolic character of border walls, as a matter of navigating our own political landscapes of
division. Rather than seeking Berlin as a site in which freedom and repression
are to be imagined as distinct formations, historically or geographically, the
reader is invited to approach the city as a means of understanding the dialectical relationship between freedom and repression as interlinked. In other
words, this book aims to unseat the relative ease with which American culture
currently incorporates the Berlin Wall into its own history of progress without further reflection on our own lines of division — whether physically or socially inscribed, historically relevant, or newly emergent since 1989. My hope
is to spotlight the enduring and urgent role of the artist, writer, or activist as
a civic actor. Cultural agents meaningfully task themselves and the rest of us
with weighing American practices of freedom, moving in and out of U.S. borders and internal sites of division, critically exploring zones of conflict, and
mapping the gaps between the nation's democratic ideals and lived realities.

The Berlin Wall emerged as a site integral to and symbolic of the Cold War
cultural imagination in the United States, but only in retrospect can we discern how integral the stories of struggle by the Wall are intertwined both with
those of its triumphant dismantling and with our current failures to imagine a world without pernicious lines of division. The Berlin Wall continues
to signify on this cyclical history, especially as leaders and state actors —

responsible for the fortifications and inhumane detention policies along the U.S.-Mexico border, the apartheid walls separating Israel from Palestine, the fences built to hinder refugees crossing into southern countries of the European Union, and the sites of climate and ecological violence, among countless other barriers—fail to learn crucial lessons from the profound violence and ignorance of bygone wall builders. The chants to "build the wall" on the U.S.-Mexico border are echoes of deep-seated white supremacist fantasies in the United States that have countered freedom principles throughout the nation's history. Berlin continues as a point of reckoning and return, once again, to measure those principles against our own practices of repression, to grapple with the weight of history and dreams of transcendence.

In the spirit of critical reflection, *A Wall of Our Own* attempts to gather the many disparate accounts of American artists beckoned to divided Berlin into a shared historical frame. This book also is meant to serve as a roadmap of creative process, moving in and out of divided Berlin, through other geopolitical sites of division, toward critical engagement and awakening. The path follows a critical and curious stance to life along our borders.

CHAPTER 1 | SEGREGATED SECTORS

Leonard Freed, the Berlin Crisis, and the Color Line

If the American found in Europe only confusion, it would
obviously be infinitely wiser for him to remain at home.
Hidden, however, in the heart of confusion he encounters
here is that which he came so blindly seeking: the terms on
which he is related to his country, and to the world.

—JAMES BALDWIN

On August 13, 1961, East German forces closed the borders of East Berlin and, in turn, encircled the allied sectors of the city's western half. Two weeks later, American photographer Leonard Freed wandered along the internal edges of the divided city. In those uncertain days of the Berlin Crisis, each side was on high alert, as the potential for conflict in Berlin between the superpowers seemed imminent, leading to a standoff and the eventual sealing of the city's western sectors. It would take the East German Democratic Republic months to fully enclose West Berlin, but within a matter of hours and days, the newly fortified boundary was beginning to take shape: barbed wire, wooden barricades, torn-up pavement, bricks, and the rudimentary beginnings of a concrete wall. In the weeks that followed, soldiers from each side drew near to protect and inspect the implementation of the closed border.[1]

Freed was fascinated by the implications of this Cold War front line. Berlin was again the epicenter of global conflict, in what he conceived as "a war of nerves" between the Soviet-led East and American-allied West.[2] By August 1961 Freed had been living outside America for more than five years. During his August travels, he spent his time close to the center of the partitioned city. With the world on the brink of war, he pointed his camera toward one of the West's last lines of defense: American GIs in the American sector of West Berlin. These new images summoned an impulse to seek out American subjects, a focus that had been only latent in his European work up to this point.

From his earliest travels to Germany in the early 1950s, Freed pondered the ways in which history and memory influenced the nation's postwar condition and, in turn, his own relationship to its people and landscapes. He wrestled with his Jewish identity in Germany and throughout Europe. Freed was born in 1929 and grew up Brooklyn, New York. His parents, Sam and Rose, were both born to Jewish families in Minsk, Russia, but met and married after they emigrated to the United States, escaping a wave of pogroms in their native land around World War I. His older brother, Milton, served as a pilot in the U.S. Air Force, flying missions over the Pacific theater in World War II. Leonard, too young to be drafted during that war, instead was compelled to leave the United States in the years afterward to encounter the legacies of global conflict. Starting in 1952, in his early twenties, Freed traveled through Europe and North Africa for two years. After going home briefly to the United States, he returned to Europe in 1956. He honed his craft as a documentary photographer and supported himself by selling photographs to local magazines and newspapers. Freed sought to further understand his Jewish heritage in the context of post–World War II Europe.

Freed had begun photographing in Germany on his first trip to Europe, focused especially on its landscapes of memory and reconstruction. On his second trip, in 1956, he met a German woman, Brigitte Klück, and his work was first published by Klück's hometown newspaper in Dortmund under the headline "Eine Amerikaner sieht unsere Stadt" (An American sees our city). In 1957 Leonard and Brigitte married in Amsterdam. He thought of the idea for his first book, *Joden van Amsterdam* (*Jews of Amsterdam*) (1958), after visiting the Anne Frank House. Early in 1961 Freed started photographing in neighboring Cold War Germany for a project that would later cohere into his second book, *Deutsche Juden heute* (*German Jews Today*) (1965). Both publications were released in Europe, accompanied by texts in their respective national tongues. Postwar Europe was a puzzle for Freed: a land of great artistic civilization, familial aura, Jewish trauma and estrangement, postwar destruction, and potential redemption. In his mind Germany was the central and most jagged piece of the whole.[3]

The legacy of conflict in Germany weighed on Freed in August 1961, when he took a train from Amsterdam to West Berlin. Freed arrived with his close friend Dutch journalist Willem Oltmans on or around August 25. Neither man had an assignment or a particular itinerary. As many around the world waited on edge for the breakout of World War III, Freed and Oltmans stepped close to the border. Freed's photographs and recollections from that trip found in Oltmans's private journals attest to their movements near Zimmerstrasse as they stalked the Wall's emergent path. Freed meandered through parked army tanks and jeeps, GIs squatting with trays of fast food, and pedestrians passing through a then-makeshift but heavily guarded Checkpoint Charlie on Friedrichstrasse. On August 27 he and Oltmans crossed the city's internal border to East Berlin, traveling down the monumental boulevard of Stalin Allee and into the Oberschöneweide neighborhood, where they sat with workers on a terrace and visited a bookstore. Later that day, back in West Berlin, Freed and Oltmans witnessed a frenzied evening scene on Moritz-platz in which U.S. military tanks with searchlights, joined by jeeps equipped with speakers, blasted Elvis Presley music near the border wall to galvanize throngs of West Berliners who had gathered to protest the still-fresh physical division of the city.[4]

Freed confronted his visions of a war-prone Germany in the American sector of a newly walled Berlin, and through his own directed movement, he pursued his own circuit of alternative cultural diplomacy. In doing so, he examined American power along the border and reflected on his own ex-patriate status. He traveled to divided Berlin to comprehend the ways Jewish history was present within a city experiencing a new wave of division. But in the majority of his images from this trip, the new wall is barely visible. In-stead American GIs stationed by the border receive his most consistent and direct focus. Many of the soldiers barely acknowledge Freed's presence, while others cast sidelong glances at him and his camera.

There is one exception to this indirect viewpoint, when Freed faced head-on both the Berlin Wall and a fellow American in the same frame. The re-sulting image would haunt Freed, beckon his return from exile, remind the expatriate of his American whiteness, and transform his practice as a photog-rapher. Here, at the nascent wall, Freed snapped a photograph of an unnamed black soldier standing at the edge of the American sector (fig. 1.1).[5] After lift-ing his finger from the shutter release, he left the scene without taking any more photographs. Freed's contact sheets from this trip confirm that, unlike his other GI images at the Wall in which he sometimes captured the same ser-viceman from several angles, this soldier image was a single shot.[6]

Taken at middle distance in black and white, the frontal portrait features the uniformed soldier in the foreground, his eyes cast downward and to the side. Freed stands near the intersection of Zimmerstrasse and Charlotten-strasse streets, between trolley tracks that dead-end in the imposing bound-ary of the Wall, seen in the background. The soldier is outfitted in full combat gear, and a helmet weighs heavily on his head, suggested by a slight forward tilt. One of his fellow GIs can be seen in an army jeep behind him, travel-

FIGURE 1.1 Leonard Freed, *Berlin*, 1961.
(Estate of Leonard Freed/Magnum Photos)

ing with another photographer, yet their attention is elsewhere, outside the frame. At the image's highest magnification, the soldier's nametag remains out of focus, but his uniform identifies him as likely in the 2nd Battle Group, 6th Infantry in West Germany. The soldier's arms jut out to his sides, and his hands rest below at his hips. This image, as an exceptional single shot, demonstrates two central and productive challenges for Freed in this period: how to identify with his subjects, and how to consider the new Berlin Wall as subject matter within a post-Holocaust European landscape.

When Freed's single shot of the soldier was later included as the opening image to his book *Black in White America* (1967/68) (fig. 1.2), Freed identified the location as "Berlin, Germany," citing the city as a whole, without distinguishing between East and West. His caption further calls attention to the soldier's affiliation and stance: "In defense of Western Civilization, an American soldier's hand rests on his gun."[7] Freed narrates the photographic mo-

FIGURE 1.2 Cover, Leonard Freed, *Black in White America*, 1967/68. (Grossman/Estate of Leonard Freed)

ment in personal terms: "We, he and I, two Americans. We meet silently and part silently. Between us, impregnable and as deadly as the wall behind him, is another wall. It is there on the trolley tracks, it crawls along the cobble stones, across the frontiers and oceans, reaching back home, back into our lives and deep into our hearts: dividing us, wherever we meet. I am White and he is Black."[8] Freed's annotation affirms the profound duality of this visual encounter: citizens of the same country stand mere feet away from each other as countrymen in an American-occupied zone in West Berlin, and yet the experience of racial division is laid bare. In fact, this image stylistically departs from his other American GI images at the Wall, as it is also the only image in *Black in White America* that presents racial division as static and impervious to interaction. Throughout the book, Freed locates fields of vision in order to wrestle with racial formation and his own whiteness. Freed acknowledges his role as a white photographer in America's racially divided society by encroaching on scenarios like this, to scrutinize his encounters with black subjects. Throughout the published book, he does so by balancing distance while moving closer to his subjects, registering their gazes in numerous directions, and marking mutual recognition without erasing social lines of division implicit or evident in his photographic encounters.

Freed's Berlin Wall images and the trajectories that spring forth from them present photography as a tool to study relationships informed by race and the legacies of repression inscribed into Cold War and civil rights–era public spaces. His tactics of perspective at the Berlin Wall are informed by technical approaches and philosophical imperatives. In a technical photographic sense, perception marks the distance between photographer and subject, determined by the angle, framing, and relative distance between the camera and the focal point of the scene. As a concept, the word "perspective" also connotes a personal viewpoint informed by history, experience, and interaction. Curator William Ewing, in Freed's retrospective *Worldview*, explains the one-word title by means of its German cognate, *Weltanschauung*, and the parallel between Freed's practice as a photographer and his philosophical outlook: "Leonard Freed saw, interpreted and transmitted in a particular way. He had a *Weltanschauung*. This term and its less-than-perfect translation, *worldview*, wraps beautifully around both Freed the man and Freed the photographer. . . . He used photography as a tool to better understand the world, first to himself (to discover who he was), and then for us (to help discover who we are)."[9] Freed's perspective as it pertains to the Berlin Wall epitomizes the way his approach to photography was influenced by his ideas of how people relate to one another and the cultural landscapes that surround them, both formalistically and historically. In Germany, he considers its status as a "nation" as a way to ruminate on the connections between its divided people, places, and epochs. In the geopolitical spaces of divided Berlin, Freed attended to a range of reflections and relationships, determined by his own photographic frame or footsteps toward encounter. Freed pursued the meaning-making of a photographic image, both at the point of capture and later in editorial selection, where he could spatially and conceptually convey questions regarding identity and mutuality. By alternately turning toward the Berlin Wall and away from its tense border zones, he intended to mark historical dividing lines while seeking recognition across them. Freed treats the Wall and other sites and structures of division as symbols of geopolitical standoff and venues for critical engagement and studied connection between otherwise divided peoples.

Most of Freed's photographs from the period of 1961–65 can be categorized by their inclusion in either his German or American portfolios; they were included in two books, *Black in White America* and *Made in Germany* (1970). Because of Berlin's geopolitical situation, limiting Freed's photographs at the Wall to only two national contexts becomes difficult. Yet by thinking through the overlapping national contexts in which Freed's black soldier image may reasonably "belong," we can trace his methodology of engaging historical dividing lines and the people who populate them. Freed maps his Berlin-based images in photobooks in order to mark and contest the Wall's simplest narratives. Freed carefully calibrated a relative proximity with his subjects, at once moving closer to identify with them and allowing for a space of estrangement to capture the multiple historical and social buffers that he attempted to comprehend or overcome by the Wall.

This chapter explores Freed's movements in and out of Berlin during the early years of the Berlin Wall, with an eye toward locating the single-shot image of a black GI within the broader currents of cultural history. While producing his respective studies of U.S. and German division, Freed would travel back and forth between the "old" and "new" Jewish worlds of Europe and America. In doing so, he produced book projects and challenged the underlying dichotomies of home and away, past and present, countryman and stranger. First, this chapter explores the larger context of the Berlin Crisis and the walling of Berlin by means of cultural productions, texts, and voices that sought to connect the German wall with the lines and legacies of American segregation. Second, it looks to Freed's development as a photographer, especially how the city of Berlin, the country of Germany, and his breaks from exile in America informed an understanding of geopolitical division and identification in the context of transnational geopolitics and cultural memory. Third, the chapter closes with a consideration of Freed's *Black in White America* and *Made in Germany*, alongside the moments he visited and viewed the Wall in subsequent trips to Germany as it further took shape in the city. Despite the separate emphases of each project, the fact that Freed took photographs across roughly the same period in overlapping territories affirms the shared productive contexts and tensions of these works. More specifically, Freed's depiction of the Berlin Wall alongside other historical boundaries — especially those along the color line in America — as well as long-term processes of reconciliation in Germany, marks these projects as products of the same emergent practice of roving perspective and identification. Understanding where Freed locates the Berlin Wall, other historical structures or figures, and himself in each of these images allows us to measure his transformation as a photographer and his evolving view of the Wall and its connotations. Freed depicted the Wall's surrounding urban and cultural landscapes, as he identified with *and* distanced himself from his subjects during these transatlantic travels. Freed's images suggest he viewed the American post–World War II democratic project as a fragile construct, while jointly documenting Germany's postwar landscapes and the color line back home.

In 1961 and beyond, as Americans were enthralled with tales of a divided Berlin in news and entertainment programming alike, the dividing crisis of segregation loomed.[10] Following the legal mandate to end segregation in public institutions in the 1954 unanimous Supreme Court decision in *Brown v. Board of Education*, the uneven adherence to the decision led to further domestic unrest and divisive, violent tactics by local authorities. In the aftermath of the case that struck down "Separate but Equal" governance as unconstitutional, the broad legal and social system of segregation continued widely across the South and the North. Through a hybrid of law, custom, and architectural design, America's own segregated sectors—including geographic places under racial rule as well as contexts of institutional discrimination in education, health, housing, and labor—reinforced the social construction of consequential racial hierarchies. In May 1961 the first Freedom Rides organized by the Congress of Racial Equality tested the desegregation of interstate bus travel. Sit-ins at lunch counters and other public venues continued to contest the undignified rituals of segregated business-as-usual. These protests also pointed to the existing barriers—both symbolic and physical—that had plagued the United States and called into question its identity as an "indivisible" nation.[11]

American cultural productions from the late summer through the end of 1961, immediately before and after the Berlin Wall's initial construction, drew focus to the city's internal border through reportage and fictional crossings, at times with attention to the interrelated dynamics of geopolitical and racial division. In a column published August 12, 1961, one day before East Berlin sealed its borders, the celebrated poet and author Langston Hughes wrote an editorial in the *Chicago Defender* titled "Beer, Berlin and Simple." The column was a pointed response to an earlier, pre-Wall address by President John F. Kennedy televised to the nation on July 22, 1961, in which he addressed the Berlin Crisis and increasingly tense communications with the Soviet Union following a July summit with Premier Nikita Khrushchev in Vienna. Hughes wrote in one of his often-used editorial forms, presenting an imagined conversation with "Jesse B. Semple," commonly known as "Simple," a fictional fellow Harlem resident. Simple's ideas reflect common but critical negotiations of domestic and global politics as they existed at that moment.

As Hughes writes from Simple's perspective, he states, "In the next war I'll have to fight for Berlin. I had rather fight for Birmingham." Simple goes on to contextualize the latest crisis in terms of his fears of recent German history

("It were but a short time ago that Berlin was fighting me") as well as America divided internally by Jim Crow laws and customs ("I'll bet Mississippi has WHITE and COLORED air raid shelters").[12]

In the days after the border was closed, and as the Wall's structure formalized, other cultural voices turned to Cold War Berlin without the switchback to the lines dividing the United States. For example, episodes of NBC's *Jack Paar Show* and CBS's *Ed Sullivan Show* and *Armstrong Circle Theatre*'s "Chapter on Tyranny: Dateline Berlin" featured a mix of reportage and entertainment and interactions with members of the military and refugees or, in the case of the latter, presented dramatized reenactments of escape attempts. A focus on the daring escapes of East Germans away from communist rule and toward the West in these productions was influenced not only by the perspective of American media—their reports were literally filed in the West—but also by American cultural figures who flocked to West Berlin to help make sense of the situation and broadcast televised images of themselves in the city. These efforts not only bridged the distance between "here" and "there" but also failed to draw reflexive comparisons. They most often were captured from within the circuits of mainstream cultural diplomacy, underwritten by U.S. military presence and support in West Berlin.[13] Others, without setting foot in Berlin, located popular expressions in divided Berlin as a means to conjure division as a symbolic condition.[14]

From the tense moments of the Berlin Crisis, some of the first press photographs of the border scene that circulated around the globe were of East German border troops, either building the border or escaping it. On August 15, 1961, Peter Leibing photographed East German corporal Conrad Schumann taking a running leap over the barbed wire blocking the border while throwing his rifle off his shoulder. A photograph showing this "leap of freedom" soon appeared on the front page of the West German *Bild* newspaper and was soon reprinted in papers across the world.[15] For western viewers, their vision of the Wall through this photograph was simultaneously one of enclosure and potential—albeit challenged—escape. Yet the full narrative of the image is not self-apparent. The civilians in the background of this iconic image, pictured in soft focus, stand casually. One figure appears to have his hand in his pocket, in contrast to the urgency of a soldier fleeing a war zone. The presence of another photographer's upheld camera in the frame reinforces the proximity and power of photography mediating views of the scene. The clashing perspectives of these two characters replicate the sense of East Berlin as decidedly strange and West Berlin as the visual norm of freedom.[16]

Within days of the Berlin Wall's construction, citizens from across the

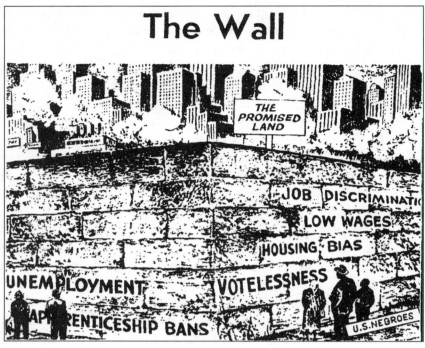

FIGURE 1.3 "The Wall," *Pittsburgh Courier*, January 20, 1962.
(*Pittsburgh Courier* archives/ProQuest Historical Newspapers)

United States went against the mainstream inclinations to treat the Wall as isolated spectacle and began evoking the Berlin boundary as a metaphor for racial barriers in America in more grassroots venues and platforms. Activists, artists, and politicians used differing forms of cultural communication to highlight the ongoing struggle for equality through the rhetoric of America's Berlin. The barriers they contested included the elusive but violently policed color line; they also referred to existing architectures of segregation in cities (including walls, fences, and pernicious "common sense" boundaries) that divided redlined housing districts from other residential areas or prohibited mobility for black citizens more ostensibly. Public speeches in late 1961 from prominent black Americans, such as State Department official Carl Rowan, NAACP president Roy Wilkins, and Fort Valley State College president Cornelius V. Troup, explored dimensions of U.S. racial segregation by relating civil rights struggles to the construction of the Berlin Wall.[17]

An editorial cartoon printed in the *Pittsburgh Courier* on January 20, 1962, also demonstrates the metaphorical grounds on which such linkages stood. Titled "The Wall" (fig. 1.3), the unsigned cartoon depicts a looming stone wall, behind which a visible skyline of a metropolis, labeled "The Promised Land," sits on its out-of-reach other side. In the foreground, figures labeled "U.S. Negroes" face blocks of stone inscribed with words such as "Unemployment," "Housing Bias," and "Votelessness." The accompanying editorial posits a forceful explanation of this scene: "The Wall that now divides East Berlin from West Berlin is as NOTHING compared to the wall that has long divided black America from white America." This symbolic visual portrayal marked the uncanny nature of the Berlin Wall, with distinction. "This American Wall is NOT insurmountable, but to MOST black Americans it SEEMS to be: and they dream of seeing it RAZED so that, like the East Berliners, they can ESCAPE to the Promised Land of freedom and opportunity."[18]

Such rhetoric boomeranged back and forth across the Atlantic, pushing politicians to grapple with this walled parallel. In February 1962, as noted, Attorney General Robert F. Kennedy addressed an audience in West Berlin to represent Cold War Berlin and the United States as a part of a "New Frontier" of democratic progress. Kennedy qualified this remark by stating, "For a hundred years, despite our protestations of equality, we had, as you know, a wall of our own — a wall of segregation erected against Negroes. That wall is coming down."[19] Along these lines, other politicians, several of them white, spoke out publicly in America about "Berlin Walls" of segregation. Illinois governor Otto Kerner told the NAACP's 1963 annual meeting that whites and blacks should tear down the "Berlin Wall of prejudice and fear . . . [and that the] walled-in bitterness we are now creating can destroy us." United Nations ambassador Adlai Stevenson spoke out that same year by saying it does "little good to demand the tearing down of the Wall in Berlin unless we tear down the wall that separates us in our own land." In 1964 Mary Tinglof, a member of the Los Angeles Board of Education, spoke of school inequities "as rigid as Berlin walls."[20] In the first years after the Wall was erected, Americans began using "Berlin Wall" as a portable, descriptive phrase to refer to specific cases of U.S. segregation, imploring officials to tear down physical color-line barriers in cities and towns.[21]

Other forms of American engagement domesticated this rhetorical map of the Wall at sites of homegrown democratic crisis. For example, in newspaper reports of protests and speeches, individuals in dozens of cities demonstrated how the "Berlin Wall" could be used to describe the boundaries in their own communities and did so for years following the Berlin Crisis. The "Berlin Wall" of Atlanta referred to the steel-and-wood barricades erected by the city on Peyton and Harlan Roads in the West End to discourage black development into a mainly white residential area. In 1962 and 1963, protestors carried signs on-site calling it "Atlanta's Wall," while others proclaimed, "We Want No Warsaw Ghetto — Open Peyton Road."[22] This incorporative form of protest sought to bring U.S. racial segregation, Holocaust trauma, and Cold War division into a shared frame. Speaking in 1963 in southeast Michigan, Rev. Dr. James Laird said of the actual Berlin Wall, "At least it is an honest wall, because it is visible, but in every city in America, including Detroit and Dearborn, there are invisible walls of discrimination and segregation."[23]

In Selma, Alabama, in March 1965, waves of protestors gathered to demand that black citizens be granted the unrestricted right to register to vote. They attempted to march to the courthouse and eventually to the state capitol in Montgomery. On March 11, just four days after hundreds of civil rights marchers were brutally beaten by state troopers at the base of the Edmund Pettus Bridge, a date ignominiously deemed Bloody Sunday, Selma's public safety director Wilson Baker tied a clothesline across Sylvan Street, cutting off the most direct path to the local Dallas County courthouse. Soon after the line went up, activists and clergy on the scene began calling the barrier the "Berlin Wall" or the "Selma Wall." They improvised verses to the tune of the popular spiritual "Joshua Fit the Battle of Jericho" and crafted a related sonic response: "We've got a rope that's a Berlin Wall, a Berlin Wall, a Berlin Wall . . . in Selma, Alabama." The crowd sang and clapped out a rhythm to guide their improvised chants until the makeshift barrier was removed.[24] In other instances, particular streets were singled out and characterized for Berlin Wall–like effect: Parker Street in Boston, Alameda Road in Los Angeles, and South State Street in Chicago. Elsewhere, in cities such as Birmingham; Deerfield; Greensboro, North Carolina; Philadelphia; Rich Square, North Carolina; Selma; St. Louis; Arlington; Wheaton, Illinois; and Newark, individuals called out the specific architecture or attributes of their city's racial dynamics through references to Cold War Berlin, referring to physical walls, social customs, and/or municipal policies.[25]

Resonant cultural productions aimed to capture these sentiments through allegory and/or irony. Hughes's *Jericho-Jim Crow*, written in 1963 and staged in January 1964 at the Sanctuary in the Village in New York, abstracts the language of structural and symbolic boundaries connected to the Cold War and focuses on the fault lines of American society. Another work, this of satire, by white author Warren Miller, 1964's *The Siege of Harlem* imagines Harlem as a fortified sovereign black capital, in sync with Cold War constructions of divided Berlin and Cuba. In his text, passersby must go through "Checkpoint Frederick Douglass," as Harlem is surrounded by a boundary made up of car parts and old protest signs. So-called privileged whites tried to entice black Americans to defect back to the U.S. side by broadcasting messages on "Radio Free Harlem." In such instances, the Wall signified more than a formidable structure; it was a social environment to be borrowed for comparative critique.[26]

As artists, activists, and political figures first made sense of Berlin's boundaries by way of American lines of division, conjuring the Wall as an uncanny structure, Freed was distant from such resonances and references, spending his time as an expatriate documentary photographer and traveler across Europe. When the Wall was built, he was in exile and largely tuned out of American culture, interrupted by his encounters at the border. But when he arrived at the Berlin Wall, he, too, sought the transnational parallels between systems and sites of division. His single-shot and Berlin images prompted his return to the United States. They informed his understanding of both the physical divides inscribed into the American landscape and the symbolic resonance of division in historically traumatized German spaces around the potential for exchange.

———

As a photographer, Freed engaged subjects at the intersection of geopolitics and history. Freed honed his connections between America and divided Germany as a matter of photographic practice and existential questioning. Freed negotiated his own positioning in relation to each of his images: how to, if at all, place himself in the same spaces as his subjects, and how to read the broader landscapes and layers of history that informed their encounters.

Freed's approach was influenced by his admiration of and affiliation with the international photography collective Magnum. Started in 1947 by photographers Henri Cartier-Bresson, Robert Capa, George Rodger, and David "Chim" Seymour, Magnum was formed as a social and aesthetic response to the human catastrophes of World War II. With offices originally in Paris and New York, this group used photography to respond to the traumas of war experienced firsthand by many of its early photographers who were victims or documenters of violence. (The word "magnum" recalls "a gun of a type designed to fire cartridges more powerful than its caliber suggests," patented in 1935.)[27] Magnum members did so by reappropriating several wartime advancements in photographic technology, including the use of portable "mini cameras" and more light-sensitive film, to rapidly restore human connection and nurture new forms of storytelling. They promoted the photographer as "the idiosyncratic mix of reporter and artist," creators who also owned the rights to the photographs they shot and contributed images to a large group archive.[28] Freed first visited Magnum's New York offices in 1955, when Inge Bondi, the German-born assistant (and later its director), welcomed him to use their facilities. Magnum advanced a transatlantic image interchange between the United States and war-torn Europe that enabled photographers to self-direct shoots on location, gain proximity to their subjects, and place themselves, even if marginally, in scenes with the people they photograph. Before Freed became a full-time member in 1972, Magnum's most acclaimed photographers had already influenced his approaches.

Rather than sticking to one place or one country, Magnum photographers were encouraged to travel among sites, to develop perspective on local matters and insights across cultures, and, when necessary, to return time and again to reassess. They often plotted their own shoots and importantly maintained ownership of their negatives, adding to their authorial position. For Freed, work that grew out of his travels to the Berlin Wall manifested in reflections on division in America and both West and East Germany. Freed attended to these countries, and their sites of border tension or proximity, by thinking through how their respective histories were reflected and made manifest in the present — most clearly through a focus on several overlapping tropes: legacies of war, rituals of mourning, and postwar reconstruction.[29]

Freed's sense of geopolitical location was balanced by another approach he employed in his work: that of mitigating access to his subjects through viewpoints in the "middle-distance." In other words, he imagined the possibility of connection between his subjects and himself while seeking to mark the social boundaries and historical forces straining coexistence. He refused the objective position and detached eye of the documentarian. As Erina Duganne remarks of another white photographer of this era but apropos Freed's subtextual practices: "[He] places his own unmediated access to [his subjects] into question."[30] In a mode of witnessing, and what Duganne deems as "intersubjective exchange," Freed shares space with his subjects in instructive moments of photographic encounter. He makes that fact known by referencing his presence in many of his images through shadows, reflections in glass, and blurred figures in the immediate foreground. He accomplishes a middle distance by balancing his own visual perspective with that of his subjects by approximating, acknowledging, and/or honoring their fields of vision by denying himself and later viewers access to what they singularly experience and see. The dynamic plays out both within scenes he photographs and in the pages of his photobooks, adding context and descriptions to augment this approach.

Among the first professional projects he started after returning home to

Brooklyn in 1954 was a series of photographs of Hassidic Jews who had sur-
vived the concentration camps and now lived in his old neighborhood. According to Ewing, Freed was drawn to them "not because he was one of them
. . . but because he *might* have been one of them had history dealt his Russian
family another hand."[31] The resulting images included Freed separated from
his subjects through glass doors and windows and behind hats covering their
faces, as they recognized the photographer with direct eye contact. (These
were among the photographs he first showed to Magnum staffer Bondi
and Museum of Modern Art curator Edward Steichen.) During this time,
he began photographing Italian American and African American subjects
as well, documenting schoolhouses and religious functions as well as street
parades and other scenes of convergence. These early images attest to Freed's
interest in framing division within social spaces of near-proximity and alienation, especially around matters of racial and ethnic identity.

Freed's move back to Europe in 1956 included his forays into freelance
photography and his first substantive, book-length projects. The first of these,
Joden van Amsterdam (1958), arrived in his mailbox on his wedding day to
Brigitte.[32] According to Wim van Sinderen, Freed and his collaborator Dutch
journalist Max Snijders "succeeded in finding a good balance between the
shame and guilt of the Dutch and resignation and reticence of the Jewish
community." This work marked a point of departure Freed would return to:
locating Jewish communities against the backdrop of a European country
that had spurned and targeted them during the Holocaust. After the publication of *Joden van Amsterdam*, Freed's focus on postwar European Jewry
shifted to Germany and to his later *Deutsche Juden heute* book. As van Sinderen adds, "*Deutsche Juden heute* did not come about easily. . . . Very few
[Jews] were prepared to expose themselves to the camera."[33] Freed did build
trust with his subjects, photographing communal and ritualistic spaces, but
he also sensed his own fraught position—as an American Jewish photographer working among a population that was hesitant to be photographed following the war.

The result, as evidenced in the images that would later comprise *Deutsche
Juden heute*, taken primarily in 1961–62, informed his evolving and roving approach. As a photographer Freed wrestled with the issue of how much distance from the lens to grant his subjects. In this case, his subjects were German Jews who had moved back to Germany or who converted to Judaism
after the Holocaust. Freed's perspective demonstrates his feeling of affiliation, although he remained cautious about identifying fully with, or as, one
of them—a discomfort that might have been tied to a sense of survivor's guilt

because his family had lived in America during the Holocaust. To balance these feelings, at times he used a shallow depth of field to garner or approach a middle distance of intimacy with his subjects. Freed often positioned his camera to evenly sync with his subjects' fields of vision or, alternatively, take the position of a complete outsider, locating himself far out of intimate scenes in which he was seeking to make pictures. Freed tried to strike a balance between having access to his subjects (by virtue of his Jewish identity), which in itself represents a form of intimacy, while also wanting to show respect and space for their privacy.

When Freed photographed away from human subjects on these excursions in Germany, he tended to isolate himself and wander around the country's bygone Jewish spaces. He tried to conjure spaces from which to locate and relate to Germany's disappeared and murdered Jews. In one of the opening images of the book, he encounters a Jewish cemetery in Worms and the burial ground's uneven terrain (fig. 1.4). Shooting from a sloped position, he gives a sense of sprawling space. Here, the zigzag layout of the tombstones and the lack of a clear vanishing point serve formally to disorient viewers, as does the lack of context to clarify whether this burial ground was desecrated during the Holocaust. The ordering aspect of sunlight, entering the cemetery at an oblique angle, turns the tombstones into daggered shadows, while the absence of a photographer's shadow in this scene denies his presence. Freed accomplishes this by standing with the sun low and to his right, maximizing the light effects on the tombstones without having to stake a presence within the frame.

If Freed depicts the cemetery landscape in Worms with a sweeping, panoramic horizon, an earlier photograph in the book, taken at a walled boundary of the Dachau concentration camp, captures the specter of the Holocaust with a more confining, though similarly isolated perspective. This image was actually made on Freed's first trip to Europe in 1954 with a Rolleiflex camera rather than his Leica. Here Freed encounters the remains of latticed wood planks left lying amid trees and shrubs along the former "blood trenches." Like the rows of gravestones, the planks angle in a number of directions, except here they form a general line toward the vanishing point farther down the boundary wall. The base of the image is in soft focus, and, as several long blades of grass creep out at the bottom corners of the frame, Freed appears to have been kneeling or squatting. By locating himself in the brush and at the outer wall, Freed pushes his own vantage point to the edge. This image powerfully catches the photographer between the two roles he played while focusing on Germany's Jews: on one hand, a "landsman" staking out the his-

FIGURE 1.4 Leonard Freed, *Worms*, 1961.
(Estate of Leonard Freed/Magnum Photos)

tory and reclaimed sacred grounds of his people; on the other, an outsider looking in, questioning his role and unsure of how to find a place for himself in post–Holocaust Germany.

Freed first traveled to Berlin in the late 1950s as part of his study of postwar Jewish communities. Of the more than fifty images in *Deutsche Juden heute*, approximately five were taken in Berlin, each taken in an indoor, enclosed space. The city's historic plazas and informal internal borders were not included within the scope of this project. Instead, he made portraits of notable Jewish families and cultural figures within their homes and spaces of refuge at a middle distance. He looked over the shoulders of people in prayer, joined across the table a family lighting Shabbat candles, and set foot outside the dedication of a reconsecrated synagogue. Only one image from Berlin depicts an anonymous sitter, and this one departs from his observational style exhibited throughout the rest of the book's public and semipublic spaces. An unnamed elder gentleman in a retirement home is presented with shallow depth of field, suggesting proximity (fig. 1.5). The man sits in an upholstered chair, his elbows craned from padded armrests; his hands form the top of a triangle, and his cane rests below. Next to him two green plants, one larger than the other, grow out of small pots, while a painting of a young man rapt in prayer, draped in a tallit as he solemnly prays, crowns the scene. The relationship between Freed and his elderly subject is complicated by the youthful figure of piety in the painting that hangs above him. If Freed seeks to identify with a figure in the scene, whom is he most drawn to, the old man sitting or the imagined young man praying? Whose role has been surrogated or mirrored, and by whom? The photographer's distance is less physical than social. As Freed gained traction as a photographer in Berlin, he struggled with the city as a space of recovery, identification, and differentiation, finding remnants of its horrific past enlivened by and grappling with stories of survival.

The next time Freed was beckoned to Berlin, it was upon receiving news that the city was being divided. His photographs from August 1961 document the random assortment of construction materials and makeshift barriers that would soon be fortified into a solid wall. In many of his earliest Berlin Wall images, American GIs are the most prominent visual feature, not the Wall. It's as if the Wall had remained outside Freed's immediate field of vision, as he stalked and moved in and out of the borders' spotlighted diplomatic spaces. He viewed the Wall peripherally, with or without American soldiers, or simply not at all. Rather than serving as a vanishing point or visual hindrance to the horizon, the Wall is actually difficult to find in many of these photographs.

Among the GI images is one close-up of three American soldiers with rifles hanging over their shoulders taken within "the first days after the Wall was erected," looking across the street toward a phalanx of opposing eastern troops (fig. 1.6). No part of the border wall is clearly visible. Instead, in this image, the soldiers comprise the immediate foreground. One stands in profile holding his weapon and looking away from the photographer, in effect appearing to glance back out and across the frame, over the top of Freed's head. The other two soldiers face the opposing phalanx, their backs and helmets facing the camera. Freed's proximity to these men suggests that he was standing directly behind the soldiers, as if to shield himself from enemy fire or advancement, as he remains extremely close to a front line of division. In this case, there is no obviously significant, imposed distance between Freed and the soldiers. It appears that the photographer is enclosed, just not by the Wall.

Similarly, in another image capturing a soldier eating lunch on the curb

FIGURE 1.5 Leonard Freed, *Berlin*, 1961.
(Estate of Leonard Freed/Magnum Photos)

FIGURE 1.6 Leonard Freed, *West Berlin*, 1961.
(Estate of Leonard Freed/Magnum Photos)

(fig. 1.7), no material components of the border system are present within the frame. Instead, an American soldier in glasses, his combat helmet shifted sideways, sits cross-legged on the curb outside a famous Zimmerstrasse *Apotheke* (pharmacy) as the central focus of the image. Freed stands several feet from the GI, hovering above him while he eats from a tray of fast food, his rifle lying on the ground beside him. Civilians chat above and around the soldier, while the presence of the Wall, less than twenty feet from the curb, is almost entirely left out of the frame. Another soldier, seated by the corner pharmacy, is barely visible. The only evidence of his presence is a black combat boot protruding from a crowd of people standing above and in front of him. Freed photographs in close proximity to the subjects but calibrates a middle distance by locating intermediate figures between them. Here again Freed locates himself in a spatial relationship that triangulates his viewpoint in relation to the American troops and the Berlin Wall. By staging his photograph from an oblique street angle and a short distance from lunching soldiers, he produces an image that reads as if he were in transit, wandering to or through the scene, rather than being a fixture along the Wall. In these images, the Berlin Wall is only a subtext, a border constituted by military might and a flurry of confused visual encounters. Freed offers no singular vision of this moment of the Berlin Crisis but instead indexes uncertainty and the flurry of activity summoned by the construction of a closed border.

Given Freed's oblique views of the early days of the Berlin Wall in which he favored shots of American GIs over direct representations of the new border system, Freed's single exposure of an unnamed black American soldier guarding the Wall (see fig. 1.1), in which both the man and the Wall comprise the main focus, stands out as distinct. Though Freed included this photograph as the opening image in *Black in White America*—and not in *Made in Germany*, despite the fact that it was made in Berlin—the origins of this singular image and Freed's own conceptualization of it connect the photograph with his other Berlin Wall images. As noted, not only does this front-facing image of an American GI and the Wall he protects differ greatly from his other photographs made in the early days of the Berlin Wall; no other image in *Black in White America* seems to so deliberately refuse the potential for the photographer to "move closer," setting up the central imperative of the photobook.

When thinking from Freed's single shot, one can sense how proximity and distance, intimacy and anonymity, play out with Freed's early depictions of the Wall. Given the middle distance established within the image, Freed reinforces the space separating him from his subjects and weighs the legacy of segregation more broadly. Though formality in portraiture can suggest co-

FIGURE 1.7 Leonard Freed, *West Berlin*, 1961.
(Estate of Leonard Freed/Magnum Photos)

operation between a subject and a photographer, here it is evidence of their strained relation and invites speculation on the curious stance of the soldier in this image. The parallel trolley tracks assume both photographer and subject are standing in a shared urban environment, though the soldier's motion toward the gun on his hip portends the possibility of friction. Freed's central framing of the soldier at a middle distance also pushes his viewers to think about what other social buffers he intends us to envision in this image. The two men are depicted as isolated from one another, though they stand in for a broader shared mapping of segregated social relations. Whether Freed invites viewers to focus on the space between the soldier and the Wall behind him or between the soldier and his distracted comrades, the converging perspectives lend this image a sense of multiple associative disconnects, underwritten by the geopolitical weight of the exchange. The downward gaze of the soldier and his hand positioned by his holster also suggest a deliberate distancing from Freed or at least emphasize the tense nature of the encounter. The prospect of mutual recognition in the American sector of West Berlin also suggests other borders beyond the Wall.

———

After Freed's initial encounters at the Berlin Wall in 1961, he returned to his home in Amsterdam. He told his wife about the single shot at the Berlin Wall and that he wanted to return to America to begin a project on race. This would differ from his work in Europe in exile, tracing the lives of Jewish communities after the Holocaust. Instead, he would step into the role of prodigal white American photographer exploring segregation and his own place within society. In the meantime, Freed continued his work on the German Jews book until after their daughter, Elke Susannah, was born, and they made arrangements to return to the United States. In June 1963, the Freeds took their darkroom enlarger and trays from their Amsterdam flat and packed them into the couple's tiny Fiat 600. They sailed with their car on the Holland America line from Rotterdam to New York. The Freeds stayed in Leonard's childhood home while his parents took Susannah to their cabin in the Catskills for the summer. After the July 4 holiday, Freed got to work. He created an itinerary on ruled notebook paper, detailing dozens of potential photo shoots, with addresses and phone contacts when available.[34] This project, which would eventually become *Black in White America*, thereby began as a series of scheduled photo shoots, portrait sessions, and explorations of his hometown and beyond.

Black in White America emerged from these shoots and other "stories" made during Freed's extended trip throughout the South from 1964 to

1965. The book-length photo-essay captured the persistence of racial division in America in the decade following the 1954 U.S. Supreme Court mandate to end school segregation and through the landmark civil rights legislation of the mid-1960s. Brett Abbott places the photobook at the start of a mid-twentieth-century photographic practice of "engaged" observation, in which Freed's "approach to photojournalism was aimed not so much at telling the details of a particular day or week, but at relating the contours of a bigger, more conceptual narrative about America."[35] Freed's image of one of the many black American GIs at the Berlin Wall is emblematic of a central contradiction of Cold War American culture: a soldier guarding the U.S.-Soviet Cold War front line abroad would, at the same moment, be denied full citizenship rights back home. Through his work on this project—beginning days after the initial construction of the Wall and extending through years of major civil rights protests—Freed captured and attempted to encroach on America's racial buffers, all the while mapping the color line and documenting other boundaries from his mobile perspective.

As a white Jewish photographer in the United States, he could not claim status or embody the role as a detached observer, so instead he considered how he might engage these scenes through close observation. Freed stated later, "[At] the time [white] Americans didn't really look at Black people. What I was trying to do was to show the faces and see the differences between them—look at what the Blacks really *look* like."[36] Freed tried to avoid visually overpowering his subjects, that is to say, to simply look over their shoulders and deny their perspective. He did feel the need to approach people, to document moments of mutual encounter. He did so not always simply to show what his subjects looked like but also to offer an affirmation or acknowledgment of their vision. No matter if they, or he, were in the way of a clear shot. Following his germinal opening image, he aimed to capture moments that lay bare the visible traces of legacies of division while approaching relational proximity.

The question of distancing, essential to Freed's work in photographing the foreign and familiar of Germany and as a white Jewish photographer in the United States, is also important to his subsequent American project on segregation. Freed's individual sense of perspective in many of these images allowed him to approach the fields of vision and the immediate physical space of his subjects (regardless of their perceived race) and around cultural landmarks, as he measured the buffers of a divided-color-line society. In the American images, he was more apt to mark his outsider status than to feign immersion. He achieved middle distance, for example, by facing his subjects while also mitigating access through indirect eye contact, locating objects or other figures between them, or including blurred figures on the periphery of his frame. The interplay between acknowledgment and dissociation underscores the racial divides in Freed's work during the years he produced images of segregation.

The photographs that would culminate in *Black in White America* locate and then invert the terms of a segregated society by shifting the focus of each image between the subject and the encroaching photographer. America is mapped here as a divided nation, not merely by North and South, but along many axes on both sides of the Mason-Dixon Line. Freed enters spaces that are rife with hostility (prisons, gatherings of unemployed men at train tracks), solemn (funerals, polls where some black citizens are voting for the first time), and quotidian (laundromats, school lectures, football games, children's summer camps) to emphasize that segregation is upheld through both violent and quietly policed buffers across all of these locales.

In two exemplary photo shoots from the project, Freed's vision of the civil rights movement emerges as he calibrates his proximity. The first involves Freed's images from the 1963 March on Washington for Jobs and Freedom. On August 28 of that year, organizers convened a sweeping multiracial coalition of over 200,000 attendees to the nation's capital to march for jobs and freedom. Freed and his wife, Brigitte, spent three days in total traveling to and from Washington. They stayed in a campsite outside the city the night before and arrived at the march at twilight. Freed took his first photographs of the day blocks away from the festivities, outside Ford's Theatre, the place where President Abraham Lincoln was assassinated in 1865. By linking this site to the culmination of the march at the Lincoln Memorial, Freed bridges the distance between the Civil War and the civil rights movement and highlights the function of deep national memory and trauma as well as the vision of democratic progress championed by the march.

Viewers can trace Freed's movements through his photographs that day, as he approached the National Mall from the federal buildings beyond Fourteenth Street and the flags around the Washington Monument. He walked around the reflecting pool, under the trees, and through the tightly drawn crowd. Whether due to the connective, crowded nature of the day, Freed's photographic approach, or both, many of his images mark a middle distance with little separation between photographer and subject. The moments where he did accomplish variable distances thus stand out, each with the monument composing the deep background's vanishing point: in one image from the early morning setup of the day, Freed looks out from the Lincoln Memorial (fig. 1.8). In the immediate foreground is a black National Park Service ranger, whose crossed arms reveal a gun holster. He faces out over the empty seats in front of the memorial, with the Washington Monument in the distance. Though there is no eye contact here, Freed stands with his subject in a shared, preemptive moment of visualization. He revisits the terms of his Berlin Wall single-shot portrait, pursuing a representation of black authority and shared space in the scene.

Perhaps more instructive of the day's historical identity is one of his portraits from the aftermath of the event. Here Freed uses the Washington Monument again as an anchor (fig. 1.9). As the day closes and the crowd disperses, he stands behind and above a man who is sitting alone at the base of the Lincoln Memorial steps, looking outward. Debris from the march is littered around him. Freed finds the figure in a moment of stillness after the march, sitting on a low marble step padded with a folded newspaper, his gaze directed toward the monument. The contrast between the unobscured view of the monument on the immediate horizon and the man photographed from the back allows the viewer a moment of reflection informed by the subject's point of view.[37]

As a postscript to his march images, more than a year later, Freed photographed its keynote speaker, Dr. King, in a congratulatory Baltimore motorcade on October 31, 1964, after King was awarded the Nobel Peace Prize. Freed had just returned from Europe, having come back to America to follow up on his work from the year before. After a summer in Deauville, France, with his family, Freed first stopped in Baltimore on a solo driving tour of the South. King, too, had just returned from Europe, where he visited Cold War Berlin.[38] His reception there—at once as a venerated visitor and a border-crossing representative of America—was paralleled in King's first celebration in America as a Nobel laureate. Freed devoted a full day to photographing King in Baltimore, including at a parade honoring him and a speech at a local synagogue.

Freed's photograph of King at the Baltimore motorcade is among the most notable images in *Black in White America* and has become prominent in itself as a portrait of King (fig. 1.10).[39] Although King is the central figure of this photograph, Freed captures many of the faces in the crowd around him. Freed's perspective conjures his approach to the march the year before, rendering the variable distances and relationships that frame the scene. When we consider where Freed was probably standing to make this picture, we might conclude that the photographer was so close he could have reached out to touch the car in which King was riding. (Freed very rarely used tele-

FIGURE 1.8 Leonard Freed, *Washington, D.C.*, 1963.
(Estate of Leonard Freed/Magnum Photos)

FIGURE 1.9 Leonard Freed, *Washington, D.C.*, 1963.
(Estate of Leonard Freed/Magnum Photos)

FIGURE 1.10 Leonard Freed, *Baltimore*, 1964.
(Estate of Leonard Freed/Magnum Photos)

photo lenses, and his other images from this day attest to the fact that he was in close proximity using his preferred 50mm lens.) Such a positioning could bring Freed "closer" to King (either physically or perceived) and allow the photographer to mitigate any notions of separation. Yet the blurred profile of a face at the far right edge of the frame suggests that Freed's position in the crowd may have been farther away than it first appears. Whether the shadowy figure on the right is standing next to Freed or simply moving into his frame is indeterminable. The effect, however, demonstrates that Freed's perspective either approximates or accounts intimately for this figure's perspective and proximity to King. On closer examination, it is feasible that this image registers King in a moment of mutual recognition with the blurred figure (or, peripherally, with Freed). If *Black in White America* was conceived as a project that set out to map American spaces of spatial division and identification, Freed's images here and throughout this body of work push for a balance between marking shared spaces of recognition and valuing African American figures' distinct fields of visions.

In the images that would later comprise *Made in Germany* (1970), made mostly in 1961–65 and concurrent with the production of *Black in White America*, Freed again favors photographing social settings. This was a way to encompass a sense of the public at large. Here, in contrast to his German Jewish and American civil rights images, respectively, he immersed himself in crowds and built spaces. These photographs show Freed attempting to come to terms with Germany and its history, face-to-face and encounter-by-encounter, but also drawing the photographer's own critical distance. He negotiates his stance by meeting people at public squares, parks, nudist colonies, schools, and industrial worksites, all of which seem to demonstrate Freed's ability to wander around freely and look at Germans. In the vein of one of Freed's photographic influences, German photographer August Sander, he set out to photograph a broad swath of Germans in their occupational or leisure contexts.[40] But as he draws attention to the many "types" in Germany, as Sander did, he also focuses on buildings that still display traces of poorly erased Nazi iconography or Holocaust memorials that go unnoticed. In each case he challenges himself and others to measure the benefits of reconciliation against the traumas of the past by negotiating the space between the particular and the collective.

Most of Freed's photographs of "Germany," presented here as a unified formulation, not as East or West, were taken in the western half. Though the Cold War had divided the country when Freed started this work, his sense of the oneness of Germany serves his greater interest in the continuities across Germany's history through numerous moments of national unification and division. Freed tries to seek out the ghosts and traces of World War II in order to grapple with Germany's dual processes of attempted rebuilding and reconciliation. In this set of images he does this in one prominent way by indexing his encounters with Germans who struggle with how to memorialize their own pasts. In his own pursuit of sites of Jewish mourning, Freed captures individuals who are attempting to handle the memory of the past, which is routed through the powerful effect of World War II on the entire nation along with the recent memory of the Holocaust. He meets Germans at moments of grieving, reckoning, and political reinvention and, in doing so, strikes a balance between suspicion and empathy. His photographic perspective gives him a self-conscious form of mutuality.

Freed's images cover multiple cities, vantage points, and landscapes of Germany. Eight images would later comprise a central subsection of *Made in Germany* devoted to the Berlin Wall—a symmetry in the book that alludes to the idea of a divided city at the heart of a bifurcated nation. The images mix the heightened tensions of August 1961 and the new normal in the following four years, as each side adjusted to life along the Wall. When Freed returned after the Berlin Crisis, he adjusted his scope to account for the evolving landscape. The section is bookended by two of his American GI images, although the image of his single shot, depicting the unnamed black American soldier at the nascent Wall, remains absent from this portfolio of images. Other images include a view of East German troops patrolling the border zone with German shepherds, children playing along the Wall with rubble from it nearby, and a memorial set up to honor Heinz Schöneberger, a border crosser who was killed near the Heinrich-Heine-Strasse crossing. One image, taken from atop an observation deck built after the Berlin Crisis subsided, shows a trio of figures descending the stairs and a long boulevard with trolley tracks trailing outward past the vanishing point. The angle here suggests Freed's ability to look over the Wall, and yet such a vantage is refused in favor of looking back at the western zone's shuttered spaces close to the border. An interpretive placard below reminds viewers of scenes along Bernauer Strasse, a street with houses that fell in both the western and the eastern sides of the city and thus was the site of numerous perilous escapes out of houses in the first days of the Wall. The middle distance here is accomplished with the placard, a reminder not just of the divided space but also of the passage of time, before and after the Wall, marked throughout the book.

Beyond the Wall and the divided city of Berlin, Freed's approaches to memory push the sense of division to other German sites in which layers of space and time continue to usher the past into the present. In one photograph (fig. 1.11), positioned at a dining room table, Freed sits across from a German antiwar activist in the Ruhr Valley. The table is covered with empty dishes, two half-empty cups of coffee, and crumpled napkins. The prongs of an angled fork point toward two propped-up photographs, each a formal portrait of a soldier. The men in the photographs appear to come from different eras, one from an earlier German or Prussian epoch and the other from a more recent time. A man in horn-rimmed glasses and a dark sweater is shown in a soft focus at the opposite end of the short table and looks down and to his side. The messy table is presented in contrast to the formal codes of the studio portraits that furnish the scene. Freed's direct view of the man and the photographs hints at complicity in this portrait; the lack of eye contact between the men also suggests strain. Like the image of the soldier by the Wall, Freed faces a subject while marking evidence of tension between them. The partially consumed cup of coffee directly in front of Freed's vantage suggests this encounter is still unfolding or paused for a moment. His subject faces obliquely toward Freed and away from his family photographs, which are propped up on the table and thus still appear to be the provenance of the man. The imperative to mourn victims of war becomes a matter of casual importance and is powerfully connected to the present. Nonetheless, the need to contend with the memory of Germany's fallen soldiers, for Freed and for his subjects, remains a complicated task.

In another photograph, Freed stands behind a short, stone wall, looking out on the road below, as an older man and woman walk from a parked car and up toward a cemetery (fig. 1.12). They wear long, dark overcoats and hats, and the woman tucks a bouquet of flowers under her left arm. Freed clearly is situated inside the cemetery walls as the two mourners approach. The stone wall separates the couple from Freed, as does a single leaning gravestone. The grave has an oval marker, bolted into the stone, with the name and an engraved photograph of a dead soldier. The same shape of the grave marker is also seen on the parked car, a plaque or oval sticker with a D (for Deutschland) on the back. Freed's perspective is not only slanted but also appears to be surreptitious. He does not face the mourners or the gravestone head-on but, instead, captures both in the same frame and thus forges several suggestive affiliations in the process—among the mourners, the dead soldier's gravestone, and the photographer connected in this scene of mourning. Freed stands behind a boundary wall, as if to cautiously stake his claim to ob-

FIGURE 1.11 Leonard Freed, *Ruhrgebiet-Frankfur*, 1965.
(Estate of Leonard Freed/Magnum Photos)

FIGURE 1.12 Leonard Freed, *Tegernsee*, 1965.
(Estate of Leonard Freed/Magnum Photos)

serve the scene.⁴¹ Unlike in his photograph of the Jewish cemetery, where it is unclear whether he sets foot in the space of the graveyard, Freed captures these mourners before they enter and uses the wall to separate himself from his subjects. Freed calibrates a middle distance to balance his sense of empathy and scrutiny. The process of moving onward from the horrors of the war for Freed, as an American and a Jew, takes place in a historical site parallel to Germany. Rather than treating this merely as a private matter, Freed makes public the rites of mourning to highlight the dilemmas of grief—his own and those of Germans in these postwar years—and the process of moving forward into a new era of democratic argument in a divided Germany.

As noted, the eventual *Made in Germany* book resembles *Black in White America* in many respects. This similarity is attributed to the fact that Freed and his wife laid out both books one after the other and had them printed by the same printing house in Holland.⁴² They also share an American publisher, Richard Grossman. But deeper and more conceptually, they read like twin photographic records of Freed's travels, with photographs used as visual maps and captions offering personalized directions. The photographs and their treatments resemble one another not only in his use of perspective but also in the way he plays with distance and proximity to his subjects. In many of them we can find the photographer at the margins of his own images, locating himself in relation to the people he photographs. Across these two nationally framed projects, Freed's photographic landscapes intersect in Berlin by the Wall. The two books, *Black in White America* and *Made in Germany*, rely on physical, architectural walls to exemplify deeply ingrained social boundaries that are also simultaneously sites of traversal and distinction.

The work of identification in *Black in White America* involves shrinking the space between a white Jewish photographer and his black subjects in varying social contexts; in *Made in Germany*, alienation is paced by an attempt to acknowledge and approach but also remain steadfast in memory. Such approaches allow Freed to move at the same time toward several goals that seem incompatible: encroach on the social buffers imposed by the legacy of racial segregation and wartime destruction; acknowledge the ongoing existence of racial strife and indifference in need of redress; seek connection with African Americans and Germans; and all the while mark the profound wounds of his people and his own nation.

The image of the unnamed black American soldier at the Berlin Wall, in effect, frames Freed's project as conditioned on a recognition of racial distances and social boundaries in Berlin. By making that frontal portrait, set at a middle distance with the Wall in the background, Freed ends up squarely facing the concrete structure at a cautious middle distance—a distance that through the rest of *Black in White America* he attempts to redress. In *Made in Germany*, he begins closer to his subjects but obscures direct views of the Wall amidst his other questions and explorations of the postwar German landscape. The relative visibility of walls and boundaries in this body of images helps Freed calibrate the social distances between him and his subjects, remapping the border and other dividing lines in the process.

————

In the years between the composition of his photographs and the production of *Black in White America*, the United States experienced a tumultuous backend pendulum swing of social change. Protest movements helped to achieve serious legislative gains in the form of 1964's Civil Rights Act and 1965's Voting Rights Act. But in 1968, the year of the book's publication, Freed's vision of a divided nation was echoed in the government-sponsored *Report* of the Kerner Commission, which famously stated that America was "moving toward two societies, one black, one white—separate and unequal."[43] Dr. Martin Luther King Jr., who was at the height of his popularity and influence after the March on Washington and being awarded the Nobel Prize, had become marginalized for his outspoken opposition to the Vietnam War and his work on behalf of unions and the poor. King was assassinated in Memphis on April 4, 1968, while campaigning for striking sanitation workers. The same sort of social unrest caused by systemic repression and brutality that the Kerner Commission investigated reescalated and exploded in more than 100 American cities after King's assassination. The slow drag of integration persisted. With military escalation in Vietnam, the assassination of Robert F. Kennedy, and new waves of social unrest, the efforts to fight the civil rights–era divisions in American society would be overshadowed by an added set of challenges. In West Germany, the welcome exchanges of "America's Berlin," faltered through increased protest aimed at confronting U.S. militarism.[44] These protests were fueled by transatlantic alliances among student activists. In American public spaces, examples of persistent segregation and reluctant integration were common fodder for court cases and protests.

During these same years, Freed found an elevated place for himself in international photography circles. His inclusion in *The Concerned Photographer*, a traveling exhibition that opened in 1967 at New York City's Riverside Museum, put his work in shared context with established photography greats such as Robert Capa and André Kertész. Freed continued to travel through Europe, Israel, and Japan over the following years, affirming his global reach

We, he and I, two Americans. We meet silently and part silently. Between us, impregnable and so deadly as the wall behind him, is another wall. It is there on the trolley tracks. It crawls along the cobble stones, across frontiers and oceans, reaching back home, back into our lives and deep into our hearts, dividing us, wherever we meet. I am White and he is Black.

Berlin, Germany

In defense of Western Civilization, an American soldier's hand rests on his gun.

6

FIGURE 1.13   Page spread, Leonard Freed, *Black in White America*, 1967/68.
(Grossman/Estate of Leonard Freed)

toward the end of the decade, as he prepared to move away from Europe with his family and back to New York City. He published magazine pieces and produced a television program for Dutch TV from his American images of race relations, all of which fueled his official entry into the prestigious photo agency Magnum.

By the time *Black in White America* was published, it was to some extent a testament that emerged a few years after its intended historical era. In other ways, it presented America's racial condition as still urgent and persistent. Absent an introduction or artist's statement, the book's epigraph carries the burden of offering an insight into what is at stake in the ongoing project of racial equality and justice. It quotes President Abraham Lincoln from an unnamed political debate: "Volumes have been written in defense of slavery, but I have never heard of any of these authors wanting to be slaves themselves."

The opening image of *Black in White America*, depicting the black American soldier by the Berlin Wall, picks up on this theme and serves its overall framing (fig. 1.13). Not only does Freed highlight the gap between language and visual experience in these opening gestures (perhaps this is also why only a handful of the images are captioned), but he suggests that acts of acknowledgment and identification carry a potential to reckon with legacies of division.[45] The layout includes several key images printed in two-page spreads with two-inch white borders reserved for captions. These include the opening Berlin Wall image and the Baltimore portrait of Dr. King. Other images are printed in close juxtaposition on pages in which groupings convey particular messages of tension or coalition, in turn aggregating Freed's visions and conveying his mapping strategies. In the final pages Freed includes an excerpt of King's speech from the March on Washington. This citation was planned before King's death, but in the printed book it appears elegiac. Freed was in Israel when King was assassinated. His brother wrote him a letter the following day telling him about the public outcry and rage in Brooklyn: "If I were a young black, I'd be with them—bitter as hell. The whites may have lost more in King than the blacks."[46] Just as King's speech and Freed's images of the march drew on the symbolic power of the Lincoln Memorial and the National Mall, Freed's placement of King's words on the concluding pages of this important photographic collection imbues a sense of melancholy within his urgent political treatment of America's racial struggles.

In April 1969 the *New York Times Book Review* published a review of *Black in White America* alongside a write-up of Eldridge Cleaver's *Post-Prison Writings*. In the review Mel Watkins imagines Freed's photographic perspective as connected to his geographic mobility. Under the headline "Diversity of His Experience" and next to a sampling of Freed's photographs from the project, Watkins writes, "The black man's experience in the United States has been shaped by . . . racial prejudice—he has been a prisoner of his own blackness. . . . [Freed's photobook's] panoramic view begins with the roots of repression in rural, Jim Crow America and moves as the black man himself has moved, to our large urban ghettos. Within its sweep, the grief, joy and rage of black America are abundantly illustrated."[47] The panoramic impulse that Watkins refers to here speaks to Freed's frequent use of blown-up snapshots printed across two-page spreads as well as the geographic and topical sweep of the collection. This review, and others published later in the *New York Times* and the *Chicago Tribune*, posits the collection as an illustration of racial division inscribed into America's built social landscapes and ghettos—and Freed as the traveling photographer who encountered them. These reports also highlight Freed as a border crosser several times over, whose critical contribution to photography was his ability to identify with and literally move closer to his subjects. His own experience and mobility are presented in tension with how he captures, in both image and text, the nagging fixedness of color-line geographies, as black citizens are denied the same freedoms he is afforded. The Berlin Wall pictured in this book, by then a fixture and symbol of a divided Germany, was only weeks old when Freed first photographed it. The photographer's subjects in this formulation are rendered as if timeless, fixed to their depictions, locations, and circumstances.[48]

For *Made in Germany*, Freed's other project from this period, the book title is branded through a capitalized, stencil-styled typeface that was used on the cover. The title thus doubles as a mantra that is echoed in the author/photographer's captioned descriptions throughout. He uses the same formulation in his introduction, in succession and in all capital letters. His repeated uses of the refrain "Made in Germany" are separated through an ongoing series of ellipses. Though the project is obviously marked by the specific historical moment of a postwar, divided Germany, Freed expresses the liminal nature of his photobook in regard to these fractures: "MADE IN GERMANY . . . let us retrogress in time and read. MADE IN WEST GERMANY . . . or still further in time and read, MADE IN THE AMERICAN OCCUPIED ZONE OF GERMANY." This sentiment is also echoed when he brings up the Berlin Wall for the first time: "MADE IN GERMANY means . . . know your history and geography. . . . Berlin, controlled by four occupying powers, has its 'Berlin Wall' running through and around it . . . stamped MADE IN GERMANY."[49]

The reviews of *Made in Germany* again reference Freed as a traveler. But the tone of his work is seen as more suspect of his subjects than their contexts. In an article titled "Pictures You Won't See in a Travel Folder," the *New York Times* writer Gene Thornton praises Freed for his mastery of the photo-text but emphasizes the discomfort and quiet menace captured there. "Instead of picturesque castles and smiling peasant girls, Freed gives us grinning mobs, somber landscapes, traffic jams, clean cut kids wearing iron crosses or throwing rocks in the streets." Thornton reads a warning in Freed's photographs and captions: "You will get the impression that they [the Germans] are all somehow peculiar to the Vriendly Volks from across the Rhine who gave us You Know Who, and You Better Watch Out, Or They'll Try it Again."[50] Although Freed cautions in his text, "what will be of Germany in twenty-five years," his images do not simply reflect a distrust of or attribute inherent danger to Germans. Freed wants to understand the profound changes of the nation and its people, set against the backdrop of Cold War division and postwar rebuilding. Freed's subjects are depicted as dynamically attached to history through the land, whichever side of the Wall they may live on. Freed roves as he meets Germans in their personal spaces, at their sites of mourning and community building, and attempts to reconcile his own struggles of religious and national identity. Again, his mobility, in contrast with the newly built Berlin Wall, which prohibits free movement across the border, creates a context for Freed to grapple with post–Holocaust Germany, his place as an American within it, and, in turn, his recognition of division back home.

Freed continued in a career of constant movement, in and out of America. Berlin was one of his most visited sites of return. Visibly displaying the scars of postwar Germany, the city of Berlin occupies a special place in Freed's work. He continued photographing the Berlin Wall from its early years through its years as a staunch border. In 1976 he lived in a flat in the artist co-op Künstler-haus Bethanien, with a window that overlooked the Wall, as he photographed for a book on Berlin published by *Time-Life*. In 1984 he immersed himself in a Turkish community in Kreuzberg for a photo-essay, including photo shoots at the border and others embedded in the neighborhood and family culture. Beyond the Cold War, the Berlin Wall symbolized for Freed the many lega-cies of division and conflict running across the different epochs of modern Germany. The Wall also continued to help Freed visualize the social barriers that defined American society.

His enduring, complex views about American culture and the Berlin Wall may be most clearly evoked in a noteworthy set of textual reflections that ap-pear near the end of *Made in Germany*. Freed's critical distancing in his books included moments when he recognized that photographs alone could not convey what he experienced. As he recalled in another caption in the book, "When the photographs do not show what [the photographer] has seen, it is not the reality but the inadequacy of the photographer and his tools to blame."[51] Freed noted that more context could be indexed beyond the frame of any produced visual encounter.

To extend this, Freed recounts a series of "traumas" (also used as the title of this section) that he experienced during his time in Germany. There are no images in this section and no titles beyond a numbered order, and none of the anecdotes in the text explicitly corresponds to photographs found elsewhere in the book. Freed did not include any photographs of concentration camps, as he had in *Deutsche Juden heute*, but instead reserves space at the back of the book for the written traumas, including two about visits to the former death camps that were later reopened as commemorative sites of memory. As the final "trauma" of this section, Freed shares a story about picking up a German student hitchhiker en route to the town of Lübeck. Freed explains that this young man "had tried" a career in the army but now wished to be a school director. Here he goes on to recall their conversation: "Then he spoke of the Wall in Berlin. [He said] the problem was the Americans; they weren't hard enough, not ready to fight." After noting that the West Germans were weak, too, and lacking national pride, Freed relays, "He began speaking boldly . . .

'one can't talk too much because here in Germany, it's such a hot topic, but other countries also wanted to get rid of their Jews. . . . Only Germany had the courage to do so.'"[52] In concluding this "trauma," Freed states, "He left and I thought . . . keep faith, one must not abandon those Germans still fighting to uphold democratic ideals. . . . German democracy is still too fragile to survive without outside support."[53]

This exchange is significant, in light of Freed's overlapping photographic projects. Across each, democracy is an ideal rendered as fragile and paradoxical, operating both as a promise and a pitfall of Cold War American culture. He shares this anecdote to suggest that the Wall is a structure symbolic of democracy's fragility in a post-Holocaust world, just as he explores it elsewhere as a place of American contradiction. Freed's images produced in Germany and its divided landscape and people are poignant reminders of the urgency of the fight for such ideals in Europe. Freed's image of a black soldier guarding a weeks-old Berlin Wall attests to a failure of American democracy to live up to its own ideals back home.

CHAPTER 2

WALLS TURNED SIDEWAYS ARE BRIDGES

Angela Davis, Cold War Berliners, and Imprisoned Freedom Struggles

In East Germany, the African American struggle for civil rights
elicited an interest at least as strong as in the Federal Republic.
The major difference to West Germany, however, was that the
East German solidarity movement was engineered and enforced
by the government. Ever since the regime's beginning, the fight
against racism was deeply ingrained in East German ideology.

—MARIA HÖHN AND MARTIN KLIMKE

By 1965 the violent border clashes and tense diplomatic relations of the first
years of the Berlin Wall had begun tempering into a sanctioned coexistence
between East and West. That summer, Angela Davis, a young African American graduate student from Birmingham, Alabama, boarded a boat, en route
to West Germany.

In the years following the Berlin Crisis, the two Germanys had negotiated
some limited, temporary border crossings, and the two sides were moving
toward steadier, if not stabilized, relations. Following the 1962 tragic shooting
death of East German Peter Fechter, whose attempt to escape was captured
by cameras and circulated in the Western press with painful and gruesome
detail, reports of instances of violent skirmishes along the border diminished.
Frederick Taylor writes, "The tunneling continued, but outside in the wider
world things were changing. The crisis atmosphere that followed the building
of the Wall slowly gave way to a kind of sullen acceptance."[1] The geopolitical
reality in Berlin moved from crisis within a divided city to a sustained, cautious, parallel existence. In 1963 authorities agreed to permit West Berliners
to visit their relatives in the East for the Christmas and New Year's holidays.
The policy of *Ostpolitik*, championed by Willy Brandt, the mayor of West

Berlin and eventual chancellor of the Federal Republic, would emerge out of diplomatic negotiations in which the two German regimes adjusted and began to openly acknowledge the endurance of the Berlin Wall.

Davis's journey to pursue a doctoral degree in philosophy at the Johann Wolfgang Goethe University in Frankfurt occurred in the midst of an emerging détente between East and West Germany. It also coincided with a critical student-led grassroots activism addressing other political fault lines in West Germany, notably stirred by a backlash to Western militarism in the era of the Vietnam War. Davis also departed for Europe during the formative years of the Black Power movement, within days of one of its watershed moments, the Watts Rebellion of 1965. Davis, who would later become one of the most recognizable and influential intellectual figures of her generation, was twenty-one years old at the time and on a pathway to advanced academic training, thousands of miles from the surging Black Power movement.

Davis was born in 1944 and was raised in the Birmingham neighborhood ignominiously deemed "Dynamite Hill" for the waves of bombings targeting black family homes, among other violent actions carried out by white supremacist vigilantes. Davis's parents were teachers and members of the NAACP, and her mother had worked on the campaign to free the Scottsboro Boys in the 1930s. Davis left Birmingham as a teenager to attend Elizabeth Irwin High School in New York City and, later, Brandeis University in Massachusetts, where she majored in French and worked with her mentor German American philosopher and professor Herbert Marcuse. During her junior year she studied abroad in Paris, where she experienced global manifestations of racism during the Algerian fight for independence.[2] On her way back to Brandeis, she stopped in Frankfurt to attend lectures by the German Jewish intellectual Theodor Adorno. Her German language skills were limited at the time, but she was aided by English and French translations. Her studies in Frankfurt thus allowed Davis to gain a significant foothold into the world of German philosophy and critical theory. During her final year at Brandeis she was awarded a German State Scholarship to return to Frankfurt for graduate school. After graduating, she embarked for West Germany.

Davis went on to study philosophy at the Goethe University in Frankfurt, one of the most highly regarded departments of its time, recognized as a global center of critical engagement. She studied with illustrious professors of the Frankfurt School—including Adorno, Jürgen Habermas, and Oskar Negt, who sought to leverage critical theory as a response to European and global politics in the years of rebuilding after the world's war.

Despite Davis's distance from home, Germany proved to be a site of awakening for her evolving social consciousness. In West Germany, Davis's education transcended school lectures and discussions. Her classmates included participants in the student movement whose reactions to repressive U.S. Cold War geopolitical policies and the shadows of Nazi fascism informed Davis's trajectories in academia and activism. In Frankfurt, she lived on Adalbertstrasse with a group of fellow students, several of whom were involved in the Sozialistischer Deutscher Studentbund (Socialist German Student Union, or sds). With this group she protested the escalating U.S. military aggression in Vietnam and the West German government's complicity in global Cold War conflicts.[3] As U.S. Army bases in West Germany served as gateways of deployment for soldiers traveling to fight in Vietnam, German universities erupted as flashpoints of protest over the war. They directed their activism toward confronting the legacy of fascism and practices of repressive governance in West Germany. These student activists drew inspiration from the civil rights, Black Power, and Free Speech movements in the United States, as well as the international struggles for decolonization. Davis studied and organized alongside fellow international students, including at least one black American former GI from Indiana and several who hailed from Haiti and South Africa.[4] While Davis was in West Germany, her graduate education in revolutionary philosophical theory fueled a critical praxis, linking her intellectual pursuits with her activism. At the same time, she was constantly reminded of her distance from black freedom struggles back home.

Davis's intellectual life and activist engagements in West Germany crystallized during one short trip to Cold War Berlin during her first spring semester of graduate school. She traveled to Cold War Berlin in the spring of 1966, with other students from her scholarship program, for a conference held by the German Academic Exchange Service, otherwise known as the DAAD.[5] By design, her school group visited West Berlin for a conference supported by a state-operated program of exchange; by choice, Davis largely separated from her group, crossing the city's border to visit East Berlin during the city's May Day festivities nourished by this alternate circuit of diplomacy. She passed crowds of Western tourists at the observation decks near the Wall at Checkpoint Charlie, leaving them behind to be able to experience a bit of her hometown of Birmingham in East Berlin. There, Davis visited her parents' friends Esther and James E. Jackson, prominent African American activists, and Robert Lumer, the stepbrother of her childhood friends Margaret and Claudia Burnham. The Jacksons, who had founded the Southern Negro Youth Congress and published *Freedomways*, a journal of African American leftist theory and culture, were in East Berlin to commemorate May Day, the

annual workers' holiday.[6] Lumer studied at the Brecht Theater and lived with members of the Cuban National Ballet.[7] While on the communist east side of the city, Davis bought Dietz Verlag printings of books by Marx and Engels and watched the May Day parade. She would later recall spending as much of her free time as she could in East Berlin on this visit.[8]

Following her trip, Davis stayed in West Germany for another year, through the spring of 1967. She left to finish her graduate work in California, citing her desire to return to the front lines of the movement in the United States and to study with her Brandeis mentor Marcuse, who had relocated to the University of California at San Diego. Soon after returning to the United States, Davis was catapulted into national headlines by her intertwined academic work and activism. Her public travails included a high-profile removal from her position as a philosophy lecturer at the University of California, Los Angeles (UCLA), in 1969–70 because of her membership in the Communist Party. Later, she spent three months on the FBI's Top Ten Most Wanted list as a fugitive, stemming from a contrived charge of aiding the kidnapping and murder of a judge in California in 1970. After she was arrested, she was detained for eighteen months in New York and California prisons, during which a widespread international solidarity movement emerged across dozens of countries, including West and East Germany, heeding the call to "Free Angela and all political prisoners." She was eventually acquitted after a widely publicized trial in 1972 in which Davis faced the death penalty.

During the trial, as sensationalizing details of her life story swirled through the national and international media reports, Davis and her legal defense committee circulated their own biographical documents and pamphlets, to support their grassroots efforts for a fair trial. They also advanced their defense of Davis by mounting campaigns for other political prisoners. The documents presented by her defense team routinely mentioned her time as a graduate student in West Germany, which directly preceded her return to the United States. They presented these details of her specialized training in academia, in part, to accentuate the international reach of her activism. Given her academic and personal connections to West Germany, solidarity campaigns for Davis also sprouted up across the country, including in Frankfurt and West Berlin. As a member of the Communist Party, she also shared a special relationship with the people and government of East Germany; before and during her trial German Democratic Republic (GDR) officials mounted sweeping solidarity campaigns in her defense, expressed in both state-run and grassroots efforts. Following the trial and her eventual acquittal, Davis left the United States on an international tour to places that had been integral to her solidarity movement for freedom, including socialist East Berlin.

As she traveled, Davis began writing her own long-form narrative, later published as *Angela Davis: An Autobiography*, which was edited by Toni Morrison and published by Random House in 1974. The book was an attempt to produce a "political autobiography," as Davis notes in the preface, to "emphasize the people, the events and the forces in my life [that] propelled me to my present commitment."[9] Writing in the two years after her acquittal, Davis used the platform to transition from her position as a philosopher writing from prison while facing the death penalty to the role of liberated author and narrative autobiographer who devoted much of her life's work to freedom movements and critical prison activism. Under Morrison's editorial guidance, Davis was compelled to adapt her writing style. As she recalled later, "When I wrote my autobiography I was somebody who was used to writing philosophy, and so I didn't think about writing in the same way. Rather than, like, writing it for me, Toni would say, 'Well, you know, what was that room like, you know, what did it look like? What was in there? What were the colors?' And so she made me understand writing in such a different way."[10]

This move, to focus on her own narrative, allowed Davis to fuse her theoretical writings with the craft of literary production and autobiography. At the time of the autobiography's writing, as one of America's most prominent figures seeking the power of telling her own story, she faced several key challenges: how to present her own personal travails for readers while demonstrating her political commitments; how to represent the barriers she faced in her life as repressive in their own right while simultaneously showing how they served as platforms for solidarity and critical engagement; and how to shape the contours of her own travels for popular readership.

Davis sought this balance by adopting walls as her autobiography's most powerful and pertinent literary symbol. She wrote about walls that divide, walls that call connections into recognition, walls that mark the boundary between freedom and repression, and walls that when toppled lead to new pathways for freedom. The book includes a dedication directed to "those whose humanity is too rare to be destroyed by walls, bars, and death houses"; descriptions of numerous prison walls and other forms of social/physical architecture; and a chapter titled "Walls." The book's closing section, labeled "Bridges," includes this epigraph: "Walls turned sideways are bridges."[11]

Amidst dozens of references to walls in the autobiography, Davis included one brief reference to the Berlin Wall, in a scene that takes place at a point of transition in her book. Davis delivers this anecdote in a section of the narrative in which she pivots from student activism abroad toward her eventual return to the United States. Davis writes,

> Each day, I walked across at Checkpoint Charlie — the border point for people with passports from capitalist countries. Crowds of white tourists from the United States would be standing in line, probably waiting to cross the border to tell people they had seen the other side of the "wall" — so they could say, in Kennedy's war-filled words, "*Ich bin ein Berliner,*" that is, I'm ready to fight communism. The tourists were always complaining about the wait. But I never had any trouble — each time I went across, I would receive the signal to go on only a few moments after I had shown my passport. This was their way of showing their solidarity with Black people.[12]

Davis locates this scene clearly without ever acknowledging the infamous wall by its most common name. Despite her reflections on Cold War Berlin — including explicit references to Checkpoint Charlie, President John Kennedy's 1963 historic visit to West Berlin, and more in later passages on the time she spent in East Berlin — the words "Berlin Wall" are nowhere to be found in the text. Instead it only appears in scare quotes as "'the wall.'" Davis's distancing of herself from other Western travelers, mostly those from America, near the Wall, reminds readers that her time spent in divided Germany was not merely an excursion away from the United States but a personal flight from Western modes of repression. Her lessons abroad were brought to a head through her time in Cold War Berlin. Later in the autobiography, she highlights Berlin two more times. In the first instance, she mentions SDS protests in 1967 around the state visit of the Shah of Iran to West Berlin in June 1967, and in the second, she describes efforts to protest the screening of *Africa Addio*, an Italian documentary that sensationalized the violence of European colonialism in Africa.[13] Her disavowal of the Wall emerges out of a significant strategy of her autobiography: to represent walls as the architecture of a dominant Western society, as well as spaces of grassroots struggle and solidarity.

From the time Davis left Europe, through her trial and acquittal, and among numerous interviews recalling her time there during graduate school, her experiences in West Germany remained an integral part of her personal and political story, told countless times in text and in public speeches; the story of her time in divided Berlin, however, has been told only a handful of times in public. Her autobiography was likely the first published instance in which she publicly shared details from her trip to the divided city of Berlin and the only place on record where she points to the structure others refer to as the Berlin Wall. In doing so she calls out the social boundaries endemic to American culture while maintaining her political affinity to socialist East Germany. Similarly, she draws attention to East Germany's programs of meaningful solidarity with people of color while turning away from their own repressive regime's pervasive border control. In doing so, she shifts a hyperfocus on the infamy of the Berlin Wall, bracketing and turning away from the Wall built by East Germans in Berlin toward addressing other physical and social walls in the United States and the West more broadly.

At first as an admiring visitor to East Berlin in 1966 and later as a celebrated returning public icon after her acquittal (and while writing her autobiography) in 1972, Davis would have also been familiar with the official German Democratic Republic mandate in regard to the Wall: from the eastern perspective, there was no "Berlin Wall," only, officially, an "antifascist protective rampart." In East Germany the word "wall" (*Mauer* in German) was not acceptable for everyday speech and, when possible, the structure was withdrawn from sight. Most citizens of the GDR were rarely able to approach the area of the Wall without official clearance. The regime saw itself as protecting citizens from what it deemed the scourges of capitalism and imperialism, which the East associated with, in part, Germany's Nazi past.[14] Though already aligned with leftist causes, Davis officially joined the Communist Party in 1968. In her autobiography, her reference to "the wall" and not "the Berlin Wall" places her in clear identification with East Berlin's refusal to acknowledge the existence of its own constructed sprawling walled border system for its own citizens. In her autobiography, she uses geopolitical terms such as "West Berlin" and "West Germany" but refers to "Berlin" as the "capital of the German Democratic Republic."[15] In turn, she becomes an American Berliner under selective and defiant terms.

To explore Davis's own evolution as a writer and an activist concerned with dividing walls, first this chapter reviews the representations of East and West Berlin in the mid-1960s and beyond, in the years after the crisis along the border, including visits by prominent Americans on both sides of the divided city. Then the chapter looks at how Davis develops and delivers the wall as a symbol, throughout the course of her writing in multiple projects and culminating in the autobiography. Finally, the chapter looks to both the production and the circulation of her autobiography, to place this reference into a broader framework of Davis's transitional activism and solidarity through circuits of alternative diplomacy. Davis does so by gesturing to but not naming Berlin's barrier, in an effort to maintain her allegiances to the GDR. She transforms the Berlin Wall from a spectacle to be viewed from the West to a symbol of Western repression. By the time she returns to East Berlin after her trial, she eventually treats the Wall as invisible altogether. In doing so, she inverts the expected tale of intrigue, danger, and despair in East Berlin toward her own political projects contesting American division.

To contextualize Davis's involvement in the representations of East and West Berlin beginning in the mid-1960s, one can look to the complex geography of divided Berlin, especially for Americans. Throughout the 1960s, the persistence of American and allied involvement in Berlin aimed to recalibrate diplomatic and military ties throughout all four controlled zones of Berlin. The incorporation of East Berlin into a Western sense of the full city was fueled by the desire by Western allies to maintain a political position of direct access to the Soviet Sector of Berlin, as per the 1945 agreements of the city's occupation. The Wall's construction served at first as provocation toward standoff and then ultimately produced a stalemate to curtail and direct tension to the border. While civilians could approach and peer over the Wall at observation decks from the West, no mirrored practice took place in the

East. As noted, for citizens of the German Democratic Republic, the "Berlin Wall" was forbidden from casual language and, when possible, from sight. Border control was tied to but not limited to the area of the Berlin Wall itself and stood in for a broader system of controlling dissent and difference. As Ladd writes, "Apart from official ceremonies, Easterners were discouraged from approaching the Wall and even taking note of its existence. Those East Berliners who lived in the streets next to the Wall had to adjust to special restrictions, intrusions, and inconveniences. Friends from outside the neighborhood could never just drop by, for example: permission had to be obtained from the police."[16]

Despite the peril in approaching the border from the East, as reflected in official messages related to border policy, many residents from both sides routinely faced interruptions and reminders of the city's other half, whether by billboard-style signage, radio and television signals, or other means of transcending the physical border. In actuality East and West Berlin together formed a whole city under the state of tense separation. As Emily Pugh contends, "East and West Germany relied on one another to define themselves, even when official rhetoric attempted to deny or ignore the other's existence and legitimacy."[17] The peace accomplished by stalemate involved shared acknowledgment and increasing bifurcation.

The circulation of mostly western-based narratives advanced ideas of the East being a connected, though often abject, part of the whole city. For a growing industry of American-authored Cold War cultural productions, a sense of West Berlin's Americanized enclaves and resurgent cultural city life highlighted that half of the city as an oasis of freedom with a massive wall as its defining endpoint. In contrast, East Berlin was cast as the foreign and forbidden urban other, epitomized by its stark wall. East Berlin existed as a space of interwoven fact and projection in American cultural accounts. The 1962 NBC production of *The Tunnel*, for example, featured actual footage of West Berlin students successfully building an underground passageway to smuggle people across the border, subsidized, in part, by funds from NBC.[18] Other fictionalized accounts imagine escaping East Berlin to achieve justice or freedom, resonant far away from divided Germany. In one example, the film *Lilies of the Field* (1963), starring Sidney Poitier as former GI Homer Smith, Poitier's character struggles to find steady work as a builder in the American Southwest when he comes across a group of East German nuns living in isolation, their escape over the Wall central to their bonding with Smith against a backdrop of a discriminatory U.S. culture. (Poitier won an Oscar for his performance, the first awarded to a black actor in a starring role.)[19] Such cultural productions frame East Berlin as a place to escape lest one be stuck "behind" the Berlin Wall.[20] Such accounts spatialize East Berlin as a place of isolation and the German Democratic Republic as a universal site of deprivation and distrust.

What was life more fully like in East Berlin? There are numerous accounts by those who lived in East Germany of the routine struggles and repressive tactics of life in East Berlin, and in the German Democratic Republic more broadly. Programs of border control, state surveillance, and restricted travel extremely impacted daily life.[21] However, if one were to encounter other accounts, western readers might be surprised to see the state-sponsored programs of solidarity and workers' protections, public support for and commemoration of antiracist and anti-imperialist causes, and various accounts of other aspects of everyday culture that had been wrongly identified as mere propaganda.[22] For example, Höhn and Klimke note, "East German leaders saw the oppression of African Americans in the United States as part of an international class struggle.... Thus they actively championed what they considered the 'other America' of black civil rights activists, focusing especially on those who shared their Marxist and socialist convictions or were engaged in international peace activities." The shared plights of African Americans and other diasporic peoples were both reflections of international counter-informational campaigns and the fabric of global networks of solidarity.

As a part of these moments of critical exchange, East German citizens regularly honored and connected with leftist African American writers, artists, and activists who made official state visits. For example, gatherings sponsored by socialist groups such as the German Peace Council (a branch of the World Peace Council) sought to protest U.S. military action in Vietnam, balancing principled critique and opportunities for propaganda.[23] This narrative is occluded from many of the Western cultural productions that fail to imagine crossing into East Berlin for reasons other than espionage, plotting escape, or reporting on stark differences between East and West.[24] Depicting the Wall as a drab and austere structure not only marked this separation but also depicted East Berlin as a metonym for the entire Eastern bloc.

Despite the decreasing frequency of overt escape attempts at the border and growing diplomatic possibilities, spy dramas were the predominant cultural mode of depicting both the Berlin Wall and East Berlin in this period. Divided Berlin was (and still is) an important site for the spy thriller of the Cold War, as the construction of the Wall brought about a cultural fascination with the transgression of the border. Siegfried Mews contends that "it may be argued that the construction and long-lasting, formidable presence

FIGURE 2.2 Robert Knudsen, "KN-C29211. President John F. Kennedy at Checkpoint Charlie along Berlin Wall," June 26, 1963. (Robert Knudsen, White House Photographs, John F. Kennedy Presidential Library and Museum, Boston)

of the Berlin Wall profoundly affected the spy novel: it confronted its authors with a new situation that required a reexamination of its generic properties as well as the underlying aesthetic and ideological presuppositions."[25] In such works, spies alternate between practices of furtive infiltration and daring escape, foreclosing other kinds of diplomatic engagements.

As the television programs and spy dramas were building out cultural maps of East and West Berlin as terrains for understanding citizenship's limits, official state visits signified the dual practices of border dwelling. For example, President John F. Kennedy's 1963 visit to West Berlin was designed to highlight Cold War citizenship, with a visit to the city's observation decks and a roaring speech to tens of thousands in front of West Berlin's City Hall: "Two thousand years ago the proudest boast was 'civis Romanus sum' [I am a Roman citizen]. Today, in the world of freedom, the proudest boast is 'Ich bin ein Berliner!'"[26]

He reinforced this declaration with the refrain "Let them come to Berlin," a rhetorical strategy that highlighted his own presence in Berlin, a front line of the Cold War.[27] Kennedy's famous "Ich bin ein Berliner," repeated in that speech and doubled when echoed by the translator moments after, was a diplomatic identification with the entire divided city, despite being delivered from within the western zone.

From a different perspective, the same year, two months after Kennedy's trip, on August 25, 1963, African American performer and public figure Paul Robeson secretly flew to Schönefeld Airport in East Berlin. The circumstances for Robeson's trip to Berlin were starkly different from Kennedy's. Robeson, the son of a minister who had been born into slavery, became an All-American football star at Rutgers and a world-renowned singer and actor. After years of widespread acclaim and popularity, as well as advocacy for leftist causes including anti-imperialism and anticolonialism, Robeson came under the vicious scrutiny of U.S. government officials during the McCarthy era. A series of publicized comments expressing his affinity for the Soviet Union on matters of racial liberation led to his passport being revoked in 1950. Nonetheless, when he was called to testify in 1956 in front of the House Un-American Activities Committee, Robeson refused to deny his position. This brought him into disrepute with the public, a dramatic fall for a figure who had been declared the nation's most loved performer in the 1940s. Richard Iton writes of Robeson, in the context of Cold War civil rights repression, "The combination of his artistic accomplishments and his political engagements made him exactly the kind of transgressive figure that would trouble, at some fundamental level, the arrangements on which the American modern depended."[28] Robeson was never convicted of any crime, but his passport was not reinstated until the Supreme Court declared in 1958 that such passport revocations were unconstitutional without due process.

Also in 1958, Robeson published an autobiography, *Here I Stand*, to counter his accusers and clarify his public perspective. His book opens with the line "I am a Negro" and then builds a few paragraphs later with the declaration "I am an American."[29] Robeson wrote his autobiography while under prohibition from international travel, but he shared the work during the same year he left America for Europe with no predetermined date of return. Robeson's career initially rebounded through appearances in Asia and Europe. In 1960 he was honored in Cold War Berlin by East Germany, received an honorary degree of doctor of philosophy from Humboldt University, and was awarded the German Peace Medal, the Großer Stern der Völkerfreundschaft (Great Star of Friendship among the Peoples]), bestowed by East German leader Walter Ulbricht.

Robeson's next trip to East Germany, after the Wall's construction, offered less of a public spectacle than a secluded rescue mission. When Robeson had returned to the international stage a few years earlier, lingering health issues and deep anxiety further plagued him. In 1961, after a suspicious turn of events in Moscow following a performance for Africa Freedom Day, members of his family suspected that covert operatives from either the CIA or the Soviet Union poisoned the performer. Robeson was subsequently institutionalized in a mental hospital in London.[30] He then disappeared from public life and was treated with episodic electric shock treatments and heavy sedatives for nearly two years, during which he remained almost entirely catatonic. After prolonged concerns about her husband's safety and distrust of his convalescence, his wife, Eslanda Robeson, furtively coordinated a change of course in his treatments.

At daybreak on a Sunday morning in late August 1963, with the help of a Polish ambassador and at the invitation of the GDR-based German Peace Council, the Robesons flew to East Berlin for alternative health treatment. Dramatic reports of this "escape" from London to East Berlin rippled across the world press. Headlines such as "Robeson Flown to East Berlin: Wife Boasts of 'Cloak and Dagger' Work" and "Departure Kept Secret" suggested an espionage angle to the story. Eslanda issued a three-part explanation in the *Baltimore Afro American* weeks later in which she detailed the circumstances of the couple's relocation to East Berlin, highlighting the circuits of alternative diplomacy that she tapped for the urgent trip. Although she made a case for the furtive nature of the transfer (to avoid a persistent press and give her husband a chance to fully recover with new treatment), the headlines adjoining her stories further sensationalized the accounts: "Why He 'Sneaked' to East Germany" and "'Escape' Reads Like Movie Thriller."[31] Despite the nuances and details of her first-person account, the press's framing of the story continued to sensationalize Robeson's travel to the divided city.

The first weeks of the Robesons' stay in East Berlin were spent out of the public eye. Paul was treated by doctors at the Buch Clinic and issued a call to be "left in peace." He was taken off the sedatives and, within weeks of his arrival in East Berlin in 1963, was able to receive visitors. He spent Thanksgiving with fellow African American expatriates in East Berlin—jazz singer Audrey Pankey and cartoonist Oliver "Ollie" Harrington. Robeson remained mostly secluded but did pose for several eastern photographers while entertaining in his home or out in the streets. Eslanda also represented her husband in public, including in at least one photograph taken days after they arrived on August 28 at the Brandenburg Gate. Together, standing with border guards, Renate Mielke of the East Germany Peace Council, and a senior state official, they were pictured at the iconic gate, adjacent to but distinct from the forbidden wall. In Robeson's archives, the caption to the photograph taken near the Wall reads, "The Wall, Brandenburg Gate, E. Berlin"; similar to Davis's approach, it fails to join "Berlin" and "Wall" in a single phrase.[32] By December, Robeson's doctors agreed he was ready to go home to the States, where he would retire from public life. But before the couple left, the process had already begun for the GDR to set up an archive of the performer's cultural and historical materials. When it opened in 1965 in East Berlin, the archive became a sanctuary for Robeson's legacy.[33] In 1976 Robeson died of a stroke in Philadelphia at age seventy-seven.

Kennedy's and Robeson's trips, when juxtaposed, clarify the complicated cartography of American cultural maps of divided Berlin. Kennedy's trip, on one hand, marked one high point of Cold War West German–American state relations. His appearances promoted the language and imagery of an American identity and citizenship that was tethered to a vision for a unified, full Berlin. He accomplished this by having his speech and presence in West Berlin widely publicized and his movements shown within paces of the border wall looking out to the East without setting foot there. For Robeson, his 1963 visit to East Berlin evinced the GDR's long-standing commitment to dissident African Americans. It also marked his troubled status as an American public figure whose family felt safest treating his illness in East Berlin after his ordeal in allied London. The Robesons did not publicly visit West Berlin. Paul's liminal and convalescent condition in East Berlin emphasized the difficulties of his making public appearances in the west.[34] Together, these trips demonstrate how divided Berlin signified a crossroads for American citizenship, in each case its marquee visitors testing its boundaries or modes of refuge on either side of the Wall.

In her own transnational account, Davis directly contends with the legacy of Kennedy's call of symbolic citizenship as an honorary "Berliner" during his visit to West Berlin in her autobiography. However, it is Robeson with whom her own life circumstances closely resonate, in and out of divided Berlin. In the United States, both withstood life-altering public rebuke and trials for their activism and turned to autobiographical writing to reclaim their own narratives. Both also spent time in East Germany, treating the country as a space of refuge. Beyond their personal protections, both received high honors from state officials. Their status as American Berliners anchored in the East differed from the status of Kennedy and other political and cultural visitors chiefly operating in West Berlin. Border crossings into East Berlin for figures like Davis and Robeson were marked by ease or fulfilment, rather than treated as flights into enemy territory either over, under, or through the Wall.

———

After returning from her trip to West and East Berlin, Davis finished another year of school in Frankfurt before moving back to America. She left West Germany in the spring of 1967, summoned by the burgeoning Black Power movement. On her way back to the United States, she stopped in London, where she attended the May conference on the "Dialectics of Liberation" with her mentor Herbert Marcuse and Trinidadian American organizer Stokely Carmichael. From there she went on to Southern California, briefly to Watts and then in the fall to San Diego, where she would continue her graduate work at the University of California, San Diego. In readjusting to life in the United States, Davis remarked on the changes in her own outlook after her years abroad and the ways in which the political climate had altered with new tensions. She encountered hostility when demonstrating against the Vietnam War and noticed intense police presence and repression encircling acts of public protest, especially around universities. Davis sensed a rise in the policing of dissidence and black liberation. She found solidarity through associations with several activist groups, including the Student Nonviolent Coordinating Committee, the Black Panther Party, the Communist Party, and the Che-Lumumba Club. In 1969 she accepted a position in the philosophy department at UCLA to teach a class on black literature as a way to support herself while finishing her degree. She was soon embroiled in a major struggle to maintain her job after articles appeared in California newspapers publicizing that she was a communist.[35] Davis had not hidden this fact, but due to an old statute of the McCarran Act carried over from the McCarthy era, university regents were permitted to fire instructors based on affiliation with the Communist Party. California governor Ronald Reagan and the regents sought to have her removed in 1969. Davis's detractors merged anticommunist sentiment with fears of black intellectual empowerment.

During this time, Davis also joined the Soledad Brothers Defense Committee, working to free a trio of imprisoned men in the Soledad Prison. George Jackson, John Clutchette, and Fleeta Drumgo, who were known for their liberation teachings from inside Soledad, had been indicted suspiciously for murdering a prison guard. In 1970 Jackson published *Soledad Brother*, his own counternarrative of his imprisonment.[36] Davis's defense of her faculty job and her involvement with the Soledad case helped exemplify and reveal challenges to her own philosophies and practices of freedom that rebuffed what she saw as the far-reaching manifestations of the U.S. prison and repressive political systems. In August 1970, Davis was charged with aiding an armed attack on a Marin County courtroom by Jonathan Jackson, George Jackson's younger brother. When it was found Jackson used firearms Davis owned, but without her knowledge, her life as an intellectual was rendered inseparable from her flight from capture and the justice system. As a prisoner awaiting trial, she formed networks of solidarity with other political prisoners and became a leading dissenting voice of the criminal justice system.[37]

In turn, prisons emerged as central sites of Davis's meaningful organizing work and critical studies. Her attention to boundaries of freedom and repression would undergird her writing before the publication of her autobiography. While the symbol of walls would more fully emerge in her book, close readings of Davis's work from the period before and during her imprisonment in 1970–72 reveal a genealogy of walls, preceding her public mention of Berlin's wall (though not by name) in her autobiography as part of her expressive repertoire. Works written by and in support of her freedom bear the imprint of the evolving symbol and lexicon of walls.

Davis joined a literary tradition of incarcerated authors and criminal justice critics who employ the symbol of walls to write from and/or about prisons. Caleb Smith argues that canonical American authors imagine space behind prison walls as a site to balance solitary forms of punishment with one's own existence against that of a larger social body. Such authors, he claims, consider prison walls as mirrors to reflect not merely on the crimes for which the individuals were convicted but also on the larger contexts for their imprisonment — including the "claustrophobic structures of modern consciousness and capitalism."[38] Lee Bernstein notes that the 1970s were an era of prison reform in which "prisons had become the center of a key ideological fissure shaping American life." He adds, "Incarcerated people during the late 1960s and 1970s hoped that the prison walls that segregated them from the larger world might reveal unseen aspects of U.S. society. Their words crossed the wall, but they also helped many people to rethink the meaning of the walls, and ultimately, the society that produced them."[39] More than a reader of this history, Davis was seen as also having shaped new approaches to such reflective, engaged writings. Dan Berger writes of the 1972 "Tear Down the Walls" Prison Action Conference at the University of California, Berkley, which cited in its circulating materials, "courageous leaders like George Jackson, Angela Davis, Huey Newton, and others [who] have stressed the need . . . to bring attention to the systematic oppression of the convict class."[40] In each instance, the prison wall is both the looming architecture of an unjust society, extending beyond its physical footprint toward other facets of society, and a site necessary to grasp and address racial and class transformation.

As Davis shaped and shared consciousness around critical advocacy related to prison and division, her life was widely portrayed through dozens of complimentary and competing biographical narratives that fueled public and popular intrigue about the circumstances of her life. While her face and image became emblematic of her life story and the political forces swirling around her case, various interpretations of Davis's life story, including her own writing, were also used as significant fodder for the shaping of her public persona.[41]

Davis's case was a fixture in the national media, including cover stories by *Newsweek*, *Time*, and *Jet* magazines, all of which used her image but also delivered stories deliberately focused on her upbringing and development as a means of understanding how she became a political radical on her academic trajectory and as if to explain her legal predicament of incarceration as jointly connected to her potential freedom. Davis's own words and writings had been unsuccessfully leveraged against her by the State of California in the trial as "political evidence." Other key evidence focused on particular books she had read and may have shared with defendant Jonathan Jackson.

Leading up to and during her trial, the National United Committee to Free Angela Davis and others turned to Davis's own words and circulated their own literature to contextualize her case around social divisions and networks of solidarity. This included copies of her "Lectures on Liberation" from UCLA, a radio interview aired on Gil Noble's program in 1970 that was circulated and released by Folkways Records titled *Angela Davis Speaks*, and the pamphlet titled *A Political Biography of Angela Davis*, circulated in 1971, which would later be included in her widely read coedited volume, *If They Come in the Morning*.[42] As she sought to define herself and the movement around her, in such texts and others that would circulate, Davis and her colleagues began analyzing walls and social borderlines around her alongside other treatments of boundaries enforcing segregation, detention, and division. Her reach and solidarity networks grew, as she embraced a variety of rhetorical and narrative approaches.

For example, in Davis's first two lectures from UCLA in 1969, in "Lectures on Liberation," she demonstrates an attention to the traditions of critical approaches to boundaries. Prepared as a pamphlet by 1971, they were sold at 50 cents apiece, with the proceeds going toward her defense. Both lectures focused on Frederick Douglass's autobiography, *The Narrative of the Life of Frederick Douglass, an American Slave, Written by Himself*. Davis's supporters frame her case as a continuation of both her struggles at UCLA and a larger history of the African American freedom struggle and abolition of slavery as demonstrated through canonical literature. This is bolstered by a letter that opens the pamphlet, written and signed by twenty-nine supporting UCLA faculty. Davis begins her lecture by citing philosophical traditions of two distinct locales: ancient Greece and antebellum America. She examines liberation as a broader theme of struggle and examines enslavement as the direct opposition to freedom.

In these lectures Davis also frames Douglass's status as a fugitive from bondage within a system of unjust laws, which merits resistance through flight to established modes of law and order. Douglass, she contends, goes on a journey of escape that encompasses his enslavement through his flight and onward to his abolition work. As Davis states, "The history of Black literature provides, in my opinion, a much more illuminating account of the nature of freedom, its extent and limits than all the philosophical discourses on this theme." Douglass's movement across boundaries—both geopolitical and psychological—draws her close attention. Davis writes: "*The Narrative of the Life of Frederick Douglass* constitutes a physical voyage from slavery to freedom that is both the conclusion and reflection of a philosophical voyage from slavery to freedom. We will see that neither voyage would have been possible alone; they are mutually determinant." She reinforces the idea that the act of writing becomes a way of problematizing and locating spaces of repression and freedom.[43]

In her first major interview following her flight from California and later arrest (an interview that would later be included in *Angela Davis Speaks*), Davis shares her first public statements about her imprisonment. The conversation was carried out by childhood friend and member of her legal team Margaret Burnham (based on questions from respondents in Harlem, published in *Muhammed Speaks*).[44] They cover issues that mainly focus on questions surrounding her court case, as well as her feelings about communism and her rationale for her flight from authorities in California. She describes the conditions inside the Women's House of Detention as horrid and inhumane: "This is a prison and the atrocious conditions that characterize virtually every American prison are present in this place. . . . First of all, this prison is filthy. It's infested with roaches and mice. . . . A few days ago, I was drinking a cup of coffee and was forced to spit out a roach. They literally cover the walls of our cells at night, crawling across our bodies as we sleep."[45] Here, Davis shares a literal description of the walls of a decrepit prison that interface and impact the bodies of the inmates, a condition of gross treatment and neglect. She constructs a shared image of the unjust conditions of detention for those on both sides of prison walls, by describing the structural and personal conditions of incarceration.[46]

During her imprisonment Davis's defense strategy was to place her individual case of incarceration in a greater context of political prisoners, all the while drawing on specifics of her own life. Her defense committee's *Political Biography of Angela Davis* drew out her life development as an intellectual and a freedom fighter. The cover features Davis in front of a poster of scholar and activist W. E. B. Du Bois, and the pamphlet opens with a preamble that cites Davis's own words: "The struggle of a true revolutionary is 'to merge the personal with the political where they're no longer separate.'" Members of her defense committee cite her words and conjure images of how division operates in the United States through tactics of segregation and surveillance. They also share her vision for reunion: "And so we stand, once more, in Angela's words, 'at the crossroads on the path of liberation.'" The contributing writers mention her time in Germany, noting its epiphanal nature for her life: "What had begun as an escape from racist America grew to seem to her an exile from the struggle of her Black brothers and sisters in America. She returned home to join the struggle." The short pamphlet closes with mention of literal walls and the symbolic connotations, around the peril she faces while in prison: "When her words echo far beyond these closed and soundproofed walls, then they seek to take her life. So for her, the life — the struggle, are one."[47] Again, the harsh, repressive structure of prison is compared to the urgent imperative to transcend such boundaries.

The political biography was one of over a dozen pieces of writing that eventually cohered into Davis's first published book collection, *If They Come in the Morning* (1971). In this book, Davis and her interlocutors more fully engage with walls in both philosophical and symbolic lexicons. Coedited with close friend and member of her defense committee Bettina Aptheker, *If They Come in the Morning* was pieced together while she was incarcerated in California awaiting trial. The book consists of writings about and from prisoners. The title was inspired by James Baldwin's "An Open Letter to My Sister, Angela Y. Davis," originally published in the *New York Review of Books* in November 1970 and reprinted in Davis and Aptheker's volume. Baldwin lets his readers know he is writing from Europe and has returned presumably to Paris from a trip to Germany: "Since we live in an age in which silence is not only criminal but suicidal, I have been making as much noise as I can here in Europe. . . . In fact, have just returned from a land, Germany, which was made notorious by a silent majority not so very long ago. I was asked to speak on the case of Miss Angela Davis, and did so. Very probably an exercise in futility, but one must let no opportunity slide."[48] Baldwin uses the example of Nazi Germany as a comparative context for the politics of incarceration. He compares her to "the Jewish housewife in the boxcar headed for Dachau, or as any of our ancestors, chained together in the name of Jesus, headed for a Christian land."[49] Baldwin evokes the memory of the Holocaust to inform perspectives on black freedom struggles in the United States. Baldwin attempts to forge connections between Davis's case and the historical relationship between freedom and repression.

Davis and Aptheker were inspired to open *If They Come in the Morning* with an excerpt from Baldwin's letter as they frame the repressive thrust of American history and its direct ties to the conditions of prisons. *If They Come in the Morning* was envisioned as an educational and fundraising tool for her case and a publication that valued intellectual creativity as a means for gaining her and others' freedom. Davis and Aptheker attempt to contextualize prison within histories of enslavement, imperialism, and the law-and-order politics of the 1960s and 1970s. They reference global coalitions to free Angela, and the potential of a "united front" in which individual cases are leveraged to make a larger point about structures of injustice—in other words, to transform the system through a "thematic unity of resistance" that recognizes the ways in which "repression cuts across ideological boundaries."[50] Walls are referred to over twenty times in the volume, including eight references by Davis and instances mentioned by others including Fleeta Drumgo, John Clutchette, Ericka Huggins, and Huey Newton. (Other allusions to barriers and other analogous symbols occur throughout the text.)

One of the book's contributors, Huggins, an incarcerated member of the Black Panthers who would later be acquitted of criminal charges, offered a poem that critically treats and then transforms the symbol of walls. In her chapter "Poems from Prison," which she penned while incarcerated, Huggins writes of the "noises / sounds / unspoken words" that were "repressed" by prison walls. She closes with a vision that prisons are "soul walls / barriers / if only all barriers could be removed." [51] Huggins exemplifies an emerging sentiment found within this collection. The spatial imagination of this poem highlights prisoners' expressive and critical thoughts in a way to call to abolish and transform prison walls into spaces of necessary connection.

In a group of collected writings, Davis's own prose in *If They Come in the Morning* structures portions of the book in which walls are rendered through philosophical and symbolic terms. Across the text, Davis is credited with ten essays or letters out of the twenty-nine featured in the book, and at least an additional eight are addressed directly to her or engage specifics of her case. The section of the book titled "Angela Y. Davis" also features the *Political Biography* credited to her defense committee and a series of transcripts from interviews between Davis and counsel Margaret Burnham in the New York Women's House of Detention in November 1970, including those released as *Angela Davis Speaks.* [52]

Davis wrote during her incarceration to fight for her own and others' freedom. She began shifting discursive approaches, fusing her political and philosophical writing with literary close descriptions of places and encounters, especially dwelling on the walls and boundaries behind which she was imprisoned. Davis, in one of her own essays written for this collection, "Prisoners in Rebellion," writes, "The impenetrable concrete, the barbed wire and the armed keepers, ostensibly there to deter escape-bound captives also suggests something further: prisoners must be guarded from the ingressions of a moving, developing world outside. Discouraged from normal social life, its revelations and influences, they must finally be robbed of their humanity. . . . In utter disregard of the institution's totalitarian aspirations, the passions and theories of Black revolution and socialist revolution have penetrated the wall." [53] Davis's biographical recollection, as well her as poetic reflection and nonfiction prose, is put forth as a significant mode of struggling toward legal freedom. Revolutionary thought and action can, in essence, describe the repressive nature of prison walls and transform them into a porous structure and meeting place.

The publication of *If They Come in the Morning* aided the defense in myriad ways. According to Aptheker, the book launched with a first print run of 400,000 copies in the United States. Additional contracts were signed soon after with foreign presses in East and West Germany, Denmark, France, Greece, Japan, Mexico, the Netherlands, Norway, Sweden, and Spain.[54] The expansive, global solidarity campaigns (including 200 officially linked U.S.-based groups and 67 in foreign countries) utilized the publication to raise awareness of Davis's case and that of the other political prisoners included in the volume.

During Davis's trial, both the widespread national and international attention influenced the case. Groups from both West and East Germany organized on her behalf, either through state-sponsored campaigns or grassroots efforts.[55] In her 1970 *Angela Davis Speaks* interview she notes, "The support from abroad has been overwhelming. All the socialist countries have lodged protests in some way or form. I was particularly pleased to hear of the activity that has been going on in Cuba and in Europe, especially in Germany, Italy and France. . . . Right now I receive from 100 to 400 letters a day, at least half of them originating from abroad, including many countries in Latin America, Asia and Africa. The thousands of letters from school children in the GDR have been tremendously moving."[56] Davis demonstrates the power of this volume and the movement around her trial to organize across boundaries, including East Germany and other places with walls and physical landscapes of division. Through this period of her detention and trial, walls enter Davis's lexicon, ahead of her autobiography's highlighting of the structure as one of its central symbols.[57]

———

On June 4, 1972, Davis was acquitted on all charges. Outside the courthouse in Santa Clara County, California, a collective gathered to support Davis: she was joined by her lawyers, family members, and other supporters from her defense committee. Davis's sister, Fania Jordan, who served as the national coordinator of the committee, read a prepared statement: "The acquittal of Angela Davis is a sweet victory for the millions of us across the earth who have supported this long and difficult fight." Jordan also referenced the immense challenges, including the construction of "a $750,000 'security network' . . . quickly erected [outside the courthouse] to create a climate of fear and danger—and to influence potential jurors."[58] Jordan also took this time to mention the group's continuing work advocating for those who faced repression behind prison walls and outside in the larger struggle for black liberation.

That summer the autobiography began to take shape. Amid continued public interest and scrutiny over her case, Davis's camp fielded offers from publishers.[59] Toni Morrison, who had visited Davis in prison in Marin County, met with Aptheker for lunch to discuss "her preliminary thoughts on the type of book Angela Davis might do." According to a letter in response, addressed to Aptheker on June 27, 1972, Morrison suggested a framing that included short vignettes leading up to an extended section on the political history of the United States, a book that was meant to be a transcendent artifact of struggle. "A series of pieces on her recent experiences in the arms of American 'justice'—subjective in approach and perception . . . the book would be personal and political (there [is] no difference anyway) but the tone would meet the requirements of each encounter, event, or reflection. The book, like its author would be both the theory and the thing, the idea *and* its manifestation. It would be so powerful—it boggles the mind. It would [be] a non-book in the truest sense—that is to say—it would never be confined to its covers."[60] By September 8, 1972, the same week Davis returned to East Berlin on her Eastern bloc tour, the first contract, for a book titled "Education of a Revolutionary," was drawn up with Bantam Books and Bernard Geis Associates. According to the contract, "Said [manuscript] will recount the experiences in the Author's life that shaped her philosophy and influenced her actions . . . [and] will also include the Author's statement as to where she stands—as a political person, as a black woman, and as a crusader for social justice."[61]

Within weeks, on October 3 of the same year, staffers at Random House, where Morrison was an editor, including editor in chief and publisher James Silberman, met with representatives from Bantam and Bernard Geis Associates. By January, 31, 1973, Random House and Bantam drafted an agreement to copublish the book. According to the updated contract, Random House would take the lead in the hardcover and "day to day editorial functions be carried out by a RANDOM editor," a reference to Morrison's engaged role in the project.[62] The title at that time remained "Education of a Revolutionary," with the first manuscript sections arriving in the spring of 1973. The book was initially separated into three sections: part 1, Flight, Arrest, New York Hail, Extradition; part 2, Childhood, New York, Europe, California; and part 3, Soledad, George Jackson, Trial.[63] Over time, Davis shifted the organization of her narrative.[64] Davis and Morrison worked closely in New York City and spent time outside the United States, including in the Virgin Islands, Cuba, and Europe. As Morrison later recollected, "There was nowhere in the United States where Angela could feel safe and write."[65]

It is not clear from available archives at what point Davis composed the section including Berlin and "the wall."[66] It is evident, however, that the book went through multiple stages of line revisions and refinement, as editor Morrison was pushed to grapple with the question of whether readers would be able to relate to this "political autobiography." For example, in early 1974 serious reservations arose about the book after a scathing reader's report arrived from Bantam. In response, Morrison wrote publisher Silberman a powerful four-page letter on February 1, 1974, addressing the charge that the manuscript contained no "sustenance" and not enough "humanness." In sharp reply, Morrison wrote, "Angela is the fiercest woman I have ever met and I come from a long line of fierce women." She added, "I must emphasize that there are no two Angela Davises. One political, one human. They are one and the same thing. She does not tuck her politics away. Never. Not even in her dreams."[67] After further detailing her own close reads of Davis's work on the biography, and demonstrating a deep care in its refinement, Morrison concluded her letter with a pointed summary: "1. I find the Bantam report wholly useless to me. 2. I am prepared to cut 200 manuscript pages, re-write a good deal for improvement in style and to add certain episodes that are interesting and amusing. I want to introduce more of the risk and joy in her life. 3. If that is not sufficient I think the work should be either assigned to another editor whom you feel can work with her and do more, or I think it should be rejected completely."[68] Despite her own reservations, which included in this same letter the suggestion of delaying the publication for ten to fifteen years, Morrison continued to push forward by keeping close tabs on the project.[69] By March 1974 Morrison had sent Bantam an updated but unedited manuscript. In April 1974 she coordinated with Random House to move the publication date to the fall, and she worked with Davis in her office or at her home in Spring Valley at least five times from May 1 to May 8 on copyediting the galleys, which were ready for review by the end of the month. As Davis finished her epilogue, Morrison continued to refine final details of the book's design. For example, she coordinated images from Angela's childhood, provided by her mother, to appear with oval edges and black outlines on the book jacket's interior folds. Once the text and images were complete, Morrison sent galleys to media influencers and cultural figures, including Ralph Ellison and Maya Angelou, while coordinating book events through the fall to broaden the reach of the book, which was published on October 28, 1974.[70]

Davis's autobiography, in its final form, reflects the emergence of Davis as a figure presented reclaiming the puzzled and problematic narratives circulating about her life, political identities, and relationships. Margo Perkins highlights the work of Davis and other black female figures of the Black Power era whose autobiographical writing "is marked by both a redefining of the self through a story of the Movement, and a notable uneasiness with the project of autobiography because of the genre's historical emphasis . . . on heroic individualism."[71] The book is structured into chapters around natural and architectural elements: "Nets," "Rocks," "Waters," "Flames," "Walls," and "Bridges." Prisons and, more broadly, the networks of the criminal justice system and state repression are woven throughout each chapter, as is the ability to work across them.

In her completed autobiography, from the dedication through the closing pages, Davis draws attention to physical and symbolic walls featured throughout the text, inviting readers to locate the author within structures of repression and networks of support. Again, this is recounted most significantly in the tales of her incarceration. Walls stand in for and/or resemble other structures that reference histories of struggle. They offer the very imaginative architecture of walls necessary to build solidarity, including the scene that takes place by the Berlin Wall. Davis uses the spatial metaphor of walls throughout the text to reengineer the terms for coalition building across boundaries and to illuminates the power of cross-border solidarity as "communities of struggle."

In Davis's first chapter, "Nets," she focuses on the three-month period when she was a fugitive and ultimately captured in New York City awaiting extradition to California. Her narrative begins with her furtive escape from U.S. authorities and then afterward moves back to a linear sense of time. The first appearance of a wall in the text, after the dedication page, is an exterior "red brick wall" of the New York Women's House of Detention. She remembers seeing this wall as a high school student in New York and recalls it in her narrative as both looming and "archaic." The exterior wall then portends her characterizations of the detestable conditions and basic rights in prisons, as well as attempts by officials to cordon off support for her from both outside and inside prison.[72] In the same chapter, as she describes being locked up in the prison's mental ward (because prison officials feared her influence in the general population), Davis uses the symbol of the wall to connote another disturbing division she encountered in this facility: "Each time I tried to help one [patient prisoner] out of misery, I would discover that a wall — far more impervious than the walls of our own cells — stood between us."[73] Davis writes of a hunger strike to call attention to the conditions of her imprisonment, focus her own energy, and match the growing support for her by those fighting for her freedom: "I would hold my own on this side of the walls while things got rolling on the other side."[74] Here, the symbol of the wall marks both her physical separation from social movements forming outside of prisons and a demarcation of psychological conditions inside. For Davis, the fortified prison walls were manifestations of larger circuits of repression.

In the chapters "Rocks," "Waters" (where she recalls her time in East and West Berlin), and "Flames," the narrative shifts back to her childhood and upbringing and moves on to her evolution away from home. She uses the language of borders and division to emphasize the violence of Jim Crow society and authority on her youth. For example, when she was four years old and the Davis family moved to a house atop a hill on Center Street in Birmingham from housing projects nearby, the reaction from her new neighbors was indelible: "Almost immediately after we moved there the white people got together and decided on a border line between them and us. Center Street became the line of demarcation."[75] Davis emphasizes being raised in networks of support and the expansive activism of the black left, and yet the dangers of the Jim Crow South and the confining nature of everyday life were everywhere: "The provincialism of Birmingham bothered me. . . . I could not define or articulate the dissatisfaction. I simply had the sensation of things closing in on me."[76] Davis also recalls her experience as a high school student in New York, where she learned to cope with being an outsider: "I could always tear away a piece of the wall and slip out to other worlds."[77] For Davis, the wall functions here as a metaphor for reality and the status quo. In each case, she uses the language of walls and borders to express the confinement of racism and segregation she experienced.

In the section "Waters," Davis describes her trip to Cold War Berlin. She tells of having spent most of her time easily passing into East Berlin during her school visit and alternately reports her reentry into West Germany afterward as being far more difficult. As she narrates, she was detained when trying to leave West Berlin for Frankfurt: "When the West German police said they were going to detain me at the airport," she states, "I was certain they were going to accuse me of being too friendly with the people in the GDR— and of course, they would have been correct." Davis goes on to point out that she was detained because she had failed to properly register her address in Frankfurt. "I could never get used to the incredible bureaucracy in which one must become embroiled merely as a prerequisite for living an ordinary life,"[78] she writes. She inverts the stereotypical treatment of East Germany as a police state, noting the repressive situation she faced in West Germany, where the physical wall was paced with a state of overbearing surveillance. That story reinforces her earlier account of housing discrimination when she was misrecognized as a Turkish "guest worker" in Frankfurt. She notes that "half the adults had gone through the experience of Hitler. And in West Germany, unlike the German Democratic Republic, there had been no determined campaign to attack the fascist and racist attitudes which had become so deeply embedded."[79] At this critical juncture of the book, she provides a sharp contrast between border crossings and life on both sides of the border, as well as programs of antiracism and denazification built into the respective German cultural systems.

By even mentioning "the wall" in reference to the Berlin border in this section of the book, as noted, Davis violates East German mandate and linguistic convention. In the book, she depicts the Wall while also nodding to a cultural rite of dissidence in the East by not specifically naming it. In this context, we see how Davis's refusal to name the Wall in her autobiography displays both an allegiance to and a violation of East German mores. Davis's reference to "the wall" is both a subtle acknowledgment and a disavowal of the shared strategies of suppression of both East and West. She does not acknowledge the repressive tactics of the East, including the building of the Berlin Wall itself. Instead, Davis positions walls as a signature structure for characterizing America and the West. She alludes to and then turns away from the Berlin Wall as a means of critically pivoting perspective in a narrative that more fully explores the repressive architecture of American political life.

In the next chapter, titled "Flames," she recounts her burgeoning activism around prisons during the transitional period of her return to America: "I became convinced that there were impending explosions behind the walls, and that if we did not begin to build a support movement for our sisters and brothers in prison, we were no revolutionaries at all. . . . The gray walls, the sounds of chains had touched not only their lives, but the lives of all Black people."[80] Later, in describing the longtime incarceration of George Jackson, she offset the designation "behind walls" between two em-dashes, as an emphatic description and geopolitical location.[81] Her treatment of walls as a literary symbol is fully realized as the central repressive architecture of society and the site of her most intense critical engagement.

In the final two chapters of the book, titled, respectively, "Walls" and "Bridges," Davis picks up with her detention in California and explains the case that the state made against her and the evolution of the legal circumstances that led to the trial. She uses an image of walls from the very first page of "Walls." The epigraph to this chapter is excerpted from "Poem with Rhythms," by Wallace Stevens:

The hand between the candle and the wall
Grows large on the wall. . . .

It must be that the hand
Has a will to grow larger on the wall,
To grow larger and heavier than
the wall . . . .[82]

Davis's autobiography highlights intertextual acts of reading and writing as ways to engage physical and social walls and to create connections between prisons and the larger society. Toppled walls often become central structures of justice realized. When recalling the preparation of *If They Come in the Morning*, Davis writes, "From the inception of the idea, we saw the book as an instrument through which people could deepen their knowledge of repression. . . . People . . . could learn what was really happening behind the walls in general."[83] As she marks the process of using writing to forge connections, she also recalls painful bouts of "profound sadness." Davis describes using the acts of reading and writing letters to fellow prisoners to salvage her focus and maintain it during her eighteen-month imprisonment: "My very existence, it seemed, was dependent on my ability to reach out to them. I decided . . . I would use my life to uphold the cause of my sisters and brothers behind walls."[84] Davis maps movement building through discourse and conveys a sense of solidarity that transcends the space and time of imprisonment.

This form of connection sets up her final chapter, "Bridges," which she opens with the epigraph "Walls turned sideways are bridges." For Davis, this epigraph serves as a mantra, a statement that also makes clear a transcendence envisioned as a literary transformation and a strategic vision. This section marks the culmination of her narrative and effectively repurposes walls as a form of transformative architecture. In this chapter she recalls the defense-team strategy and multiracial and transnational solidarity campaigns that contributed to her acquittal, as Davis suggests. Just as she displaces the Berlin Wall in the earlier section, in this chapter she re-envisions the prison wall. This displacement is emphasized on the final page of the chapter, where she uses a metaphor of deconstruction to explain the circumstances of what is next for her and the movement. Rather than ramparts or barricades appearing, pathways open in Davis's formulations: "Work. Struggle. Confrontation lay before us like a rock strewn road. We would walk it."[85] The path resembles debris from a tumbled wall, and Davis writes as if the limits of her incarceration have yielded a new outlet for an activism built through networks of solidarity over and through walls.

The framework for engaged political identifications she lays out here is furthered in her book's epilogue, in which she recalls travels she had taken since her acquittal, including trips through the Eastern bloc and Central and South America—including nations closed off to the West but seen as protective spaces for her. The language of autobiographical recollection segues into the present tense as she marks her own timing in the writing of the book. In one of the final pages she mentions the freshness of recent cases and her collective view of the future: "My freedom was not yet a week old when I left. . . . An enormous political responsibility has been thrust upon me. . . . Our ability to keep the movement alive offered the only hope to our sisters and brothers behind walls."[86] She also details more of the activism that she would continue to carry out with the momentum from her case. Such unity, emblematized by a wall turned sideways, powerfully includes prison walls as well as other social boundaries that recall deep historical divisions, not just the one in divided Berlin. She does recall the "hundreds of thousands" of GDR citizens who greeted her upon her return to East Berlin after the trial, but there is no mention of "the wall" again in this section, as it does not fully exist in the public perception and ideology of an honorary citizen of East Germany, as Davis had become. Instead, she crosses borders and turns walls sideways through critical forms of displacement and continues to find refuge and connection behind the Wall's borders in the Eastern bloc.

———

Davis presented her life story in its final, published form in *Angela Davis: An Autobiography* in 1974, with her own national press campaign and numerous reviews, at a time when America was in the midst of several challenges to territorial legality and paradoxes of official state narratives. The Watergate scandal brought to light the illegality of President Richard Nixon's administration and government, and the recent pullout of troops from Vietnam occurred amidst further inquiries into the ground actions of combat troops, especially after details of the My Lai massacre were revealed to the public. Davis's publication also coincided with a major referendum on American political constructions of truth: the passage of the Privacy Act and Freedom of Information Act.[87] The broader realization that members of governmental agencies gathered surveillance on American citizens and conducted covert missions abroad yielded legislation aiming for redress and transparency.

Similarly, the Black Power movement was at a crossroads. Jeffrey Ogbar writes of the "radical spirit of black nationalism" that had started to transform national consciousness about issues of social justice and power. This led to a spike in the election of black government officials, the sprouting of black studies and ethnic studies departments at universities and colleges, and cultural and commercial appeal for Black Power's messaging. Ogbar also details the "daunting and complex web of government repression [that] undermined radical black organizations."[88] The extent to which the government surveyed and curtailed such activist circles they deemed "radical" through COINTELPRO counterintelligence measures is still being discovered by contemporary historians today.[89]

Davis remained in the public eye after her trial, and her autobiography extended the widespread knowledge of her case. Several books about her trial were released before or around the time of her own autobiography, including Regina Nadelson's *Who Is Angela Davis? The Biography of a Revolutionary* (1972), J. A. Parker's *Angela Davis: The Making of a Revolutionary* (1973), and Marc Olden's *Angela Davis* (1973). A former member of the jury at Davis's trial, Mary Timothy, published *Jury Woman* (1974), and Davis's friend and member of her solidarity committee, Bettina Aptheker, detailed courtroom proceedings in *The Morning Breaks: The Trial of Angela Davis* (1975).[90]

Davis's book was widely reviewed, sometimes multiple times by the same national publications. Many reviewers made reference to Davis's development within the black freedom struggle and her global pathways. An anonymous reviewer for *Publishers Weekly* wrote, "Angela Davis' life is a uniquely American odyssey."[91] Reviewers noted the artful rendering of her prose but took up the nature of her autobiographical intervention. The question of the genre of political autobiography drew scrutiny from several reviewers. Christopher Lehmann-Haupt wrote in the *New York Times*, "The autobiography seems to be direct, simple, and relatively personal in style. So presumably we are afforded a glimpse at the author's character. . . . As it turns out on closer reading, however, her character isn't especially conducive to the autobiographical mode. As it turns out, she is successful in not 'individualizing' herself."[92] Others echo the travails to her travel, often mentioning of her time in Germany. Gwendolyn Osborne, writing for the NAACP's *Crisis*, saw such movement as indicative of larger stories of African American experiences in the nation: "The autobiography of Angela Davis begins — complex and paradoxical. It is the story of a black woman born in the South, and educated in the world's finest institutions who remained bound to her roots. . . . It is also a collective biography — of black life in white America."[93] Her border crossing was seen as exceptional and a vehicle for growing identifications among people.

In the ensuing years, Davis would return to East Berlin habitually, making at least three trips, in 1972, 1973, and 1975, enshrining her role as a dissident American Berliner.[94] From her first trip to her last, she went from being a

FIGURE 2.3 Peter Koard, "Berlin: Erich Honecker received Angela Davis. — The General Secretary of Germany's Socialist Unity Party (SED), Erich Honecker, received American civil rights activist Angela Davis on October 11, 1972. During this meeting, he invited her, as representative of a different America, to the World Festival of Youth and Students in 1973 in the East German capital." (Bundesarchiv, Bild 183-L0911-029)

young graduate student to a hugely popular and celebrated public icon. During an official state visit in September 1972, soon after her acquittal, she was greeted by tens of thousands of East Germans, some of whom had written letters and sent telegrams on her behalf to the judge presiding over her case, to officials in California, and to Davis herself. Höhn and Klimke note that *Time* magazine referred to the atmosphere at the time as "Angelamania." Like Paul Robeson before her, East German general secretary Erich Honecker bestowed her with a Great Star of Friendship among the Peoples (fig. 2.3). She was also given tours of historic sites to much fanfare, including Soviet sites of mourning such as the Soviet War Memorial in Treptower Park and Neue Wache on Unter den Linden. Official state publications and photographers captured her movements and appearances in large public gatherings. Davis returned to East Berlin several times after 1972. In 1973, she was a featured guest at the Tenth World Festival of Youth and headed the American delegation. She also returned in 1975 for the World Congress of Women and in 1981 for the Children and Youth Sports Festival. Through this time, she finished her doctoral studies through East Berlin's Humboldt University.

FIGURE 2.4 Klaus Franke, "Davis, Angela, East Berlin: Visits East German Border with West Berlin," September 1972. (Bundesarchiv, Bild 183-L0912-412)

Davis's ability to convincingly displace the Berlin Wall in the American imagination worked to reaffirm her networks of solidarity. She almost completely bypassed the American cultural fascination with the Berlin Wall and attempted to reorient people toward other divisions: in particular, the liberation politics of struggle against Cold War strategies of containment and, with greater focus, the harsh, politicized, and racialized contours of the U.S. prison system. On subsequent trips or in public discourse, Davis was not recorded pondering or directing a self-conscious gaze onto the Berlin Wall or East Ger-

FIGURE 2.5 Peter Koard, "Davis, Angela, East Berlin: Visits East German Border with West Berlin," September 1972. (Bundesarchiv, Bild 183-L0911-030)

man border control. The Wall proved to be somewhat of a haunt to Davis, a topic of non-acknowledgment lurking in public exchanges about her time in Germany, even when she was physically close to the Wall on subsequent visits. Davis bracketed the Berlin Wall in a sense, with an intended focus on other sites of division.

Visual artifacts from her 1972 visit to the GDR reflect her perspective on the Berlin Wall. During her 1972 trip, following her acquittal and on a tour of Eastern bloc countries, her appearance and words indirectly acknowledged the Wall's presence. On that visit, Davis was followed by state-affiliated photographers and writers. They documented her moves throughout East Berlin in official state events, visits to memorials, and at prominent spots close to the border. In one image, within steps of the Wall (fig. 2.4), she stands with hands clasped together in front of her while speaking to border guards. Davis stands with her back to a nearby guard tower and the border's internal wall. There, as

Davis faces away from the Wall, the photographer captures the border system as a vanishing point beyond the crowd exploring the area with Davis by foot. Images such as this could not convey the full scope of Davis's movements, conversations, and glances that day by the border, but their place in state archives can demonstrate imperatives to document and explore the scene with a particular point of view.

Another image at the border (fig. 2.5) depicts Davis as she stands in front of the Brandenburg Gate, holding a bouquet of flowers and meeting with border guards and activists. The image is shot from below, capturing the grandeur of the gate behind Davis. A GDR-produced pamphlet titled *Peace, Friendship, Solidarity: Angela Davis in the GDR* reported her meeting with border guards there who told her of their responsibilities and conveyed the story of Corporal Reinhold Huhn, a fellow border guard who was killed ten years earlier by a man fleeing to the west. According to the pamphlet, Davis committed to carrying this message back to the United States: "We mourn the deaths of the border guards who sacrificed their lives for the protection of their socialist homeland," Davis said. "When we return to the USA, we shall undertake to tell our people the truth about the true function of this border."[95] Davis demonstrated the potential for social coalition as she conversed with border guards. There, at the Brandenburg Gate, she again stood close to the Wall — without gazing in its direction, heeding its hazards, or calling out its infamous name. Instead, she directed her words toward other boundaries of repression.

CHAPTER 3 | **SCALING THE WALL**

Shinkichi Tajiri, Exiled Sculpture, and the
Reconstruction of the Berlin Wall

At its center a violent, lethal non-place; an alluring, pitiless
obstacle course; a forbidden zone with nothing but the silence
before the shot. The actual designers were no longer in control
of the architectural result of their work. . . . The Wall enjoyed a
career as a thing of its own making.

—OLAF BRIESE

Within a decade of the initial construction of the Berlin Wall, the sprawling barricade aimed at keeping intact both the social vision and the citizenry
of the German Democratic Republic, the ruling regime eyed improvements
to its border system. The GDR intended to secure the permanence and ele-
vate the esteem of the infamous structure. Sculptor Shinkichi Tajiri, a new-
comer to West Berlin in 1969, was compelled by the Wall's vast footprint
and uneven surfaces under revision. The renovations of the late 1960s and
early 1970s meant that the Wall, by design, would be in a state of constant
change for several years. As the period of détente with the West unfolded,
GDR officials tinkered with the massive overhaul of their byzantine border.
They ordered reconstruction of the wall system through a "robust mandate"
to address the structural and aesthetic concerns over a border wall that had
been hastily constructed, improvised even at its most significant and visible
locations. Olaf Briese cites a 1965 internal document from the city command
that stated, "The technical barriers are non-standard and maintenance intensive. . . . They often do not increase the prestige of the German Democratic
Republic on the world stage."[1] In addressing such concerns, the GDR aimed
to remedy the function as well as the aesthetic reputation of a border wall that
from its beginnings was as unwieldy as it was menacing, with built components placed clumsily in the interest of expediency. Briese explains that the
East German regime carried out this first round of extensive revisions in the

late 1960s and early 1970s, during which "the wall became the foremost element of a refined, graduated barrier system: an interior wall, a border alarm fence, antitank barricades, dog-patrolled areas (mainly on the edges of Berlin), observations towers, light arrays, patrol paths, plowed or raked strips of ground, trenches to prevent vehicular breakouts, and finally, at the outermost point, [a] strip of wall."[2]

The revision's most prominent feature, its outer western wall, consisted of a repeated sequence of prefabricated concrete horizontal slabs stacked into interlocked steel-supporting frames. The result was a wall that approached full standardization only after nearly a decade of existence.

From the perspective of Tajiri and others, the so-called wall was an amalgam of many intersecting structures of border control, on both sides of the divide. For Tajiri, an American expatriate of Japanese descent and veteran who had left his home country twenty years earlier, moving through divided Berlin brought him in contact with traces of U.S. military occupation. As he prepared to begin a teaching post at West Berlin's Hochschule der Künste, the border, in its state of partial construction, was too monumental to ignore.

At the time of his first trip to divided Berlin, Tajiri was already an internationally recognized sculptor and multimedia artist who incorporated a wide vocabulary of surrealist strategies into his work. Fashioning small models by hand, he made many of his large-scale sculptural works in his own foundry, located within a rehabilitated castle in which he and his family resided in the Netherlands. His works included intricate bronze fortresses and towers poured into carved brick molds, large metal war machines with giant legs and protruding weaponry, assemblages from metal drippings, and oversized hardened fiberglass and polyester knots. Many of his sculptures from this period constituted reflections on the relationship between violence, militarism, and technological advancement during the Cold War. As an artist in what he deemed a "self-imposed exile" from the United States, he viewed his country of origin from afar, with a posture of engaged and wary critique.[3]

Specters of American war and division followed Tajiri throughout his life. The son of Japanese immigrants, with Samurai ancestral traditions on both his mother's and father's sides, Tajiri was born in the Watts neighborhood of Los Angeles on December 7, 1923. He turned eighteen on December 7, 1941, the day of the attack on Pearl Harbor. Less than a year later, when President Franklin Roosevelt signed Executive Order 9066 calling for the removal of 117,000 Americans of Japanese descent from their homes, the Tajiri family were living in San Diego within a designated civilian "exclusion zone." With the executive order, the Tajiris were subject to forced relocation and criminal charges if they refused. Within days, the family were removed from their home and told they had to leave most of their belongings behind. After spending five months in makeshift, cordoned-off containment facilities at Santa Anita racetrack, they were moved to the Poston 3 Relocation Camp in the Arizona desert. Tajiri later recalled of the camp facility in which his family were forced to live: "Encircled with barbed wire and watch towers with machine guns . . . . we were imprisoned, our freedom denied."[4] Months later, after being given an option to join the war effort to gain freedom from the camp, Tajiri enlisted.[5] He went through basic training in Shelby, Mississippi, a town under Jim Crow rule, and joined the 442nd Regimental Combat Team of Nisei soldiers.

On May 1, 1944, Tajiri shipped out to Europe with his segregated unit, led by white officers.[6] Shortly thereafter, he was seriously wounded in combat in Italy. After a six-month convalescence, he was transferred to limited service and worked as an army artist in a village near Mannheim, Germany, where he drew portraits of detained political opponents of the Nazis for the army. He identified with such a category of "displaced persons." After an honorable discharge in 1946 and a brief stint spent studying at the Art Institute of Chicago, he decided to leave the United States rather than contend with postwar racial aggression against Japanese Americans. Tajiri recalled, "I reminded people of their recent enemy."[7] In 1948, he received GI bill support for art study in Paris and left the U.S. without a plan for permanent return. In Paris, he studied with Fernand Legér and Ossip Zadkine. He later moved to Amsterdam, ultimately settling with his family in Baarlo, where they purchased an old village castle, refurbished the historic building's crumbled sections, and placed his studio in one of its wings. Other than occasional family visits and brief arts residencies, he never again lived in the United States.

In October 1969, Tajiri accepted an invitation to meet with officials about a guest professorship at the Hochschule der Künste in West Berlin. He was summoned at the request of students who had seen his work at the prominent Documenta IV arts festival in Kassel, Germany, the year prior, at one of the international art world's most prominent venues, and petitioned him to join the faculty. Tajiri accepted the position under unorthodox conditions: he would teach almost continuously for two weeks a month, live in a tent in his studio, and make himself readily available to students (fig. 3.1). The other two weeks, he would return to Baarlo and family and work on larger commissions. Tajiri's own reasons for accepting this position in West Berlin had much to do with the tragic death of his wife, Ferdi, a Dutch artist and frequent collaborator, in a household accident in February 1969. A week before her death,

FIGURE 3.1 Shinkichi Tajiri in his West Berlin studio, ca. 1969.
(Shinkichi Tajiri Estate)

the letter of invitation arrived from West Berlin but was ignored. Months later, when searching for his next steps, he rediscovered the letter. He decided to take intermittent time away from large sculptural works while mourning Ferdi and turn to the teaching position in West Berlin to support his family.

For his first meeting with administrators, Tajiri drove his speedy white Lotus Elan 2 from Baarlo to West Berlin. There he encountered the Wall and was immediately intrigued. He later recalled, "Once in the city center, I began to feel a low throbbing vibration, like a transformer plugged into the mains supply, but without a machine to relieve the current load. Driving towards the university, I was suddenly stopped by the Berlin Wall at the Brandenburg Gate. Walking along the Wall, it occurred to me that the vibration I had felt earlier might be energy that had been trapped within the city. . . . The air felt electric."[8]

Between teaching spurts, this experience by the Wall beckoned him to embark on a new artistic undertaking. He set out to photograph the Wall in its entirety as a study in sculpture, focusing on the portion coursing through the middle of the city, from its southernmost point to its northern edge. Over a six-month period, he photographed in West Berlin after school or during

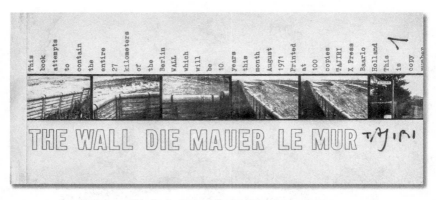

FIGURE 3.2 Shinkichi Tajiri, *The Wall Die Mauer Le Mur*, 1971.
(Shinkichi Tajiri Estate)

his commute back to Baarlo, driving to a location, surveying the landscape, and shooting multiple frames. He eventually produced over 550 sequential negatives. While his goal was to grasp the sweeping, routine nature of the border wall system, he grappled with moments of variation, due in part to the Wall's unwieldy path and his own desire to track particularly curious attributes or angles. In addition to viewing densely populated urban areas and checkpoints with border guards then familiar to global audiences, he located the Wall on the city's margins: coursing through fields, cutting off access to bridges, jumping back and forth across waterways, and running into ruined buildings swallowed by the Wall's path. In the artist's view, the Wall constituted an evolving construction site and an embedded piece of architecture within a city steadily accustomed to its own division.

In 1971, to commemorate the wall's tenth anniversary, Tajiri compiled his images in a small book that he printed on his own offset press in Baarlo. The title, *The Wall Die Mauer Le Mur* (fig. 3.2), is a nod to the three languages featured on much of the signage of the Western allied sectors of West Berlin. The book comprises the artist's exposed negatives, rendered in facsimile strips, and covers his entire view of the Wall. Tajiri's survey prints begin on the cover and segue into the bound volume. Each frame is printed as a transparency but remains sized at the same scale as its negative — the size of a postage stamp — and thus is discernable only when brought close to the naked eye. The only text appears on the cover, with no punctuation and only one word on each line, oriented vertically. Tajiri writes, opposite the title, "This book attempts to contain the entire twenty-seven kilometers of the Berlin WALL which will be 10 years this month August 1971 Printed at 100 copies TAJIRI x Press Baarlo

Holland." Tajiri's *The Wall Die Mauer Le Mur* tempered the megalithic scope of the Wall with a close-up documentation, barely discernable to readers and presented with limited public reach. Tajiri's steering of his work away from broader public review sparks a productive tension, given the engaged, public character of his study. For a sculptor who regularly placed finished large installations in city squares, on bridges, and in museums—including several that were sited in the United States—this project stands out for its intimate scale, limited print run, and status as remaining largely unknown in his country of origin. Tajiri shared single images of his survey and expanded its scope in multiple formats throughout his career, under revision as a concept for documenting the Wall, but did not print the entire body of work from his study until 2005, when he published the project in a book titled *The Berlin Wall*. Even in this version, he suggested that his work was unfinished and future editions would be forthcoming.

Within Tajiri's oeuvre, the Berlin Wall project functions as both an aberration and a cipher. Scholars of his long-running Wall project have alternately referred to it as a photographic survey, a historical documentation, or land art, among other distinctions. Christoph Schaden contends that Tajiri's project renders the Wall's "[metamorphosis] into an unintentional work of art."[9] Helen Westgeest suggests that in Tajiri's work "the wall appears to move like an endlessly long and monumental sculpture through and around the city."[10] Tajiri spawned a series of Wall projects that he would continue to revisit throughout the rest of his career. Though he never created an obvious monumental sculpture in relation to the Wall, his concerns and nuanced observations were deeply tied to his study of divided Berlin's physical contours. The survey allowed him to balance large-scale work at his foundry in Baarlo with a more mobile approach to contend with the massive border wall in Berlin. Further, though he began with this study a longer-term exploration of photographic techniques, he did not view himself as a fine art or documentary photographer. As Els Barents suggests, Tajiri was "not concerned with *pure photography*. . . . [He] only began to experiment with photography when he felt sure of his position as a sculptor."[11] Tajiri's other photographic undertakings regularly involved building physical devices for enhanced public viewing or adding layered inscriptions on his own prints.

As a whole, Tajiri's Berlin Wall project does powerfully share many aspects of his other artworks, including his reflections on technologies of war, his unpacking of a deep memory of internment, and his ongoing critical relationship to his status as an American. Tajiri never explicitly stated that he saw the Wall as related to his experiences in the internment camp or the segregated army. He did, however, continually insist that creating artwork was a mode of self-reflection and discovery and that he would spend the rest of his life processing the loss of his family's home and status as an American expatriate. Barents adds, "An immaterial quality of emulsion on a piece of paper was, for him, not a goal in of itself. . . . It was sooner an adventurous tour through the dark alleys and ghettos of the subconscious, which, as he now knows later in life, all end up in one point, that of the recollection."[12] Tajiri produced his photographs as a sculptural study of the Wall and, in turn, while moving through the geopolitical American borderlands of Berlin, mapped the meandering path of his own circuits of alternative cultural diplomacy.

A closer examination of Tajiri's process also sheds light on a significant, often understudied period of Berlin Wall history: the more than two decades during which both Germanys and their allies adjusted to the fact of its existence without knowledge that it would one day fall. For the Western powers, this meant not withdrawing the goal of free access to the entire city but, nonetheless, shifting away from the contest over the Wall as the focus of their Berlin policy. For the GDR's leadership, the fact of the Wall's endurance affirmed the goal of making the structure alternately more functional and estimable. The signing of the Four Powers Agreement in 1971, and its implementation a year later, also affirmed the Cold War détente in Berlin and affirmed the vision for cooperation in the walled city.[13]

Concurrently, more artists began making sense of the Wall's shifting and embedded physicality as well as the geopolitical terrain on which the border was situated. Artists aware of continued American military presence in West Germany, discerning the festering pockmarks of past conflicts, and those taking advantage of emergent cultural programs pondered the ways such an insistently violent border could be approached. They turned to conceptual and site-specific projects dealing with its material existence at a time of sublimated violence and border tensions. While the Wall's inner and outer layers were in a state of near-constant repair, continued sublimated terror, and routine bureaucratic watch, artists took the lead in publicly reflecting on its increasingly but loosely standardized conditions. German artist Joseph Beuys served as a catalyst to this emergent rite, suggesting that the Wall be raised five centimeters to correct its aesthetic proportions.[14] Beuys, a practitioner of "social sculpture," an expression of the conceptual art movement that placed the experiential elements of viewing or making art over its material value, continually merged performance and installation to comment on German history and division.[15] His call to tinker with the Wall's height was a provocative gesture dually concerned with the physical and the symbolic adaptations of the border.

Tajiri, too, was among a cohort of international and American artists in West Berlin who took on the question of how to approach and represent the Wall as a blunt geopolitical border and a structure deeply in flux. Such cultural figures aimed to make sense of the Wall by attempting to imaginatively "scale" it to a workable size, not to ignore it or to flee its confines, but to bring it to a form and view amenable to critique. This included scrutiny, of its builders, divided citizens, and allied forces across the Wall, all of whom were responsible for the border's daily enactment, negotiation, and improvisation. As Tajiri approached the Wall to capture its fine details and full materiality, divided Berlin also became a place to weigh his own history and status as a self-exiled American.

As a new guest professor in West Berlin, Tajiri surveyed the Wall with an eye toward its unwieldy structural qualities and an exploration of his own artistic and expatriate identity. This chapter explores how this, in turn, led Tajiri back to considerations of American power and presence by the Berlin Wall. Such an approach drew on the interlinked historical experiences, artistic practices, and architectural evolutions of the border. The chapter ends by exploring Tajiri's multiple approaches to documenting the Wall, including film and varied images practices. Ultimately, Tajiri's long-standing project of approaching the Wall emphasizes the way his methods of geopolitical exploration and visual excavation were connected rites for the artist. In particular, his recurrent focus on the border signage of the American sector brings his experience as an expatriate artist and soldier in relation to the ripple effects of U.S. militarism. American artists, like their colleagues in Europe and elsewhere, reconsidered the scope and scale of the Wall as an artistic and geopolitical dilemma: to attempt to reconcile strategies of confronting the border's pernicious state while at the same time approaching the border as a venue for artistic inquiry and exploration.

––––––

The Berlin Wall's first major renovation coincided with an emergent status quo in which the divided city's Cold War status evolved further from potential battleground to site of simmering tension. In its early days, Berlin's division seemed to position the city on the brink of a global battle. Despite the later period of Cold War diplomacy and East-West acknowledgment, American presence in Berlin was nonetheless volatile. The American occupation of

Germany officially ended in 1955, but the U.S. military presence continued there through the Cold War. Following a high point in American–West German relations in the early 1960s, the escalating conflict in Vietnam and the rise of student movement protests in West Germany led to a fraying of identification with the legacy of the Americans as liberators. Martin Klimke notes, "The U.S. government's prestige began to change among the perceptions [of] the young generation both in the United States and Europe. . . . The notion that the United States, once seen as a democratic model, guiding spirit, and leader of the supposed 'free world,' was waging an ever-escalating and questionable war in Southeast Asia led many to revolt against what they believed to be a cynical version of democracy."[16]

Opposition in West Berlin to unchecked American military power occurred alongside grassroots global uprisings in Paris, Prague, Mexico City, Chicago, and other cities. In West Berlin, in 1965, the first prominent Vietnam War protestors gathered and threw eggs outside the Amerika Haus, a building designed for cultural exchange through state-sponsored cultural diplomacy. In 1967, dissenters amped up their pushback as several activists associated with West Berlin's Kommune 1 were arrested in conjunction with a plan to stage a symbolic "pudding assassination" on visiting vice president Hubert Humphrey with confectionary and flour. The harsh arrest of the planners of this action fueled massive protests that merged with others held around the visit to West Berlin of the Shah of Iran, a Western ally who claimed power during a CIA-assisted coup in 1953. (Angela Davis remarked on the latter protests in her autobiography, and future students of Tajiri's were incensed by the overwhelming repressive backlash in this period.) During the Shah's visit, protestors were met with violent reproach from the police, with one student, Benno Ohnesorg, shot by authorities. Such confrontations reflected the fragile relationship between authorities and younger residents in West Germany, which spiked activism directed at U.S. and allied institutions. This fueled a growing counterculture of dissent and radicalism in the city and the shift away from the Wall as the primary site of conflict in West Berlin.[17]

Such shifts in political attention and cultural attitudes about the Wall also coincided with a surge in artistic experimentation in West Berlin around the actual space of the border wall by the likes of Tajiri, Allan Kaprow, Christo and Jeanne-Claude, and a host of others. The evolving nature of the Wall, viewed as both a structural monstrosity and an environment inviting close-up exploration, was ripe for artists looking to question its contours. Claudia Mesch suggests, "A number of artists in West Berlin, several Americans among them, based their work on the material aspects of the postwar city space and of the objects and detritus that littered it."[18] The heightened attention to a standardized walled separation contrasted with loosened attitudes about direct or nearby engagement with the western area adjacent to the Wall. Though illicit, casually sanctioned graffiti on the Wall became a visual staple in the mid-1970s, a cohort of artists who encroached on the Wall did so with their eyes on its materiality and strange landscape.

A new cohort of conceptual artists aimed for institutional political critiques of social systems and the art world beyond their immediate composition, eager to work in and on Berlin. The Wall's sprawling context compelled them to incorporate it into projects amenable to conceptual art's broad, pointed aims. Tony Godfrey notes, "Conceptual art challenges the traditional status of the art object as unique, collectable, or saleable. Because the work does not take a traditional form, it demands a more active response from the viewer."[19] Godfrey distinguishes four classifications of conceptual art—ready-made or found object, intervention, documentation, and word-based—which artists take on singularly or in tandem. In Berlin, the physical and symbolic contours of the city compelled conceptual artists in all four of Godfrey's registers, as they set sights on the strata and stories of Germany's division, as well as previous eras of conflict laid bare in the city. The Wall was alternately considered a ready-made, a revised object, a site of beckoned interactivity, an observation tool, and a structure inviting cultural dialogue.

The range of opportunities for exploration often occurred with the financial and programmatic assistance of state-sponsored or mainstream American and German institutions. An anchor of this scene was one of its chief sponsors, the Deutscher Akademischer Austauschdienst (German Academic Exchange Service), or DAAD, which supported a steady rotation of international artists' projects in Berlin each year, including many proposed by Americans. The DAAD's artist program was originally funded in 1963 with a three-year, $3-million grant from the Ford Foundation and was later operated with support from the Berlin senate and the German government. Grantees were not limited to visual art but ranged in discipline from literature to performance. Among the first grantees were abstract painter Shirley Jaffe and poet W. H. Auden, a then-recent transplant to the United States from England. In West Berlin, a range of cultural institutions became venues with which the DAAD artists routinely showed and collaborated. The Free University, which opened in 1948, routinely hosted visiting scholars and in 1963 inaugurated its John F. Kennedy Institute for North American Studies. The Goethe-Institut also adjusted its outlook and methods across its network of language schools to include cultural programming appropriate to a time of dissent. Despite these larger, significant supports, other artists chose to break from the rhythms and constraints of grant cycles. The Galerie René Block began hosting visiting artist shows and performances in 1964, in coordination with the DAAD. Smaller grassroots organizations such as Künstlerhaus Bethanien, which fully opened in 1974 in an abandoned hospital in Kreuzberg, provided workspaces and residencies to international artists, including those from the United States. Overall, subsidized and supported artistic exchanges between Americans and West Germans were increasingly available to those seeking outlets in West Berlin through official networks. Such programs incubated a culture of experimentation and critique in proximity to the Wall.

Out of this period, even with an infrastructure of state-funded programs, Berlin gained the distinction of being both a wasteland of historical memory and an artists' dream destination, pushing the outer limits of formal circuits of cultural exchange. Artists responded to the city's aesthetic influence and physical landscapes and interiors. They made frequent trips across somewhat relaxed borders to East Berlin, and powerfully, the experience of living near the Wall, the ritual of living in the city, spurred American critical thinkers and cultural producers to seek West Berlin as a personal refuge, a pressure cooker, or both. Habitual West Berlin denizen Iggy Pop, who recorded albums with David Bowie in the abandoned-Nazi-ballroom-turned-recording-studio Hansa at the Berlin Wall, near Potsdamer Platz, recalled 1970s Berlin as "a city you could go to get lost in, or be forgotten and still get something done. A good and dangerous place for lunatics and the artistically minded."[20] The view from Hansa inspired Bowie's "Heroes," an anthem spotlighting insistent lovers who embrace at the Wall despite the risk and violence that surround them. The Wall's looming condition elicited numerous creative responses provoked by its evolving form, footprint, and shifting geopolitical realities.

In November 1970, performance artist Allan Kaprow visited West Berlin on a DAAD grant to pursue a site-specific project along the border. In conjunction with the Rene Block Galerie, Kaprow carried out a performance on Köthener Strasse in Kreuzberg titled *Sweet Wall*. Known for his "happenings" in other cities in which banal activities with minimal staging became vehicles for performance art, Kaprow referred to this as an "activity" in an advertised flyer. With a small group of collaborators and a location of an empty lot near the border wall, Kaprow fashioned a wall of cinder blocks held together with bread and jam as its mortar. Soon after constructing this analogous wall, the group toppled its own creation. *Sweet Wall* was neither a work of resolute mirroring nor fully disconnected from the idea of playfully and feasibly commandeering the physicality of the wall. Kaprow reflected on this project, stating, "As a parody, *Sweet Wall* was about an idea of a wall. The Berlin Wall was an idea, too: it summed up in one medieval image the ideological division of Europe. . . . Like the wall with its bread and jam, symbols could be produced and erased at will. The participants could speculate on the practical value of such freedom, to themselves and others. That was its sweetness and irony."[21]

Without expressing a blunt political critique of either side, the location of the project and its attempt to forge a proxy wall presented the border as an area ripe for site-specific interventions that questioned the parameters of Cold War cultural understandings. According to Mesch, Kaprow levied an engagement with experiences that were denied comparison by the Wall. She notes, "*Sweet Wall* examined a 'natural framework' for the materials being manipulated in the performance, and made reference to the actual Wall, constructed of Soviet concrete. . . . . Kaprow examined the collectivized labour process contained in both state socialist and capitalist models."[22] The collective aims also included a call to draw close to the abandoned urban core along the Wall. West German police, who functioned as unforeseen and unknowing participants in the performance, questioned the staged disruption but ultimately deemed it beyond reproach. Kaprow later released an activity booklet of the project, presenting his claims as parody. The resulting *Sweet Wall*, though reduced in scope and size from its referent border wall, nonetheless existed within an orbit of scrutiny, surveillance, and play along the actual border. Kaprow attempted to scrutinize and mitigate the effects of the Wall through a performative duplication.[23]

A year later, in 1971, Christo and Jeanne-Claude, married artists responsible for immense environmental and site-specific artworks, began realizing a massive artistic undertaking to address Berlin's traumatized past and divided present: to wrap the ruined remains of the Reichstag, located just steps away from the Wall. The two artists, though born in Bulgaria and France, respectively, had resettled in the United States in 1964. The first idea for the Reichstag project came at the suggestion of an American historian, Michael Cullen, who lived in Berlin. Cullen sent Christo and Jeanne-Claude a postcard in August 1971 while they worked in Colorado on their *Valley Curtain*. They met several months later and began working on this idea for Berlin. According to Christo, the notion of the Berlin Wall also inspired him to consider the ramifications of the hardened border: "I was still a stateless refugee, without a passport or nationality, and I was dead scared."[24] Their first idea was to construct a fabric fence to run parallel and thus mirror the Berlin Wall, titled *A Curtain for West Berlin*. The project proposal was reminiscent of their *Running Fence* (1972–76), a twenty-four-mile zigzagging installation of a monumental but permeable boundary also made with fabric, running through the coastal hills of northern California to the Pacific Ocean.[25] In 1972, they envisioned *Wrapped Reichstag (Project for West Berlin—Der Deutsche Reichstag)* to temporarily envelop in fabric the destroyed former seat of German government next to the Wall. The pair had previously issued a manifesto of sorts toward wrapping monumental buildings as a form of artistic intervention.[26] Christo and Jeanne-Claude created a vision for this project remotely with the help from city residents, until they visited divided Berlin for the first time in 1976.

The selection of the Reichstag as the project site was a way for the artists to engage the division of the city while pursuing a project that could be visible on both sides. The Wall was not off-limits for smaller artistic disruptions, like Kaprow's, but Christo and Jeanne-Claude imagined a much larger civic intervention. The decision to wrap the Reichstag called into question the practical dynamics of Berlin's fragmented governance. Jennifer Mundy notes, "The Reichstag was then under the jurisdiction of both East and West Berlin authorities. It was scarcely used, but such was the tension between the two governments, and the political sensitivity of the site, that the project to wrap the building was rejected three times."[27] The ruined iconic stone facade of the Reichstag was to be consumed by massive unfurled spools of fabric, visible from both sides, which simultaneously would conjure and withhold its sculptural form. Wieland Schmied adds, "The state of a wrapped object not only has negative aspect that the object is withdrawn, estranged from us; it also contains its formal qualities."[28] Along the wasteland of central Berlin's hardened border, Christo and Jeanne-Claude imagined an added visual system intended to treat the traumatized structure of the Reichstag and the Wall adjacent as a call to heal both monumental structures.

For three decades, Christo and Jeanne-Claude's Reichstag project lived solely in multiple iterations of large collages, before its eventual implementation years after the city's reunification in 1995. The first iteration, credited to Christo in 1972, is an assemblage that incorporates "pencil, charcoal, pastel, wax crayon, fabric, staples, photographs, map and tape," a diverse materiality that as an artistic proposal mirrored the space near the Wall, too, as an ensemble of material components. Later versions of collages also included fabric, twine, wood, and paint; the images incorporated representations of the outermost barrier of the Berlin Wall but dwarfed in comparison with the enormous Reichstag. Other additions involved alterations of the name of the work itself—for example, changing "West Berlin" to "Berlin" in 1977. The Wall could not be enveloped through artistic intervention, but its adjacent traumatized architecture could embody the division through an act of reconcilia-tion.[29] (Christo and Jeanne-Claude eventually and famously carried out their project in 1995, after reunification, attracting millions of viewers.)

The range of American artists who worked in or on Berlin during this period included others who did not look to the Wall as a primary site of en-gagement, at least not explicitly, but instead benefited from the increased networks and cultural resources for artistic exchange.[30] Such artists included John Cage, Nam June Paik, Carolee Schneemann, Edward Kienholz, and others who ventured to West Berlin and produced significant artworks less directly focused on the city's division. Nor did the location of Berlin bind the production of representations of the city to its actual terrain. For example, Lou Reed's 1973 album *Berlin* is a woeful and spiraling narrative about de-structive love in the shadow of the Wall, recorded before Reed ever set foot in the city. Later, as shared by biographer Anthony DeCurtis, Reed noted, "I love the idea of a divided city. . . . It was purely metaphorical."[31] But for other artists, those officially invited and those who ventured there on their ac-cord, the Wall became a more embedded architectural facet of the city. West Berlin emerged, too, as a well-known space of creative refuge and tension.

By the late 1970s and early 1980s, other self-exiled or visiting American Berliners followed suit. Lindy Annis, Jonathan Borofsky, Allen Frame, Nan Goldin, John Gossage, Keith Haring, Gordon Matta Clark, Adrian Piper, Lawrence Weiner, David Wojnarowicz, Bill Van Parys, and many others visited or relocated to Berlin toward their own productive ends. Such identi-fications with Berlin included a relationship to the Wall as both a border site and a cultural meeting place and occurred without knowledge or insistence on the eventual Wall's end. Instead artists increasingly treated the city's divi-sion, at the Wall and elsewhere, as part of its despondent and chic identity, reflective of Berlin's emergent reputation as a postapocalyptic urban labora-tory where anything goes as geopolitical conflict simmers.

————

Before arriving in West Berlin and prior to his Berlin Wall survey, Tajiri had in his previous projects considered militarized division as a foil of freedom. But divided Berlin's own border zones offered him new source material to explore such landscapes. Tajiri, Leonard Freed, and Angela Davis were com-pelled to come to divided Berlin, and, in turn, the city became a productive space for confronting and testing the limits of freedom and their American identities. However, whereas Freed and Davis were prompted to return to the United States for their creative and critical productions, Tajiri's divided

Berlin project would remain in exile, as a closely held reflection on themes, places, and modes of representing the Wall and its cultural analogues. While traversing the city, Tajiri shifted and honed his previous methodological approaches to deal with the context of the Wall's reconstruction. Many of his other artworks differed in recognizability and levels of abstraction but shared in his approaches to mine personal or historical experiences through the symbolism of material traces. He outlined his working ethos: "The student, the artist, has to discover some sort of individual expression. I always have this idea that the artist or the student has to be a kind of an archaeologist and he has to pick as if to reign himself, and out of himself he has to produce these artifacts which tells me and tells themselves who they are. It's all a process of selfrealization [*sic*], and i think that's something you can't teach but you have to sort of encourage and guide."[32]

Tajiri worked out themes of excessive militarism, technology, and aggression—historically found within nuanced artworks pertaining to his home country's history and the Cold War between the United States and the USSR. Though he relocated to Europe, he kept a U.S. passport throughout his life, to ensure his ability to heal hinged on his desire to speak out against the violence and dislocation that haunted his youth and continued into his adulthood.

Tajiri's sculptural and conceptual works often reframed American national mythology and symbolism around dialectical pairings of spatial presence and absence. He cited American sculptor Gutzon Borglum as one of the few artists who influenced his practice, because Borglum "blasted the heads of 4 presidents out of the granite slopes of mount rushmore [*sic*]." (Borglum also contributed to Confederate Stone Mountain outside Atlanta, Georgia, and *Wars of America* in Military Park in Newark, New Jersey.) Tajiri understood the parallels between calculated destruction and Borglum's notion of "emotional value of volume" to use new methods to fathom monumental projects about American history, regardless of size or scope.[33] He viewed American geopolitics and constructed artworks by proposing visions and forging sculptures that presented material form with suggestive voids, membrane surfaces, visible negative spaces, and inferred connections.

For example, Tajiri named his sculpture *Wounded Knee, 1890* (1953) after the nineteenth-century U.S. Army's clash with the Lakota at the Pine Ridge Indian Reservation, which resulted in the massacre of more than 200 indigenous civilians. His chosen nomenclature conjures land theft, border conflicts, and the importance of the date in a history of national violence. Tajiri's surrealist ironwork has the surface of a cell membrane, climbs to over three feet to nearly resemble a small tower or satellite, and stands on three talon-like legs. Sharp objects including arrows, thorns, and scissors are abstracted as menacing spikes protruding off its top-half surface, with a hook engulfed in its visible midsection. When he later carved a representation of this sculpture on scraperboard for a retrospective book, he placed a black-and-white American flag under its base to conjure a military coffin.[34]

In 1958, in another set of sculptures called *Tower of Babel* or *Columns for Meditation*, Tajiri reflected on the "gap in communication" between the superpowers during the Cold War. He had pioneered a method of carving an inverse design into porous bricks. He sculpted not to build out, but through the reduction of form, effectively making a mold inside the bricks. He then poured a molten material into this cast to form the artwork, creating a complex representation of an upwardly built structure that is more allegorical than historically specific. Each tower comprises stacked levels that look like rooms, each one unique, leading to a top that resembles a rooster feather or a wilted leaf. Each level appears sturdy when all are viewed as strata on top of one another, and yet as a whole the towers are ashen, brittle, and suggestive of an impending crumble.[35]

Tajiri's *Made in USA* series, built in conjunction with a yearlong teaching residency at the Minneapolis Institute of Art (his longest return to the United States since the 1940s) consisted of over a dozen sculptures and related "machines." He reflected on the U.S. role in Vietnam and the ways technology is oriented to conduct war without face-to-face human interaction. Within this series, the sculptures carried either names like *Fortress* or *Tank* or just identifying numbers. Each had legs, as if to anthropomorphize them, but they also looked like hybrid figures, composed of abstracted, recognizable features of insects, leaves, high-tech weapons, and robots.[36] Tajiri wove together expressions of technology and grotesque nature. He pondered human intentions in leveraging creative energies toward violence and made them to help him confront the legacy of war in his own family and his life. The artist recalled, "They expressed the need to purge myself of the horrors of the war. . . . I meant them to be a protest against the excessive amounts of money spent by governments to wage hot and cold wars."[37] Tajiri was upset to learn that exhibitions of this work, like that held at Amsterdam's Stedelijk Museum, were perceived by visitors as glorifying war. He proceeded to look for other ways to explore themes of war, rethinking matters of abstraction and recognition.

Responding to the reception of his own antiwar artworks, Tajiri created a series of monumental sculptural knots. He aimed for a recognizable symbol, forging it in varying patterns in polyester or bronze in his home foundry. Against the misreading of his antiwar messages and wariness over the art world's turn toward conceptual art that at times privileged ideas over materials, Tajiri saw himself needing to fashion works of immediate perceptibility and territorial distinction. He stated of the series, "Put a knot in the middle of a jungle, and everyone knows what it means." However, his knots, as Lambert Tegenbosch writes, do evoke the traces of hidden meanings and conceptual aims beyond their shape: "A knot joins one thing to another. Tajiri, however, leaves one and the other thing out, thus depriving the knot of its function and primary meaning." Instead, Tegenbosch suggests that a "wealth of meanings" stem from recognition, as well as his titles, placement, and productive links with other works in his oeuvre.[38] Tajiri's first in this series, *Granny's Knot* (1968), was over eleven feet tall and resembled a partial bisection of a double helix. The knot conjured balance without symmetry, and solidity without continuity. (The sculpture was shown at Documenta IV, purchased by Nelson Rockefeller, and seen by students at the Hochschule der Künste, initiating their invitation for him to join their faculty.) The name of the piece refers to a common type of knot and offers a nod of familiar respect and remembrance of Tajiri's own family. This knot was crafted as a possible gesture of reconstitution in the face of insecurity and loss.[39] He built on this by producing hundreds of other knots, each with both obvious recognition and layers of visual riddles.

As a sculptor, Tajiri found in his Berlin Wall project a space of experimentation outside his studio that was process-oriented and materially focused. While many of his projects involved intensive processes of design, mold building, casting, and installation, he deferred these in the production of his Berlin Wall survey. He sought reflection over fabrication, as he carefully focused on material components of the Wall. Though he detoured from his usual practices, he pursued on-site study of such components of the Wall's renovation to further explore the themes of his larger body of work. Tajiri's images offer an extensive and ostensible visual inventory. Across the produced images that he captured in 1969–70, Tajiri presents an abundance of disparate building materials, border components, and social circumstances of division that together exploded the notion of a singular Berlin Wall. Specifically, Tajiri views the intended and unintended elements of concrete, steel, brick, wood, water, wire, debris, trees, gravel, sand, shrubs, rubble, and trash on the scene. He encounters multiple forms of machinery and modes of transport, including boats, excavators, trains, bicycles, trolleys, and cars, routinely parked perpendicular to the Wall in mundane fashion. He challenges notions of isolation along the border by playing between the physicality of the Wall and the social activity around it.

To locate a starting point days into his project, Tajiri drove to the southeast edge of West Berlin's American sector. There, he ascended an observation deck and pointed his 35mm camera downward at the wall system's outer barrier. Tajiri did not reach out to touch the Wall for fear of rebuke from the border guards, but he could explore the tangible components and contours in other ways, drawing close enough to fully observe and render his surroundings. He began to register a sort of "emotional value of volume," in Borglum's terms, without sculpted touch or formal casting. He varied his perspective, beginning with a view at the Wall from the top down. Tajiri was enthralled not only by the Wall's spectacular form, but also, and perhaps even more so, by its total environs.[40]

In these opening frames, he glimpses three uppermost concrete slabs placed directly onto one another, the steel support beams that reinforced the barricade and sent rust marks to its stone surface, and a pair of rounded cylinder tops that crowned each stack, unevenly but in tandem. The ground level is not visible on the western side, but a strip of dirt over the Wall is within prominent view. Tajiri indexes the smoothed dirt of the death strip but also includes patches with rocks jutting out on the ground. As a single image, this would offer an inversion of the political reality of the Wall, a structure seen chiefly from above and as placeless in its perspective. But in the beginning of an ensemble of views, he scoured the Wall's presence for the same sort of physical qualities he would see in the middle of the city—a range of structural feats that are foreboding and repeated emphatically to discipline the landscape and its people, as well as a plethora of instances in which shoddy workmanship and obvious cracks of a recently updated structure already dominate the view. Collectively, Tajiri captures dynamism and movement at the Wall. The rhythm of the artist's movements to document the Wall was more generatively staccato than exclusively even, incessant, monolithic, or standardized, in contrast to its builders' intended designs.

Through his study, Tajiri makes sense of the border in a way that opens understanding of the Wall as under renovation. Overall, he experiences the Wall as a social structure pertaining to the day-to-day enactment and negotiation of the border in both material and immaterial ways. Though he strives for completeness, or at least an accurate sampling, he never operates with a clinical totality. He forges a path, his camera as compass, to bring him closer to calibrating the Wall's sprawling architecture and acute curiosities. He weaves through the city to question how this structure functions as an outcome and technology of war and a scene of sublimated violence. He views land as mostly demarcated into clear distinctions of East and West, but in

FIGURE 3.3 Shinkichi Tajiri, *The Berlin Wall, 1969–1970*. (Shinkichi Tajiri Estate)

many streets boundaries are blurred, due to either the construction in process or the existing topography. In turn, the landscape holds the capacity to
disorient the artist. He easily glimpses the residential balconies, backyards,
and other habitual border crossings into East Berlin, at times surveilled by
border guards who pointed cameras and binoculars at him. Alternately, he
encounters places in which the ghost architecture of East Berlin by the border looks forlorn and frozen as a wasteland. As noted, graffiti at this time was
not a common feature on the Wall, as we see its dull, gray facade, though a
handful of central spots bear the marks of border guards' erasures by way of
covered paint.

But through his attention to materiality and the surrounding social scenes,
Tajiri comes face-to-face with his exiled American status. His path through
the city starts with images at the rural southern edge of West Berlin, as noted,
in the city's American section. Soon after, Tajiri brings this area's primary
geopolitical landmarks—"American Sector" signs denoting exit and entrance
along the borderline by the Wall—into dozens of frames of his study (fig.
3.3). Originally, the signs were placed throughout the middle of Berlin, following the occupation of the city after 1945, by all four occupying powers, the

FIGURE 3.4 Shinkichi Tajiri, *The Berlin Wall, 1969–1970*. (Shinkichi Tajiri Estate)

United States, Great Britain, France, and the USSR. They remained littered across the landscape as the border was fortified, even at locations without obvious checkpoints. Among the most recognizable instructions included "You Are Now Leaving the American Sector of Berlin / *Sie Verlassen Den Amerikanischen Sektor*," which would be read while facing east, denoting the end of the allied border zone. From the other side of the sign, which often had to be viewed from the very edge of West Berlin's territory, the text read, "You Are Entering the American sector / Carrying Weapons Off Duty Forbidden / Obey Traffic Rules." Other variations include those warning lines in French and Russian, or an abbreviated version in German that reads simply *Achtung!*[41] Over the course of Tajiri's project, the clear emphasis and repetition of the allied sector signs refuse to affirm the geopolitical layout of Berlin as logical landmarks. They become staggered question marks for Tajiri, to ponder as a possible element of the wall system or a reminder of this Cold War American frontier.

Tajiri encounters the first of these American sector signs outside the Waltersdorfer Chaussee crossing point, near his opening images (fig. 3.4). Taken from the middle of the street, the image shows a juxtaposition of messages: one sign announcing the end of the American sector and the other marking the beginning of the Soviet sector. Subsequently, in other takes close by, the signs are viewed from their side or from fifty feet away. In each case, the Waltersdorfer Chaussee checkpoint is viewable, with its low white dividers and mazelike routing system. No signs of border guards or imminent danger are immediately clear. Tajiri evidently sees more holes in the Wall, again, behind the signs and at the top of the Wall, beyond which he views the pale sky. The signs' variations match the uneven structure of the Wall itself.

From there, Tajiri follows the path of the Wall northward, toward the section of Rudow and the Teltowkanal waterways. He is mostly uninterrupted by obvious human interaction, other than checkpoints, for what seems like several miles. The Wall, when close to him, in many cases appears as rudimentary as it did in 1961. When the next three American sector signs are rendered visible in images by bridges over the Teltowkanal, they nearly disappear into the imaged backgrounds, including several bridges that are intact but fenced and off-limits in Tajiri's explorations. Instead, cars parked in the foreground (including Tajiri's own Lotus) or leftover accessories of the canal's previous life, such as life preservers set out for swimmers of a bygone era, mark the scene's geography as marginal, if not also forlorn.

As he moves onward, Tajiri alternates between exacting location through his camera and abstracting the Wall and the space around it. For example, at the Sonnenallee checkpoint, Tajiri captures two images that appear as a continuous panorama when placed side by side. From left to right, we see guarded fencing and light posts beyond the Wall and, in the West, preparatory guided driveway for crossing and a decorative garden gnome atop a tree stump in the foreground. In the next image, we find a parked car and an American sector sign obscured by a tree. But, as Tajiri moves to the next site of imaging, we see the continuous landscape has been disrupted. This view, taken from an observation deck, shows two American sector signs along this crossing, which means the artist must have moved it out of his frame, along with the observation deck in the previous series. Later, at the intersection of Wegastrasse and Planetenstrasse, the street sign and an American sector sign are both unobstructed. All four languages of the occupied sectors are clearly noted, including Russian. The Wall behind comprises a bottom quarter of the frame, while the rest is composed of the open sky.

In the Treptow district, Tajiri encounters updated sections of the Wall behind elements of the older built border. Trees, shrubs, and property fences also clutter the view of this architectural revision by the East. Tajiri continues to use the American sector signs as visual landmarks, but their plotted positions are inconsistent in relation to the border structures around them. Whether posted in repeated fashion at crossing checkpoints or in desolate areas beyond the purview of clearly demarcated pedestrian footpaths, these signs continue to evoke something elusive and ghostly about the American presence in Berlin. While neither subject nor fully subtext of the artist's explorations of the city, they comprise a landmark in reference to the long arc of U.S. military intervention and occupation. If the signs are both explicit and redundant with the walls behind them, do they attest to military strength, a competing claim of sovereignty, or a woebegone claim to American power over this geopolitical space? Are these signs functional or obsolete relics? Tajiri does not offer a clear answer. Like his knots, they give the appearance of completeness without an anchor or clear functionality. In the early years of Berlin's division, the signs may have made sense as a means to demarcate the landscape, but in the years of a maturing border system, Tajiri picks up on their enduring, odd placements. They have become a part of the scenery as border structures have been built despite them and flora has grown around them.

Tajiri's compositions in the center of the city focus less on the negative spaces around the Wall and more on the death strip area and construction zone of the borderline. He views materials that sit close to the Wall that are left in the temporarily deactivated death strips and the machinery once aimed to reinforce the border but now in a state of disuse. Instances of heightened activity and architectural makeover are visible as the circumstances of a renovation in progress, alongside others of disrepair and disregard. West Berliners are seen nonchalantly gathering, playing, or moving through the city, all near the Wall. For example, one man, whom Tajiri captures in several frames, walks his dog and peeks through a gap in a newly placed concrete barrier to view the construction activity on the other side. Within several blocks, at the intersection of Zimmerstrasse and Lindenstrasse, Tajiri finds a Wall area nearly finished in its reconstruction (fig. 3.5). At least five strata of the border systems past and present can be seen here, from wire fencing around the border's guard post to the tank traps in the death strip to an updated interior "hinter" wall to the elements of a new outer wall nearly raised to include new concrete slabs. But from his view, Tajiri focuses on traces of the previous generation of wall building and a sandy area in the foreground with a parked excavator with no workers in sight. Two American sector signs are visible: one has been ungrounded and lies atop a pile of building materials, while another, beyond the sandy construction zone, is still upright. The presumption, if one follows the rest of the strange logic of border zone sign-

FIGURE 3.5 Shinkichi Tajiri, *The Berlin Wall, 1969–1970*. (Shinkichi Tajiri Estate)

age, is that the sign will be placed back into the ground upon completion. If not, its full disposal, one could imagine, will only nominally address the geopolitical situation. Together these two pairings epitomize a key observation of Tajiri's imaginative and multifarious wall "sculpture": in the former, the American sector sign is situated in a central city wasteland, a border of alternating hyperactivity and disregard, a sense that both the East and West are working against nature to uphold a border without a true logic; in the latter, a toppled American sector sign conjures a mundane tinkering at this stilted but nonetheless fortified front line. Neither image clarifies the position of the American presence in Berlin or affirms the success or failure of the Berlin Wall, but, rather, they hint at the unresolved status of the city, its border, and its divided people. Tajiri spotlights the arbitrary and purgatorial nature of the Berlin Wall as an illogic of war, the by-product of a longtime military occupation, and an inverse vision of American power abroad. His place, as his own stated method suggests, is as an artist digging to question and comprehend his exiled surroundings.

Tajiri took the majority of the images from this survey in the city's internal American sector, the largest of the three allied zones. But he does not stop at its internal allied sectors, and he moves beyond Checkpoint Charlie near its northern interior edge, toward the bombed-out and untouched ruins of central Berlin, to the British and French sectors. Tajiri first travels on the margins of Potsdamer Platz, which, located at the bottom of the British sector, he views as a nearly empty void. The traces of previous eras of hyperactivity rise to the surface, including abandoned subway staircases and a void left across their surface. Next, Tajiri looks at and through the Brandenburg Gate as a window into East Berlin and varies his stance farther back, a fair distance west on Strasse des 17 Juni. With the gate and East Berlin's Fernsehturm visible on the horizon, he balances out the scene with a view of a nearby Russian World War II memorial, strangely located on the west side of the Wall, a by-product of the zigzagged nature of the city's division. The memorial is another oddity in the divided landscape, a strained space of symbolic and actual sovereignty in the midst of the western side of the city.

If Tajiri's previous sculptural projects were balanced commentaries between traditions of violence and technologically enhanced manifestations of war, his Berlin travels also shed light on the duality of willful militarism and arbitrary, even absurd, geopolitics. In these allied sectors, he views the Wall as a site of spectacular violence and mundane management, a structure that cuts up land as it follows and creates tense spaces and illustrates formidable battles between human control and nature's reclamation of such dividing lines. The artist initially felt the Wall as a magnet drawing him into its resurgent urban core, but he also understands it as embodying a duality, its paired repellent force. Just north of the Brandenburg Gate, still within the British sector, he encounters the ruins of the Reichstag, where a couple and their child walk through the sprawling field beneath its steps. There is little natural overgrowth here, as the lawn looks recently trimmed, but neither is it a hub of activity. Tajiri's view of the other allied sectors builds out his sculptural view of the Wall with additional adjacent and ghostly structures, partially ruined architecture, and nature's role in the reclaiming of empty spaces along the border.

In the northernmost allied French sector, for the final steps of his study, Tajiri finds more of a border and surrounding landscape under continued identity crisis, between calm and the impinging calamity of the border. Among the first scenes, he locates a tennis court and set of matches near Chausseestrasse. Without the Wall comprising the primary horizon line in his image, one might easily mistake the gentle scene for a country club. The lamps above the court are meant for nighttime play, not simply borrowed from the adjacent, illuminated death strip. The chosen image highlights the juxtaposition of urban leisure with the infrastructure of division. This oddity is matched in others he sees nearby, with children playing in the dirt at a French sector construction zone, a line of newly planted trees perhaps better suited for an orchard than a would-be war zone, and lines of cars casually parallel-parked near Bernauer Strasse.

In the French sector, Tajiri's status as neutral observer is tested in ways he had not accented previously. Tajiri climbs the slight incline of Bernauer Strasse and offers close-ups of four memorials dedicated to people killed while attempting to escape East Berlin. He hones in on the names inscribed—Ernest Mundt, Rolf Urban, and Ida Siekmann—and an inscription that commemorates a fourth, unidentified slain border crosser. Tajiri varies his approach with each but hones in on the materials used in the vernacular memorials themselves, which clearly incorporate elements of the border system, including barbed wire and wooden planks. The memorials do not float out of context of their western production, though they are nearly subsumed into and overshadowed by Tajiri's treatment. In a subsequent frame, his lens captures a nearby border guard in lockstep who looks back at him. Simultaneously another observer on an observation deck photographs that same border guard from above. These relationships between observers mirror the relational components of the Wall. This stage of the border's development is another study in looking for the tools of war; rather than overwhelming efficiency, power, or speed, the Wall and the forces of its adjacent allied sectors appear enmeshed in a moment of adjustment and disassociation. The fear of imminent conflict segued into status quo acknowledgment and stasis, but the shadows of violence remain. Whether as landmark allied signs or haunted traces of conflict, Tajiri's images adapt the border components into traceable abstractions themselves.

Tajiri took the last two dozen frames of his photographic sculpture in the northernmost region of West Berlin. Here, train tracks in the Pankow section become the predominant structure between East and West. In most instances, one gets the sense that Tajiri is riding the S-Bahn train, perhaps disembarking occasionally to view the scene. The images are in soft focus, as if we are viewing the artist and the elements around him in motion. There is no clear rendering of the Wall as sculpture here, in Tajiri's view or in the logics informing the border area. The final images offer no denouement for the project or the structure. The fact that Tajiri rides the train around this section to view the Wall signals the difficulty of traversing this part of the border zone, its obliteration of the natural form of the city, and the artist's own desire to move beyond it. Perhaps this also marks an attempt to satisfy his interest in a structure without a perceptible end. The Wall here is physically more distant from

Tajiri than it has been previously, but nonetheless it is shown as interconnected, staggered, and deliberate. With the inner core of the city behind him, Tajiri moves through the outer region of the allied sectors. Overall, his photographs exist as fragments, but as a study in sculpture they conjure or approach a vision for critical reflection. The artist varies his distance, perspective, and approach. As an artist in double exile, he finds the border to be a threshold, a productive space to observe and experiment, and where he withholds a final place of closure or return.

———

Tajiri's 1969–70 survey of the Berlin Wall was a study in the border's standardizing form and simmering geopolitical surroundings. Other than the official images made by GDR border guards for private record-keeping and their commanding officers, Tajiri's study happens to be the only known comprehensive record of the wall system as the structure in construction, a study in the sprawling divided city's architecture of the period.[42] But Tajiri did not arrive at any one final outcome for his project. As opposed to most of his physically constructed sculptures, which once installed were considered complete, his conceptual photographic and sculptural study allowed him to rework his raw materials and to continue tinkering with his image archive of the Wall.

Despite immense efforts, the Wall's architectural evolution was not finished during this stage of revision. Although there was a major overhaul in the late 1960s, the GDR leadership decided to proceed with another redesign several years later. As Tajiri's images attest, after the prefabricated concrete slabs were installed, they could not escape their shaky foundations and difficult-to-manage standardization, resulting in further need for extensive repair. Plans for the fourth generation, Grenzmauer 75, were released in 1975, with construction beginning the following year. The iconic Berlin Wall of prominent historical recall (and later post-1989 salvage) included over 45,000 individual concrete segments with L-shaped bases, smooth surfaces, and coats of light paint, which when lined up in sprawling sequence made for a compelling canvas ripe for artists and commenters from the West.[43]

Tajiri, too, returned to reimagine the scale of the Wall shortly after his ground survey. The frustration evident in his final images led to a varied mode of visual observation. In 1972, with the permission of the Berlin senate, Tajiri flew over the city and captured a continuous, twenty-minute film of the Wall while he was strapped into a British "Sioux" helicopter. His idea was both conceptual and attentive to pragmatics of the border. He filmed from 200 meters away from the border, 200 meters in the sky, and with 200 meters of Sony Portapak tape held in a connected rigged backpack. Tajiri again attempted to see the Wall as one long sculpture. The footage, low-resolution by today's standards, was a technological achievement for its time, not to mention a feat of geopolitical balance. Tajiri uses a transcendent media: he could temporarily overcome the Wall and pursue a scope unimaginable from the ground. He makes the Wall, the border system, and the landforms around on both sides visible as a continuous set of interlocked structures. But rising above the earth, he misses the rich detail he achieved during his wandering through the city. Despite the poetry of flying above Berlin's wall, the distance is lacking in what the photos offered: an attention to close-up form, as well as the disruptions, variations, sublimated violence, and broader contexts of what division wrought on the terrain of the city.

Three years after Tajiri self-published his *The Wall Die Mauer Le Mur* in 1971, he resumed work with his negatives of the Wall survey. He began to produce daguerreotypes using a nineteenth-century photochemical practice that produced ghostly keepsakes, a process nearly as antiquated as the notion of a walled city itself. He fashioned nearly 100 small daguerreotypes in an alchemic process; six featured scenes by the Wall, including images of Checkpoint Charlie and the Brandenburg Gate.[44] Tajiri ended this experiment with daguerreotypes after a doctor advised him of potential mercury poisoning. In this iteration of the project, his Wall visions are self-evident artistic oddities, unwieldy and precious objects. They propose a renewed reading of the Wall by producing its likeness as an artifact, more rarified than the palm-sized self-published book. After making these daguerreotypes, Tajiri put his negatives in storage. He lacked the immediate interest or necessary patience to print the series in full, but he continued revisiting the Wall project in new ways every few years. Tajiri's sculptural study had stalked the Wall's transformation from monumental front line and then adopted it as an object of reverence and experimentation.

Despite Tajiri's extensive work in divided Berlin's American sector, he did not pursue the same level of public engagement back in the States as he did in Europe. His works remained largely outside American purview, as he focused on his teaching and life in Europe. But he continued to interact with American artists who visited Europe, such as Leonard Freed, Kenneth Snelson, and Keith Haring, as well as others like Dorothy Iannone, who resettled in West Berlin from the United States. Tajiri found a passion for teaching at the Hochschule der Künste, which he continued through 1989. When he took his students on an international trip in 1985, the destination was not his home country but another famous wall: the Great Wall of China.

While most American viewers would have to wait years to see Tajiri's Wall works, one brief glimpse of his vision did make it back to art audiences in the States. Some of his aerial shots of the Wall were embedded in Yvonne Rainer's 1980 psychoanalytic art film *Journeys from Berlin 1971*. Rainer, a feminist choreographer and filmmaker, made the film in conjunction with a 1976–77 DAAD fellowship. She combs the contexts of Berlin's division for a film that is neither linear nor limited to the city of its titular framing. Even the inclusion of "1971" in her title, not the year of the film's production, mis-directs. As Mesch suggests, "Berlin is a point of departure and not a desti-nation for Rainer, and therefore the title of her film. . . . It is quite difficult to describe the film given its disparate quality, particularly in terms of the dis-junction between sound and image." Tajiri's shots feature in this cinematic assemblage, with aerial footage that shows the Wall as elusive, not presented with the goal of comprehension, and appearing alongside other aerial foot-age of Stonehenge and street shots of Berlin and New York. Mesch adds, after "one of Stonehenge, which becomes increasingly legible . . . the other [is] an almost unrecognizable view of the Berlin Wall, slightly out of focus and difficult to make out or place."[45] Rainer credits Tajiri, but the work as pre-sented disavows an apparent connection to Tajiri's extensive traversing of Berlin. Instead, the clip appears as disassociated footage, without the context of his creative or critical imperative to look closely at and scale the border to a workable view. Much of Tajiri's Wall works remained in limbo, too, far from the public squares and museums he was used to installing in, until he felt ready to reveal this work beyond its points of process.

Outside his time spent as a teacher in West Berlin, Tajiri made brief visits back home, as short interruptions in his longer exile. For Tajiri, the Berlin Wall remained a site of prominent contact, where he continued to treat the city and its border area as a forlorn transnational American space. In 1981, for the wall's twentieth anniversary, Tajiri took 360-degree panoramas of twenty-four prominent intersections. On Snelson's advice, he used a Widelux F7 camera and, rather than moving upward through the entire city, found a way to hint at the contours of shape in an image. The newest generation of the Wall, Grenzmauer 75, bears signs of a descent into disrepair, new graffiti, and on its periphery, the continued presence of American sector signs (fig. 3.6). In one photo, the sign is covered in a dried glob of paint. The sign has been absorbed into the blank canvas imagined as the Wall. In another, Tajiri is able to capture the "other" side of the typical American sector sign, still from the west, marking entrance as opposed to exit. Set against a bleak, up-close view of the Wall, plain without graffiti, cropped to avoid its rounded top, a Christ-

FIGURE 3.6 Shinkichi Tajiri, *The Berlin Wall, 1981.* (Shinkichi Tajiri Estate)

mas tree cast aside at its footprint, at its walkway at its base, the sign is the telling detail of the far right-hand side, the far end of the 360-degree image (fig. 3.7). The signs reads, in English, "You Are Entering the American Sector / Carrying Weapons Off Duty Forbidden / Obey Traffic Rules." Tajiri's approach gives a view of the border scene from inside out. This seems to be the first time he has documented the view of the other side of the sign in any of his images, which would have been seen in a previous era upon exiting East Berlin, but then faced the Wall instead. However, he provides no significant views of the American sector beyond this one, or a clear view of the sign. He prefers to stay on the city's margins, perched almost at the point where the sector signs are located, close to the Wall. Of his panoramas, he made prints, on both paper and linen (which he called "Berlinens"), and intended to build a room for viewers to walk into — not a sculpture of the Wall but a monumental form to share his perspective.[46]

That same year, 1981, his installation of a pair of identical castings of his *Friendship Knot* sculpture underscored his American identity as a balance between distant connection and chosen exile. One version of Tajiri's knot was included in the exhibition *Amerikanische Künstler in Berlin* at the Amerika Haus in West Berlin, the institution in Schöneberg established in 1945 to promote cultural exchange between Berliners and Americans and the site of the Vietnam protests in the 1960s. The show was held semiregularly with a rotating cast of artists and was sponsored by the Initiative Berlin-USA e.V., and its director wrote in the 1986 catalog that Tajiri was among the eight artists selected "from among the nearly one hundred who currently work in Berlin. . . . They all allow us to experience the effects this city had on them."[47] Tajiri's knot stood outside the building, and a photograph of its installation in the catalog depicts a wooded scene outside, akin to the notion of the knot in the jungle. Here, a sculpture made by a self-exiled American, outside the West

FIGURE 3.7 Shinkichi Tajiri, *The Berlin Wall, 1981* (detail).
(Shinkichi Tajiri Estate)

Berlin Amerika Haus, reaffirms a location of creative exchange and critical distance, against the long shadows of war and its reconciliations.

The same year, another casting of the *Friendship Knot* was given a permanent placement in the United States. Standing over twenty feet tall, the work was fabricated and shipped from the Netherlands to Tajiri's hometown of Los Angeles. This *Friendship Knot* was placed in Little Tokyo on Weller Court, outside the previous home of the Japanese American National Museum. In a rare occurrence, Tajiri returned briefly to America for the dedication ceremony. Family members from Europe and the United States joined Tajiri, as did such luminaries as Los Angeles mayor Tom Bradley and actor George Takei, himself a former resident of the internment camps. As a new landmark of the Japanese American section of the city, the *Friendship Knot* was dedicated as an icon of survival, resilience, and renewed civic participation. In the tradition of Tajiri's knots, it also served as a space to question and explore reconciliation in the face of traumatic loss. That day, as part of the festivities and a gesture of gratitude, Tajiri received a key to the city, a symbolic artifact that opens no doors but harkens back to the divisions and loss of home in his American past. Tajiri brought the key back to Baarlo. He hung the commemorative key in his Dutch castle, in the hallway outside the wing that housed his studio, where he would see it whenever he returned from teaching, between his back-and-forth commutes to West Berlin.

CHAPTER 4 | MIDNIGHT CROSSINGS

Audre Lorde, Intersectional Poetics, and the Politics of Historical Memory

A border is a dividing line, a narrow strip along a steep edge.
A borderland is a vague and undetermined place created by
the emotional residue of an unnatural boundary. It is in a
constant state of transition.

—GLORIA ANZALDÚA

"During these first days of 1984, I would like to share with you and the people of the world my thoughts on a subject of great importance to the cause of peace: relations between the United States and the Soviet Union," stated President Ronald Reagan from the White House East Room in advance of a summit on European disarmament in Stockholm. In this speech, President Reagan shared a New Year's message intended to promote greater communication with his Cold War adversaries. Delivered in the wake of in his own administration's spike in aggressive, anticommunist rhetoric and directives, President Reagan publicly pivoted as he prepared for a new series of diplomatic meetings. A year earlier, President Reagan had deemed the Soviet Union an "evil empire" in the midst of policy initiatives and military interventions aimed at the aggressive Reagan administration "rollback" of socialist governments and forces around the world. He sent U.S. troops or financial support to anticommunist forces in Afghanistan, Nicaragua, El Salvador, Angola, Cambodia, Grenada, and elsewhere.[1]

Divided Berlin further slipped as one of the reaccelerated Cold War's central hot spots, as the leaders from each side of the Wall adjusted the landscape and their policies toward further acceptance of a walled reality. With its newest Wall renovations in place, the GDR removed the tank traps and ground spikes, previously nicknamed "dragon's teeth" and "Stalin's lawn," from the death strip, due, in part, to their harsh appearance and seeming obsolescence. Part of the balance achieved along the Wall was underwritten with covert exchanges between the two Germanys. With options for temporary visas growing, the GDR secretly sent 35,000 migrants across the border for permanent resettlement to help cover economic shortcomings, including paying down loans of over 1 billion deutsche marks (DM) issued to the GDR by West Germany. Frederick Taylor writes that the GDR "basically set up a completely alternative, secret economy that it didn't have to account for" to deal with a shrinking economy and increased defense costs. This included sales of weapons, antiques, and black market goods and a "blatantly criminal source of foreign currency [that] came from the GDR's sale of its political prisoners to the West. Political prisoners as 'export items.'"[2] The East Germans received upward of 100,000 DM per political refugee, and the exiled refugees in turn helped support their economy. The border area along the Wall remained a pernicious and even lethal locale but with increased opportunities for cross-border interaction and management. Due to both internecine and external pressures for reform across the Soviet bloc, the geopolitical focus of the Cold War once again shifted toward sites dispersed around the globe.

Meanwhile, also at the dawn of the New Year, poet Audre Lorde faced several pressing uncertainties that coincided with the weeks surrounding her fiftieth birthday. She had just returned from her parents' Caribbean homeland of Grenada, shortly after the Reagan administration directed U.S. troops to invade the island following the ouster and execution of Prime Minister Maurice Bishop. Lorde went there to survey the aftermath of the occupation and drafted her troubled response in the essay "Grenada Revisited: An Interim Report." Her observations were a late addition to her first book of collected prose essays, *Sister Outsider*. In the first weeks of the year, she wrote the Grenada essay while she reviewed the manuscript's final edits on typeset pages. An accomplished writer and National Book Award–nominated poet, Lorde had recently authored a reflective opus, the autobiographical "biomythography" *Zami*. But her rationale for publishing her first collection of essays was in part to increase availability to wider audiences and to ensure that more of her work would survive beyond her lifetime. Two weeks before her February 18 birthday, Lorde also began weighing options, as her doctor had discovered a tumor in her liver following an acute gallbladder attack and recommended a biopsy.[3] Already a breast cancer survivor, Lorde elected to put off immediate treatment. She was wary of invasive medical approaches to treating liver cancer and thus avoided getting a firm diagnosis. Amidst these profound exigencies, Lorde kept working and followed through on a commitment she had made the year prior: to serve as a guest professor for the summer semester at the John F. Kennedy Institute for North American Studies at the Free University in West Berlin. She opted to travel, holding off on a liver biopsy that may have prevented her journey to West Berlin. "I'm asymptomatic now except for a vicious gallbladder," Lorde wrote in her journal. "And I can placate her. There are too many things I'm determined to do that I haven't done yet." She included on a short list of unfinished aims to "see what Europe's all about."[4]

Lorde's early life and writerly output had previously inspired forms of identification across borders. She was born in 1934 after her parents had settled in New York City. She published poetry from her teen years onward and eventually worked as a professor to supplement her writing. In her early twenties, she visited Mexico, and international travel became a common mode and theme of her later work. Trips in the 1970s and early 1980s to Ghana, Barbados, the USSR, and Grenada greatly impacted her life and work, as did her activism on behalf of women writers of color and the antiapartheid movement in South Africa through the group she cofounded, SiSA (Sisterhood in Support of Sisters in South Africa).

Lorde's first trip to divided Berlin in 1984 occurred in the midst of swirling turmoil but initiated a significant period of personal and communal transformation. She arrived in April and settled in an apartment on the ground floor of Auf dem Grat 26, outside the city center near the Free University in Dahlem. Lorde lived across from Thiel Park, a green space with meadows and a pond surrounded by willow trees. She explored the city with her partner Gloria Joseph, moving between circuits of mainstream and alternative cultural diplomacy. She led readings and discussions, including one at West Berlin's Amerika Haus. She met with women in East Berlin.[5] At the Free University, Lorde taught three seminars: Contemporary Black Women's Literature, Contemporary Black Women's Poetry, and The Poet as Outsider.[6]

During her three-month stay, Lorde faced persistent health problems due to her ailing liver, including an inability to consume solid foods. Dagmar Schultz, the Free University instructor and women's press editor who had invited the poet to West Berlin, found a homeopathic doctor who began treating Lorde's cancer with injections of Iscador, a remedy derived from mistletoe. This form of therapy soothed her illness and energized her to write. By June 7, she had already written in her journal of the treatment, "I feel less weak," and when she returned home later in the summer, she added, "Saints be praised! . . . The tumor has not grown, which means either the Iscador is working or the tumor is not malignant! I feel relieved, vindicated, and hopeful."[7] Lorde faced a terminal outlook and daily challenges to her health

FIGURE 4.1 In the park, 1984. (V/N-47/227, Audre Lorde Archive, John-F.-Kennedy-Institut für Nordamerikastudien, Freie Universität Berlin Archives)

but continued to surpass personal and professional aims for her visit. In the company of Schultz, Joseph, and other friends, Lorde found places to thrive: flower markets, dinner parties, and lesbian nightclubs such as Die Zwei and Pour Elle. By June 16, as the summer solstice approached and sunsets in Berlin extended deep into the evening, she wrote in her journal that dancing was a source of catharsis and joy.[8] This journey to Berlin also fueled the expansion of a broader diasporic consciousness specifically honed in Germany. Lorde was prolific in the divided city, despite her fragile health, fears of mortality, and distance from home. She routinely documented both her struggles and triumphs: "Sitting here in this lovely green park in Berlin," Lorde wrote in her journal, while sitting in Thiel Park, "I feel I still have enough moxie to do it all, on whatever terms I'm dealt, timely or not. Enough moxie to chew the whole world up and spit it out in bite sized-pieces."[9] Lorde expanded her diasporic consciousness with teaching and writing poetry as her most powerful tools of navigation and survival.

After she returned to the United States in July 1984, her health remained stable for several months. She began publishing numerous poems, essays,

FIGURE 4.2 Dagmar Schultz, "Party in Begine," 1984. (Audre Lorde Archive, John-F.-Kennedy-Institut für Nordamerikastudien, Freie Universität Berlin Archives)

and journal entries drafted during, related to, and inspired by her time in Berlin. The imprint of Lorde's first trip to Berlin, including her three-month guest professorship at the Kennedy Institute for North American Studies at the Free University, would become most publicly legible to readers of *Our Dead Behind Us* (1986) — a collection of poems that includes "Berlin Is Hard on Colored Girls," "This Urn Contains Earth from German Concentration Camps: Plotzensee Memorial, West Berlin, 1984," and "Diaspora" — as well as in *A Burst of Light* (1988), a book of essays and edited journal entries written in the months surrounding her trip to Europe. These public modes of literary production evince Lorde's self-revealing, interdisciplinary poetic methodology. But they also hint at a cache of Lorde's unpublished drafts of poems, journal entries, photographs, and audio recordings left outside her readers' seemingly transparent access to the circumstances of her life.[10] This first 1984 visit and other trips to Berlin continued to profoundly shape Lorde's personal and published personae. But if such a constellation of works marks her moments of public productivity and healing in divided Berlin, it also lays bare her moments of difficult translation, skepticism, and persistent challenge, especially around legacies of racism and militarism evident in the city. Lorde's relationship to the city was as productive as it was fraught with com-

FIGURE 4.3 Cover, Audre Lorde, *Our Dead Behind Us*, 1986. (Norton)

plex negotiations, especially as she considered her sense of being alternately at home and on edge in Cold War Berlin.

Lorde's creative methodology for writing poetry sheds light on her own previously stated theoretical formulation that poetry is an imaginative form of historical record and intervention. Lorde's primary identification as a poet did not preclude her pursuing multiple genres of political and critical writing or engaging in nonpoetic forms to deal with the political potential of poetry and reckon with structures and sites of division.[11] Consider her critical assertion in "Poetry Is Not a Luxury" (1977) that poetry is the "skeleton architecture" that forges "a bridge across our fears of what has never been before," in which she conveys a connection between poetics and political reality. She expresses her conceptualization of this idea in the form of an essay, merging prose and poetic lines to justify her argument against abstract reason and expression without grounding in existing struggle.[12] For example, in one conversation following a reading at Café Araquin, she tells audiences, "books . . . make bridges between people."[13]

Emblematic of Lorde's relationship to her poetry, and to the divided city of Berlin, was her ambivalent treatment of the Berlin Wall. Lorde engages the Wall in numerous writings to ponder its geopolitical relevance and its symbolic weight. She presents the Wall as both a spatial and temporal divide and a poetic manifestation of division to be countered with diffusion. From 1984 onward, the Berlin Wall would enter Lorde's poetic language as a complex symbol of history and memory through which she addressed Cold War–era issues of division and difference, and solidarity and survival. At times, she would treat the Wall in abstract terms or turn her gaze to the broader implications of a divided geopolitical terrain; at other times, she would face it squarely in order to critically engage the structure and its implications. The fact that she returned to Berlin annually from 1986, while the Wall was up, through her final trip a month before her death in 1992, after reunification, affirms her strong connection to the city, as do the traces of German division included in all of her subsequent published projects. Throughout her work, she drew from her rituals and routines of exploring the divided city, imparting both her peaceful thoughts and her more volatile experiences.[14]

Lorde's rendering of the Berlin Wall in her poems demands attention because she captures multiple forms of division on both sides of the divided city and eventually on both sides of the 1989 historical threshold. How she accounted for the Wall in language depended on the relative connections and sense of historical timing she wished to forge through her interdisciplinary modes of recollection. Bridging Freed's and Davis's often deliberately oblique reflections on the Berlin Wall, and Tajiri's on-site excavations, Lorde adopted a range of similar tactics to underscore her poetic explorations of division, in and outside Berlin, navigating through official and alternative circuits of cultural exchange.

Lorde's poems from *Our Dead Behind Us* and other writings from *A Burst of Light* forge connections between her Berlin-based self-reflection and her work across lines of difference and division, toward a practiced understanding of identity. The poet's revisions of her writing, in and of the city of Berlin, offer a compelling case study for exploring her creative process, as well as her personal projects of healing and diasporic connection. As Lorde powerfully wrote, "Poetry is not only dream and vision; it is the skeleton architecture of our lives," the divided city offered the author a poetic architecture of what Lester Olson terms "transnational sisterhood" and a creative space to continue working across lines of division despite her ambivalence.[15] Such a vision of "skeleton architecture" works in divided Berlin for Lorde, as she employs

multiple forms of construction of and revision to her poems there to reimagine borders of Cold War geopolitics and to delve into matters of political
complexity, personal estrangement, and survival.

The Cold War context for Lorde's poetic self-exploration can be best
understood through her mixed and flexible treatment of the Wall. She brings
the Berlin Wall into reflection with other global sites of division and shifts
her emphases based on the historical and geopolitical focus of her respective
evocations. She engages with the division of Germany closely in *Our Dead
Behind Us* and builds out additional reflections in complementary poetic
writing, prose, journals, and open letters. This chapter reads her publicly circulating work, as animated with readings of revised poems, journal entries,
and photographs and recordings from archives devoted to her oeuvre, to
view how multiple layers of revision and editorial selection inform her geopolitical views: how, when, and if Lorde depicts the Berlin Wall in order to
reflect on broader thematics and moments she encounters around her time
in divided Berlin. Thus Lorde's poetry can also be understood in conversation with broader discourses on memory and border politics, including those
that contest the Reagan administration's reaccelerated Cold War policies and
other cultural actions envisioned or enacted by the Berlin Wall.

———

The Reagan White House's call for Cold War peace in early 1984 immediately
followed several proxy instigations directed at its Soviet Cold War antagonists,
including the invasion of Grenada. Together, both forms of politicking served
as mutual, if not befuddling, counterpoints of strategy to simultaneously en-
flame and pursue dialogue with the Soviet Union. In spite of the pendulum
shifts in policy concurrent with multiple sites of proxy conflict around the
world, Germany's political status continued to inform the American political mindset. Even as the Wall diminished as the prominent point of standoff between and among Cold War powers, its symbolic weight continued to
hold a significant place in American culture. For example, during the weeks
leading up to the fortieth anniversary of the end of World War II in April
1985, President Reagan announced a plan to commemorate the occasion with
a visit to Bitburg, West Germany. Allied bombing in 1944 had decimated the
Rhineland town near the Luxembourg border. Bitburg was transformed into
a NATO airbase during the Cold War, eventually under the supervision of the
U.S. Air Force. Reagan's mission would include a visit to the Bitburg airbase
and a ceremony at the Bitburg Military Cemetery with West German chancellor Helmut Kohl. Reagan was to lay a wreath to honor German soldiers

buried there. At first, his plans did not include ceremonies in any other allied countries or other prominent sites from the war. Upon the announcement of the trip, the fact that the Bitburg cemetery included burial plots for forty-nine Waffen-ss Nazi officers was made known to the American public. Immediately, members of Congress and prominent Jewish Americans criticized the selection of Bitburg for this commemoration, given that no former concentration camps or sites of Jewish trauma were included in Reagan's itinerary.

Reagan addressed critics at a press conference, clarifying his decision as a matter of forging further reconciliation with West Germany, one of the United States's "staunchest allies," which in the early 1980s had supported NATO efforts to station major components of its Pershing missile system throughout the country despite its own domestic "Euro Missile" protests. Reagan also mentioned the ss soldiers, whose particular combat histories became fodder for his defense of the planned trip. Reagan claimed, "Those young men are victims of Nazism . . . drafted into service to carry out the hateful wishes of the Nazis. They were victims, just as surely as the victims in the concentration camps."[16] Elie Wiesel, Holocaust survivor and Nobel laureate author, who happened to be visiting the White House the following day at a ceremony in which he was bestowed with a congressional medal, addressed the president directly: "May I, Mr. President, if it's possible at all, implore you to do something else, to find a way, to find another way, another site. That place, Mr. President, is not your place. Your place is with the victims of the ss."[17] Following the public outcry and Wiesel's appeal, the White House amended the president's agenda, adding the Bergen-Belsen concentration camp to his official itinerary, though the president kept his commitment to Kohl to appear at Bitburg. The decision did not fully appease critics and further incensed those who saw Reagan's visit as a form of hastened closure and forgiveness, an offering of shared identification with both victims and perpetrators of World War II.[18]

On May 5, President Reagan laid two wreaths 220 miles apart: one at the base of an obelisk at Bergen-Belsen and another above the tombs of buried German soldiers at Bitburg. Reagan issued remarks at the Bitburg airbase later in the day, to put his two gestures of commemoration in perspective. After making brief remarks to address "veterans and families of American servicemen who still carry the scars and feel the painful losses of that war" and "survivors of the Holocaust," Reagan defended his overall mission to honor U.S.–West German post–World War II relations. To accentuate his point, his speech sampled a famous declaration of identification with Berlin, conveying the importance of this transatlantic diplomatic relationship: "Twenty-two years ago President John F. Kennedy went to the Berlin Wall and proclaimed that he, too, was a Berliner. Well, today freedom-loving people around the world must say: I am a Berliner. I am a Jew in a world still threatened by anti-Semitism. I am an Afghan. And I am a prisoner of the gulag. I am a refugee in a crowded boat foundering off the coast of Vietnam. I am a Laotian, a Cambodian, a Cuban, and a Miskito Indian in Nicaragua. I, too, am a potential victim of totalitarianism."[19]

Reagan's rhetorical approach was to conjure myriad identifications through equivalence and, like Kennedy, claim status as a Berliner. But Reagan extended the identification with Berlin to accommodate a host of other Cold War strategic alliances and disputes through the series of "I am" statements. By mentioning the Holocaust and the Berlin Wall in the same statement and joining them with other geopolitical identities, he attempted to personalize and stand in for a litany of "victims" in Cold War hot spots—without identifying his own administration's participatory or aggressive role in cultivating these global conflicts. Further, he did so without defining the particular forms of suffering and culpability evident in each context. Beyond reconciliation, West Germany was to be affirmed publicly as a crucial military partner in the Cold War and as a site of valid American and NATO armament. To be at once a Berliner, a Jew, a Vietnamese refugee, and a prisoner of a Soviet gulag is an appeal to identification without difference and a justification for increased military action in and through West Germany. Leveraging an identity as a symbolic Berliner—in presence or rhetoric—can be viewed here as mode of political maneuvering confused with memorial recognition.

In addition to Wiesel, American cultural figures responded loudly to Reagan's visit to Bitburg. The trip inspired at least two musical rebuttals: the Ramones' "Bonzo Goes to Bitburg" and Frank Zappa's "Reagan at Bitburg." In an interview with *Spin*, Joey Ramone (otherwise generally a supporter of Reagan) said, "We had watched Reagan going to visit the SS cemetery on TV and were disgusted. . . . We're all good Americans, but Reagan's thing was like forgive and forget. How can you forget six million people being gassed and roasted."[20] In another visual cultural response, African American expatriate cartoonist Oliver "Ollie" Harrington, who had lived in East Berlin since 1961, drew two editorial cartoons on the subject for the Communist newspaper *Daily World*. In the first, a grinning Reagan walks toward a gravestone with a wreath labeled "from Ron." Under the ground, one uniformed skeleton with SS paraphernalia rises to attention. In the second, another skeleton, again in combat gear, stands up from his grave and reads an official-looking decree titled "Full Pardon" and signed by Ronald Reagan and Helmut Kohl.[21] The cultural reverberations across the Atlantic revealed the problematic nature of historical memory and prevailing fears of ethnic violence in Germany underlying the intended act of commemoration.

If the president's stated goal was commemoration and furthering reconciliation in West Germany, such an action occurred in the wake of two currents in the United States. The first was a reacceleration of the Cold War through U.S. foreign policy actions. This resulted in a segue from Cold War détente following the end of the Vietnam War to the policy of "rollback" of direct military intervention or covert operations in nonaligned or socialist-led countries. This was propelled, in part, by President Reagan's concept of the Soviet Union as an "evil empire," even as possibilities for peace talks emerged. In 1983, Reagan announced the speculative "Star Wars" missile defense system and partnered with NATO to station 572 Cruise and Pershing II missiles across Europe, including 108 in West Germany. During this period, the United States also carried out military aggression or intervention through the support of counterrevolutionary forces in the Caribbean, Latin America, Africa, and the Middle East, due to fear of containment and to secure valuable commodities. This diverse and far-reaching group of foreign interventions points to the ways the view of a reexacerbated bipolar Cold War with the Soviet Union during the Reagan years underwrote a large expansion of the U.S. empire around the world and a redeployment of cultural fears of a communist threat barely tempered by occasional calls to thaw relations between the United States and the USSR.[22]

The second current that set the stage for Reagan's rhetoric was the boom in memorial culture. Political struggles of the Cold War were publicly routed through debates about "sites of memory" and questioned legacies of World War II freedom and repression. Pierre Nora's landmark essay "Between Memory and History: Les Lieux de Mémoire" (published in French in 1984 and translated into English in 1989) identifies "sites of memory" at odds with "real memory." In some cases, such sites are where "hopelessly forgetful modern societies . . . organize the past," yet for Nora, "sites of memory" also beckon the potential for a cultural memory that approaches "critical history."[23] Spikes in contested national expressions of cultural memory were also fueled, in part, by increased economic and social rootlessness, amidst swirling questions and debates about national identity, impacted by race, gender, sexuality, and class. Marita Sturken writes, "Cultural memory is a means through which definitions of the nation and 'Americanness' are simultaneously established, questioned, and reconfigured." Sturken discusses official memorial projects as measures to bring "cohesion" and "closure," as opposed to cultural memory, which seeks to democratize modes of historical representation and re-flection.²⁴ Given Reagan's rhetoric at Bitburg, especially his "I am a Berliner" remarks, his overlapping memorializing and Cold War strategic alliance missions become clear. He laid bare a U.S. agenda that sought to rescript national identity along the imperatives of rollback foreign policy, in this instance by routing a global American identity through Germany and the transnational cultural imaginary of the Berlin Wall.

Reagan was not alone in testing the expressive boundaries of Cold War rhetoric and policy. As discussed previously, American artists and writers had explored the Cold War "borderlands" of Berlin since 1961 to make sense of U.S. Cold War policy as well as to test the limits of American identity. Joyce Carol Oates's collection of short stories *Last Days* (1984) was inspired in part by her 1980 trip to Berlin. Oates writes about Cold War division along the Iron Curtain in stories about Germany, Poland, and North Africa, among other locales. Two of her stories, "Ich bin ein Berliner" and "Our Wall," take place on opposite sides of the divided city. In Oates's journals from the period of her own trip, she reports she was "haunted" by the Berlin Wall. She writes in the following year, as she was drafting her stories, "I swing back and forth between too much awareness of certain insoluble problems (I mean on a larger scale — society, the world, Reagan, our new mood of meanness and suspicion in America) and what must be too little."²⁵ In the first story, she personalizes "the danger of being an American in Europe" through a somber, defeated spin on a spy tale. The protagonist is the younger brother of a Fulbright scholar who claims the body of his sibling. The deceased brother's obsession with the Berlin Wall led to his fatal shooting at the border. Though the younger brother claims to reject identification — "for the record, I am not a Berliner" — he returns to the city and is tempted to reenact his brother's suicidal journey, to approach the border wall again from the West.²⁶ The result is a sense of doomed repeat by the Wall.

In the second story, "Our Wall," Oates reimagines the 1962 murder of Peter Fechter by border guards as he tries to cross the border from the East. She writes again as an imagined younger brother and employs a grammatical sense of shared identification ("our") with the Wall. The personal and political crises Oates writes about in her journal entries from Berlin are reflected in her own alternating close descriptions and dreamlike approaches to the Berlin Wall in the final pages of the work. She writes, as her protagonist approaches the forbidden, militarized border from its east side, "Someday it is whispered, we will overcome The Wall." Within several lines she ends her story, however, and pursues a detached narrative point of view. Oates concludes with a declarative statement: "Come closer, have no fear, long before you were born The Wall was, and forever The Wall will endure."[27]

Perhaps the most poignant rebuttal of the problem of American-German memory in the era of Cold War reacceleration can be found in Lorde's poems from *Our Dead Behind Us*. Inspired in the year before Bitburg (1984) but revised and published the year following (1986), the book of poems tasks itself—and the genre of poetry—as an ambivalent yet critical form of historical reflection. While Oates's short fiction is transfixed with the Berlin Wall, compelled by its totality and aura of alienation, Lorde purposes Cold War divides in Berlin and elsewhere to call for working with and across boundaries as a means to undermine them. As Sagri Dhairyam notes, *Our Dead Behind Us* "is a testament to 'the burden of history,' the overtly political freight that the poems carry. . . . The poems in [*Our Dead Behind Us*] resolutely stitch threads of various extraliterary discourses in the poetic."[28] While Reagan's trip to Germany sought to reaffirm U.S. global power through calls to memory and an extension of "I am a Berliner" identifications, Lorde's poetic explorations of diaspora in Berlin and elsewhere acknowledge difference as a meaningful source of identity; her work imagined or informed by divided Berlin also operates as a mode of interrogating U.S. empire and hegemonic notions of national authority by locating sites of diasporic consciousness that were also sites of U.S.-fueled conflict. In preparing to release *Our Dead Behind Us*, Lorde reflected on her own strained identification with Reagan in press interviews surrounding the project, as well as her need to relate. As she told West German journalists, "I cannot say I am black and so Ronald Reagan has nothing to do with me. . . . The personal and political are entwined; they are not the same, but they support each other."[29] Many of the book's poetic scenes occur in or refer to a litany of American Cold War hot spots and sites of grassroots activism: Germany, South Africa, and Grenada or within the United States at sites of racial, gender, sexual, and economic violence.

The book's title, based on a line of her opening poem "Sisters in Arms," is an invocation of memory and forges a language of shared belonging. She does not attempt to distance herself from the "dead" to whom she refers but, rather, create space for memorialization and collectivization.[30] Further, the "us" in the title *Our Dead Behind Us* conjures multiple potential meanings. The title announces a call for collectivization but marks division and difference as the ground for solidarity. The "us" could also stand in for "U.S." and refer to Lorde's own wrestling with her identity as American at a moment of Cold War reacceleration, which she made public through alternate, lowercase spellings of "america."[31] In this sense, Lorde's poetic approach bridges the geopolitics of the Cold War and memorial culture—just as Reagan did at Bitburg—but in ways that allow diasporic consciousness to be forged across lines of difference, with poetry enacting open-ended reflection instead of closure. As Lorde writes in a poem in *Our Dead Behind Us*, "Home," she follows a path to seek out meaningful spaces of mourning and belonging. Grenada is conjured as "her mother's island," and in the poem she weighs kinship through and beyond a "name in the stone." She seeks connections that live beyond violence and disruption of military conquest, as well as state-sponsored and traditional forms of memorialization. Adding a purposeful spatial pause, a signature of Lorde's work to be explored throughout this chapter, she calls for alternate forms of inscription: "we did not need to   go to the grave-yard / for affirmation."[32]

———

Upon her arrival in West Berlin in April 1984, Lorde promptly wrote in her journal that within a week's time she found an emerging sense of balance and new possibilities for her life.[33] Lorde was taken in and taken aback by Berlin, a city that led her to new paths of recovery, haunted her, and became a site of immense productivity. Berlin offered an archive of poetic imagery and ideas. Lorde drew from her relationship to the physical environment of the city in all of her writing about her experiences there. There, she was aware of how her multiple intersecting identities (black, lesbian, poet, and American, among other distinctions) marked her as an outsider but also gave her opportunities to work across difference on both sides of the city's internal divides. She encountered active silences about racism and anti-Semitism maintained in the long shadow of Nazism encoded in the city's public spaces, and she at once repurposed them as sites in which to speak out against injustice. Lorde turned to divided Berlin as a space of self-fulfillment, homeopathic treatment, critical confrontation, and habitual return for poetic work, and those close to her contend her trips to the city added years to her life and new layers of meaning to her work.[34]

Lorde's initial encounters in the divided city prompted poetic exploration. For example, the unpublished, free-verse poem "First Impressions"—which she began as a journal entry on May 2, 1984, a month into her first trip to Berlin, and then typed out and revised in three iterations on May 15—exemplifies how Berlin's historically traumatized urban spaces served as poetic points of reflection for her. In the poem, she captures her observations of life in the divided city through a series of pairings in which she addresses the concepts of home, health, and longing. Her observations are not centered on West

Berlin's sprawling layout or central divides but on its confined spaces. Here Lorde conjures Berlin as a space of intimacy as well as strained refuge. Comparable to the contemporaneous Berlin-based work of American photographer Nan Goldin, who included her portraits of women in bathrooms in *The Ballad of Sexual Dependency*,[35] which premiered the same year, Lorde begins her poem behind the locked door of a bathroom stall in West Berlin, where she processes the cultural distinctions and her challenges within this new city. Lorde represents Berlin as an alluring and bewildering domestic space within which she experiences both estrangement and comfort. Lorde conjures Berlin as neither an open city nor limited to just east or west. Against the backdrop of Lorde's professorship and exploration of Berlin, her first poem focuses on subtle observations, urban rhythms, and German turns of phrase that catch her attention.

She closes the poem with stories outside in the city, alluding to women she meets and how she moves with and around them as she navigates the city. The women in this poem are not sought here for simple solidarity or generative dialogue. They allow Lorde to hide, a form of restraint not usually attributed to a poet known for her outspoken nature and coalitional thinking in Germany.[36]

In her drafts of "First Impressions," she experiments with the placement of a refrain locating herself "in Berlin" to bridge and blur distinct observations between the lines of the poem. For example, the phrase does not appear as the ending line of her untitled journal version that provided the initial lines for this poem. She added the phrase two weeks later to the final line of the poem when she first typed up the work. This first typed draft includes the refrain on its own line at the end of the poem, only to be crossed out in a handwritten edit. The next draft and the final unmarked version retain the phrase, though she removes the line break and joins the final two lines with modified wording,[37] functioning as what Amitai F. Avi-Ram refers in relation to Lorde's work as an "apo koinou," a word or phrase that through enjambment shares meaning between two lines.[38] Whether the handwritten edits on the typed-out drafts are Lorde's or another reader's, the poet's questioning of how to deal with being in the city stands out. Lorde mined the physical and cultural makeup of the divided city as a surface of reflection and turned to poetry as an outlet to consider such observations. The fact that this poem remains unpublished, while much of her other writing about Berlin was prominently revised and published, reemphasizes the productive tension between Lorde's site-specific prolific output and purposeful exile in the divided city.

Outside of this early poem, Lorde also explored the complex landscape of the city, moving between public spaces of reflection and her own intimate sites. While clearly evinced in her poetry, a cache of photographic snapshots taken on the trip also lays bare these dynamics of public inquiry and personal refuge. Most of the photographs were taken within or at the edges of her apartment. In one, Lorde stands outside by a door, a large bouquet of flowers clutched to her spring jacket, her bag leaning against her door, as if she had paused momentarily before reentering. Most others revel in small details of the apartment, including her desk from multiple angles, open windows and doorways, furniture she has rearranged within the apartment, and a sight line from her desk and a rose in a vase facing toward the greenery outside (fig. 4.4). (On the back of another print, an inscription reads, "As you can see, I tried to decorate the drab out, first thing.")[39] In the images taken in public spaces, Lorde appears as a figure making sense of her surroundings. In several photographs, each taken with varying angles of the unmistakable cobblestone patterns of German streets (fig. 4.5). According to Schultz, she was transfixed by this fine detail of the city's common street areas. Here, the poet traces and indexes the rough edges and intricate designs of the city's built environment, the perspective suggesting that the camera is inches off the ground but varied in each image.

Other images, however, focus on the multiple facets of divided Berlin and its transnational character. One likely taken from a car in West Berlin (fig. 4.6) features a street corner with a long view down a residential street. From this vantage, a message displayed on the tall firewall of a building reads, "EIN VOLK BRAUCHT FRIEDEN / HANDE WEG VON NICARAGUA" (A People need peace / hands off Nicaragua), bringing American geopolitics back into her frame. Another photograph (fig. 4.7) is a detached shot of East Berlin's Alexanderplatz, the only visual artifact from the city's eastern half in this cache. The image captures the socialist public square from its edges, and the iconic World Clock is pictured in the middle distance. The clock, dedicated in 1969, contains an embossed world map and lists world capitals, including those from the socialist bloc. A yellow sign is inscribed with the designation "BERLIN" without naming its location in the East. Lorde's image is taken from a considerable space from these elements and other people, marking a distance to take in the full scene. In each of these images, she encounters text in public spaces that map geopolitical resonances and connections beyond the limits of the divided city.

As Lorde explored the cultural and topographical contours of historic Berlin on both sides of the Wall, much of her poetic and literary work focused on dialogue and interaction with women writers and activists. She conducted regular poetry readings and discussions with West German feminists about anti-Semitism, homophobia, lesbian identity, and racism, in venues such as Technischen Universität Berlin, Café Araquin, and Schokofabrik. As noted, Lorde, her partner Gloria Joseph, and Schultz visited with a group of lesbian writers in East Berlin.[40] According to Schultz, "We were at the time working with them; we were going to publish something they were writing [but it] turned out to be too dangerous to transport the material back and forth across the border."[41] In West Berlin, she joined an Easter Sunday demonstration against the U.S. deployment of Pershing II missiles, which led to the Amerika Haus. On the back of another picture from the day, the inscription reads, "Easter Sunday march — America House with police and moveable barricades drawn up in front to protect them from us."[42] Weeks later, in June 1984, Lorde read onstage at the Amerika Haus, including poems such as "Solstice," "A Woman Speaks," "Yankee Women," "Harriet," and "A Litany for Survival," before answering a question from the audience about the invasion of Grenada. She opened her question-and-answer session with an invitation: "A poetry reading is not a performance, it is something that is circular, it passes between us."[43]

To be sure, Lorde's time in Germany spawned a series of poetic possibilities, both for the German women she encountered and for herself. Lorde became a key figure in the emergent Afro-German movement, through and growing outward from her teaching. At the outset of her trip, she posed a question in her journal, "Who are they, the German women of the Diaspora? Where do our paths intersect as women of Color . . . [and] what can we both learn from our connected differences that will be useful to us both, Afro-German and Afro-American?"[44] Some of these women, as Lorde would learn, had African heritage that dated back to Germany's colonial occupation of Africa before World War II. Others were born to German mothers and African American GI fathers who had been stationed in Germany following World War II. In each case, these women were without identifying nomenclature or solidarity, often isolated or referred to by pejorative names such as *Mischlingskinder* (mixed brown babies) or "war babies." Lorde's time in Germany sparked an emergence of the very notion of "Afro-Germanness." Michelle Wright notes, "Afro-German activists most often point to Audre Lorde . . . as one of their most inspiring leaders and organizers."[45] Tina Campt also writes, "The thoroughly diasporic, cross-cultural exchange between [the movement] and Lorde contributed substantially to their articulation of their identity as Afro-Germans."[46] Lorde is credited in part for coining the term "Afro-German," and her encouragement in numerous dialogues, correspondences, and solidarity movements with women from this community led to

FIGURE 4.4 Snapshot, "Audre Lorde's Trip to West and East Berlin in 1984." (Audre Lorde Papers, box 66A, courtesy of the Spelman College Archives)

FIGURE 4.5 Snapshot, "Audre Lorde's Trip to West and East Berlin in 1984." (Audre Lorde Papers, box 66A, courtesy of the Spelman College Archives)

FIGURE 4.6 Snapshot, "Audre Lorde's Trip to West and East Berlin in 1984."
(Audre Lorde Papers, box 66A, courtesy of the Spelman College Archives)

FIGURE 4.7 Snapshot, "Audre Lorde's Trip to West and East Berlin in 1984."
(Audre Lorde Papers, box 66A, courtesy of the Spelman College Archives)

ongoing, reciprocal friendships with a number of them, including May Ayim and Katharina Oguntoye. It also led to the production of the movement's foundational 1987 literary text, *Farbe Bekennen: Afro-deutsche Frauen auf den Spuren ihrer Geschichte* (*Showing Our Colors: Afro-German Women Speak Out*), an anthology of autobiographical and poetic writings for which Lorde wrote the foreword, which included fragments drawn directly from this previous journal entry. As Lorde worked alongside these women, she posited Afro-German women writers as connected to a larger constellation of communities of African diasporic women and women of color.[47]

Wright and Campt note Lorde's foundational impact on the women writers of the Afro-German movement; what also emerges in an exploration of Lorde's poetic archives is the reciprocal effect that Berlin had on Lorde's vision of herself. This includes her modes of coping with her own evolving ideas about her work and life. The effect of divided Berlin on Lorde's sense of self is especially evident given her fragile health and homeopathic treatment, but it can also be seen through her wrestling with her identity as an American in divided Berlin — and the geopolitical complexities of being a traveling black lesbian writer from the United States who forged transnational solidarities and lodged critical inquires through poetry. In the same journal entry from before her trip, she notes, "We are hyphenated people of the Diaspora. . . . We are an increasingly united front from which the world has not yet heard."[48] Her mixed grammars of "we" and "they," along with the presumptive "I" of the journal form, epitomize Lorde's approach to both poetic and diasporic consciousness — exploring possibilities for connection across lines of identified difference especially through poetic writing. In addition to her significant contributions to Afro-diasporic communities in Germany and elsewhere, Lorde's own evolving process of creation included self-reflection and poetic revision helmed in divided Berlin.[49]

The profound transformation Lorde experienced in Berlin, from unsteadiness to a sense of purpose, can be traced to the way she interacted with the material contours and physical landscape of the city and translated them into her writing. In one edited journal entry, listed as June 7, 1984, printed from *A Burst of Light*, she meditates on her own struggle for survival. "I am listening to what fear teaches. I will never be gone. I am a scar, a report from the frontlines, a talisman, a resurrection." She weighs her own mortality and seeks legacy beyond her own time, as narrated from her vantage at that point in West Berlin. Lorde lingers on the themes of fear and survival while nodding to the geopolitical currents of divided Berlin and her place there. She writes, "And what does that war teach when the bruised leavings jump an insurmountable wall where the glorious Berlin chestnuts and orange poppies hide detection wires that spray bullets which kill?"[50] For the first time, she offers the Berlin Wall in her writing in the city. By introducing the Wall in her journal, she locates the divide as a place to weigh legacies of war she encounters in the city and to consider the transcendent forms of nature in which she is immersed while navigating the traumatized urban landscape. In this entry, she aims to shape her legacy and fight for survival, pushing ahead to heal herself and others, by looking at the Wall.

Confronting fear is central to Lorde's mission in Berlin, and the backdrop of the walled city becomes a venue for engagement with this emotion. But in unedited versions of this journal entry contained in her archive, "the wall" was pluralized, listed as "insurmountable walls" in both the entry of her personal journal and page proof from the book.[51] Both her original phrasing and her revision suggest the actual wall system's intricate and myriad modes of border control, including its multiple walls, but she also powerfully alludes to other lines of division she encounters. Lorde's understanding of her experience, living in Berlin across such multiple lines of division, may also include moments of refracted mirroring between lines of private and publicly edited poetic work. Lorde uses revision as a regular facet of her creative process. She treats the Wall as a formidable structure, though rarely as "insurmountable," as read through her revisions that frame the divided city as a space of strained coexistence and potential connection across multiple divisions.

After she returned home to New York from her first trip to Berlin in 1984, Lorde prepared poetry for publication that would ultimately appear in *Our Dead Behind Us*. She writes about this period in journal entries included in *A Burst of Light* (and in other pieces in her archive, including unpublished journal entries and drafts of poems) and presents this time from late 1984 through 1986 as one of revision and continued reflection about Berlin, a city she renders in descriptions of textures, both rough and soft. She collected several poems for a preliminary collection, initially titled, "POEMS from OUT TO THE HARD ROAD."[52] Lorde published some of her poems to be later included in *Our Dead Behind Us* in journals and magazines such as *Black Scholar*, *Ikon*, and *Parnassus*. She submitted the book-length manuscript, with forty-three poems, to her publisher Norton no later than December 1985, and in January 1986 she received page proof. The book was published in late 1986.

Given the centrality of divided Berlin to the book's conceptualization and production, Lorde's poem "Berlin Is Hard on Colored Girls" is an integral poem through which the author highlights her experiences of Berlin in poetic complexity. According to her archive, Lorde began drafting this poem in her journal on May 8 and 9, 1984, while teaching in Berlin. The typed drafts of the poem that survive are dated February 11, March 31, and April 1, 1985.[53] At each stage, Lorde tends to her draft around choices of language and line spacing. The poem features an intermingled use of recognizable symbols and sites from both sides of Berlin, as well as coyly presented private images and memories that transcend the divided city's limits.

Scholars have suggested that Lorde represents the plight of Afro-German women in her poem. Melba Boyd, who attended Lorde's reading at West Berlin's Amerika Haus, contends that the poem "embodies [Lorde's] identification with the plight of Afro-Germans and women of color in Berlin, as 'woman' is coded as the city, with forbidden borders and American influences."[54] The "American influences" Boyd mentions should also be read to include Lorde's own experiences in Berlin. To be sure, Lorde's poetic rendering of Berlin as a "strange woman" opens the poem around notions of identity and estrangement for her observations of the city but, importantly, also about herself. The title of the poem signals the Afro-German community's strained relationship with the city, but it also deploys the term "colored" to convey a potential connection with U.S. racial discourse; in this way and others throughout the poem, Lorde opens herself up as an additional, if not central, subject of the piece.[55]

Lorde begins her poem in the time-space of a dream and in the geopolitical reality of divided Berlin. The poem opens in a dream state, with the word "Perhaps" announcing its beginning and serving as a refrain throughout the remaining stanzas, as a " strange woman" sneaks into her bedroom at night, "wasps nest behind her ears."[56] In this poem, Lorde introduces this woman, and Berlin, through a matrix of diasporic images. The symbols in the first stanza — "kittiwake" birds, "lizard," and "gray whales" — conjure the tropics by the sea and thus connect readers to Lorde's other non-American homespaces, in Grenada and Saint Croix. The poem stands in as an encoded diasporic map, including divided Berlin. The possessive "my bedroom" stages an interaction that starts with an intrusion and cedes to acts of shared movement and translation.[57]

As the poem progresses, Lorde imagines ways to approach and transgress the Berlin Wall. The internal border of the Wall functions here along several lines as a divider: it marks the spatial divide between the poem's two stanzas, the introduction of the narrative "I," and the divider between one day ending and the next beginning.[58] By the second stanza, the speaker traverses the city's internal border at the Wall, and the narrative perspective changes to the first person: "I cross her borders at midnight / the guards confused by a dream." Like Angela Davis before her, Lorde conjures a scene of border cross-ing without mentioning "The Berlin Wall" in this poem. In addition to resist-ing the Wall's monumental nomenclature, Lorde finds several ways to locate and then transgress the poem's alluded boundary. She accounts for the Wall not through direct naming or its concrete architecture but instead through the language of "borders," "guards," and temporal and geopolitical trickery.

Midnight as a poetic time of liminality is crucial to this poem. The night-time offers a charged temporal space, as it suggests uncertainty, ambivalence, and possibility, while signaling intimacy between women.[59] In Berlin's geo-political time, midnight is significant, as it is a clear reference to the actual East German policy in which all sanctioned daily visitors from West Berlin would report and return back across the border-crossing checkpoints. The poem's travel after midnight suggests that border control ultimately fails to keep the city's division intact. In crossing the borders after midnight, in the poem Lorde imagines going against accepted protocols and gestures to understand that the Berlin Wall is as porous. For example, Lorde writes the woman is "selling a season's ticket to the Berlin Opera." In a city with two opera houses—East Berlin's Deutsche Staatsoper and West Berlin's Deutsche Oper Berlin—Lorde opens up the East as a site of habitual ("season") re-turn.[60] Ultimately, she undermines the normalcy and logic of division in the dream space of the poem.

Further, Lorde's use of the word "perhaps" throughout the work accentu-ates its liminal contexts and her own ambivalence about the city. Given her free-verse style, her poetic structure comes not from meter or rhyme per se but from the rhythm created through line breaks, stanzas, repetition, and spacing. The poem begins with the word "perhaps," which then reappears six times, either by itself after a line break or with extra space separating it from other words on the line. Mimicking the actual zigzagged path of the Wall, the word acts as an unsteady refrain and snakes through the poem, offering the work a sense of structure. Thus Lorde undermines polemic division and sin-gular political meaning, all while making sure the actions she explores in the poetic dream are both purposeful and conditional.

Contrasting the surreal realm of dream border crossings, her attention to extremes of tactility and texture is also important through both stanzas, as ex-pressed through a litany of images suggesting what she deems "a tender for-giveness of contrasts," including an interplay between the "hard" of "a gran-ite bowl," "a stone," "metal," and the soft of a "half-ripe banana," "Mother Christopher's warm bread," "silken thighs," and the "american flag." These contrasts ground the dream and poem in the city's material conditions—

including military occupation and fortified borders—even as they summon ethereality and a forgiveness akin to letting go. Among these "contrasts," Lorde's rendering of "american" without an uppercase "A" offers an implicit troubling of her national belonging and conjures Alexis De Veaux's formulation that Lorde selectively dropped the uppercase when traveling abroad.[61]

In the final lines, Lorde writes, "perhaps / A nightingale waits in the alley," conjuring the nightingale. The bird, an important poetic symbol from antiquity to the Romantic period, embodies and negotiates a number of divisions explored in poetry, including expression and silence, masculinity and femininity, and the threshold between life and death.[62] For instance, John Keats's "Ode to a Nightingale" looks to the bird, like a poem, as a way to transgress these boundaries.[63] Lorde reimagines and places her nightingale in Berlin's Cold War urban context.

Lorde's wall crossing is imagined through undermining the systems of border control in a dreamed excursion that culminates in another moment of potential flight. By previously spatializing and grounding her poem with closing mentions of the nightingale near a street "corner" and "the hair-bouncing step / of a jaunty flower-bandit" (an opaque reference to Dagmar Schultz),[64] the nightingale pauses for her in the alley, symbolizing escape, restraint, and comfort. Here, the city's hard edges—of history, of the Berlin Wall—make stone and concrete important material referents to Lorde's poetry in and of Berlin, as does the potential for soothing, softness, comfort, and flight from that very haunted and politicized urban topography.

Part of Lorde's complex and haunted relationship with Berlin was also connected to the public memory of the Holocaust. The city is where Lorde suggested she was "listening to what fear teaches" and remained as a "scar" in a place in which hatred and the afterlife of war remain as forces in the landscape. As in the poetic navigation of "Berlin Is Hard on Colored Girls," Lorde extended her own exploration of the divided city in another poem, "This Urn Contains Earth from German Concentration Camps: Plotzensee Memorial, West Berlin, 1984." Located on a lake in northwest West Berlin, Plötzensee was a former Nazi prison and execution house. In 1952 it was dedicated as a memorial to those persecuted by the Third Reich.[65] During Lorde's 1984 trip, the Plötzensee Memorial was West Berlin's most prominent remembrance of the Holocaust. As Lorde's title suggests, the site marks memory of the Holocaust by incorporating earth from each German concentration camp into a large urn at the entrance with an inscribed plaque in German from which the name of the poem is based. Lorde visited the site and retained copies of the memorial's takeaway pamphlet in her records.[66] It was one of the only sites in West Berlin in which she could discern public inscription to Holocaust trauma and memory. She began drafting her reflections as a journal entry while considering her own comforts and reservations at the close of her time in Berlin. On July 29, 1984, she wrote in her unpublished journal of the bland character of the memorial site. In particular, she located the urn as an unintentional symbol of the site's silences and disavowals regarding anti-Semitic violence. Lorde's identification with Jewish victims of Nazi tyranny was also connected to her concerns about contemporary racism in Germany.[67] Lorde connects her close exploration of this site of Holocaust memory to the plight of diasporic people of color in Germany. In doing so, Lorde connected her reflection on the history and memory of the Holocaust in Berlin to her Afro-diasporic consciousness.

Inspired by this journal entry and shared identifications, Lorde typed out drafts on February 2 and February 19, 1985, and continued to revisit the concept and edit the poem toward publication.[68] In the poem, Lorde marks this memorial as a site of contradiction rather than resolution. Lorde's poem conjures Claude Lanzmann's film *Shoah* by placing her vision of the site of memory around the "overgrowth" of nature and amnesiac cultures over sites of Holocaust trauma.[69] She also uses geographic space to signify historical time. Lorde's earliest drafts carry the titles "Plotenzee Memorial to the Resistance: Berlin 1984" and "Plotensee Memorial_Berlin 1984."[70] In the final draft, she makes two key changes: the primary title is a translation of the actual plaque inscription at the memorial ("Diese Urne Enthält Erde aus deutschen Konzentrationslagern"), which she had also cited in an early draft of the poem, and the geopolitical descriptive "West" is added to Berlin in the title. In the latter case, she recalls the specific location of the site, as well as how Germany's post–1945 division created spaces of historic estrangement and sublimated traumas of the recent past. Through all the iterations, her use of the year in the title reminds readers of the influence of her first trip but also resembles an inscriptive timestamp often found on historical markers or printed photographs, as if to retrieve the site from a frozen past and bring it toward an active present.

The poem opens with a tension staged between remembrance and erasure. Lorde begins with a recounting of the memorial's architectural features (a "stone wall," and parts of the memorial's actual inscription in her poem) set against memorial elements added to the site ("self-conscious wreaths/ the heavy breath of gaudy Berlin roses") in order to convey the gaps between what is presented and what is rendered silent in this historical scene. Her references to a "stone wall" and "self-conscious wreaths" also conjure the Berlin

Wall and place President Reagan's 1985 Bitburg cemetery controversy within the context of the problematic nature of Holocaust memory. "The heavy breath of gaudy Berlin roses" further suggests the empty expressive gestures of beauty in the face of a misremembered history. She compares the stone wall to the height of her daughter, personalizing her view of the historic site. The memorial, Lorde characterizes by the word "neatness," a contrast to what see senses as the pervasive haunting and lack of reckoning within the historic site.[71]

As a motif, Lorde again uses extra horizontal spatial gaps to emphasize the disjointed character of the scene ("Neatness / wiping memories   payment / from the air") to convey rhythmic structure, as well as to suggest gaps and silences in the imposed rhythms of historical time and memorial reparation. Rather than granting "neatness" as a simple observation, the spacing and phrasing together conjure a vision that is off-kilter and out of control. Society rushes to move on rather than healing or necessarily talking about its losses and tolls of the past.

Lorde goes on to describe her picnic in the park and lake area that encompasses the memorial park. The bucolic scene becomes eerie and features several juxtaposed images of reproduction and destruction. For example, Lorde describes sitting to eat: "beneath my rump / in a hollow root of the dead elm / a rabbit kindles," conveying at once a litter of baby rabbits and burning fire. Subsequently, as Lorde ends the picnic, the haunting does not cease. The appearance of a "writhing waterbug," a roach flicked but split open in her food, symbolizes through interruption the degradation and loss of life, as well as the potential for survival as deterred. As the bug appears, the picnic is halted. Lorde's line breaks and extra spatial pauses in this stanza convey an unsteady rhythm to this moment. The caesuras in this stanza—between "I stand   pick up my blanket" when the bug appears and "cracked open   her pale eggs oozing" after the picnic is disturbed—double as physical descriptions of stepping away and breaking open.

In the poem's final stanza, Lorde marks and pushes the limits of memorial practice, both at the site and in her own poetry. Here she distinguishes between "earth" in the urn and what is not brought forth, "the unremarkable ash" of human remains. She reminds her reader that commemoration cannot fully stand in for the loss of human life. She highlights how this site's appeal to nature as a form of rebirth doubles as a funereal absence and hinders critical dialogue about violence and history: "careful and monsterless," she recounts the site's central memorial vessel, "this urn makes nothing / easy to say." The collected earth contained in the urn perpetuates a harmful silence. Themes of fractured speech and silence coexist in these lines, as does her clear question-ing of sites of cultural memory like Plötzensee. The murdered people she ac-knowledges, in particular, are Jewish infants and teenage girls. Her gendering of the murdered Jews is carried out again in her reference to Ravensbrück, a predominantly female concentration camp outside Berlin. In relation to her work with German feminists, this serves as a call to identification through critically addressing their pasts. Her final lines, "careful and monsterless / this urn makes nothing / easy to say," respond to both the urn at Plötzen-see and perhaps her own urn poem as limited in ability to find the utterances appropriate to encounter such a violent history. Further, like her reference to a nightingale in "Berlin Is Hard on Colored Girls," the final lines conjure another classical symbol of poetry, the urn, and Keats's canonical "Ode on a Grecian Urn." Keats's poem also mediates the gaps between speech and silence but owes its culminating lines to a lesson "spoken" by an urn and conveyed in quotation marks: "'Beauty is truth, truth beauty,' — that is all / Ye know on earth, and all ye need to know."[72] Lorde's ending signifies and challenges Keats's ode, akin to her formulations within her "Poetry Is Not a Luxury" essay, to remind her readers of the aesthetic limits of memorial ges-tures, be they poetic and/or material. The past can be localized into poems, aesthetic objects, and memorials, but true loss extends beyond speech acts made evident in sites of historical reflection. Overall, Lorde revisits the the-matic extremes of soft and hard materiality in divided Berlin — the tensions between the inscription of the plaque and the physical traces it references, the offering of tangible earth that was sealed in the urn. Against these two material extremes, and between fine-grained detail and a bigger picture of the spaces wrought by division, Lorde conveys her own and a larger shared sense of divided Berlin as a simultaneous refuge and site of potential danger.

Finally, Lorde's poem "Diaspora" in *Our Dead Behind Us*, departs from and extends outward visions of these previous poems that are clearly sited in Cold War Berlin. Lorde mined the city's emergent diasporic identities and memorial displays and, in doing so, created a body of work that mapped the divided city into a larger, transnational vision of struggle incorporating mul-tiple political hot spots of the period. But the site-specificity of some of her divided Berlin poems was also balanced by the abstracted Berlin imaginary from which she continually drew. For example, a different poem, "For Jose and Regina," was titled in earlier drafts "Growing Up in Berlin."[73] The poem "Diaspora," however, bears the traces of her experiences of the divided city while expanding and confounding its city limits and symbolic landscape. The concept of diaspora is for Lorde tied to notions of danger and flight, as well as to connection across lines of division and difference. Modes of fear and survival are staged in Berlin in these works. Several other poems in *Our Dead Behind Us* have these themes or foci, some of which cloak allusions to Berlin in poetic imagery or were altered in the revision process. Lorde appears to have begun writing "Diaspora" in the United States; her drafts appear in an unpublished journal entry on January 30, 1984, before she left for Berlin.[74] Here she writes a clear vision for her forthcoming poem to confront the different manifestations of fear and what happens to the emotion when it passes.[75] The critical study and transformation of fear was an integral theme of Lorde's work and travels to Europe. Typed drafts of this poem appear in her papers dated May and July 1984. Here, as the poem eventually titled "Diaspora" emerges, readers understand the connections Lorde draws between fear and difference, American identity and exile, while conjuring and revising the poem in divided Berlin.

Lorde worked on "Diaspora" in West Berlin, and she imagined her experiences extending to her other travels in and beyond the spaces of U.S. military intervention, which included Cold War Germany. The term "diaspora" is recognized not only as a dispersal that transcends modern boundaries, but also as a form of militarized or politicized division that, once recognized, can be mined for creative and political projects.[76] She begins the poem with the line, "Afraid is a country with no exit visas."[77] In "Diaspora," Lorde problematizes national belonging. By referencing exit visas, she also nods to a key concern of East German activists working to achieve internal reforms of increased cross-border mobility. The Berlin Wall is both implied and extrapolated from here: the official state documentation and the controlled national borders delineate the hybrid country Lorde describes, but so do its horizons, outward stretches, and assembled topos. The adjoining of "Johannesburg Alabama" without extra spatial pausing or punctuation places the cities together in the shared space of the poetic line and thus joins them as mutually constitutive sites within Lorde's diasporic imagination and geographic rendering of repression. Lorde spends the poem naming and creating a roll call of other places, some actual and some imagined, to offer a vision of struggle, including the Shatila Refugee Camp in Lebanon and the "Braceras Grande." The latter is a wordplay on the Rio Grande but also the word *bracero*, or male manual laborer. Lorde offers the *bracera* as a female worker to present a womanist workforce in the context of the U.S.-Mexico border.[78] The rituals of return and flight here are accented by Lorde's poetic imagery and form, especially in one instance when she uses an extra spatial pause to add another site, this time of destination and return: "Washington bound   again." Notions of fear and leaving are enacted at the center of the American capital as well as along the margins of its militarized borders in Mexico, Germany, and elsewhere. Lorde suggests diaspora as a means of finding home while on the verge of or in the midst of the state of exile.

A nightmare in this poem, like the dream in "Berlin Is Hard on Colored Girls," is again a location of furtive movement, albeit in pronounced danger. But rather than the return to slumber or potential for intimacy, in "Diaspora" she pushes toward a state of chaotic and exigent movement at its close, leaning toward self-preservation. Her linkage of escape and movement across national borders incorporates numerous geopolitical contexts and courses of escape. Lorde blurs distinct geographies toward a mapping of the shared conditions of global division. The poem closes as its unnamed protagonist wakes and "gulps carbon monoxide in a false-bottomed truck" as she finds herself transgressing borders and fording rivers, "grenades held dry in a calabash / leaving." The image of a grenade hidden in a hollowed-out gourdlike fruit implies impending doom as well as a strategic form of resistance—and the chance of nourished liberation through flight. The last line as a single word, "leaving," enjambed and left hanging, pushes for further ambiguity. Leaving becomes a mode for Lorde in the poem to imagine movement without closure, a way of pointing and directing readers' attention beyond the poem, out into the world. To do so, she conjures a collective vision of a woman furtively crossing national borders to be cast into limbo, who interacts with Lorde through a dream. Diaspora is conjured through modes of border crossing and identification, dreams and geopolitical maneuvering, which bring about possibility through uncertainty, a recoding of the borderlands and practices of survival.

————

Between the writing and publication phases of *Our Dead Behind Us* in 1986, U.S. Cold War policy and the question of militaristic reach across national borders were matters of significant political debate. Reagan worked with newly appointed general secretary of the Communist Party of the Soviet Union Mikhail Gorbachev on missile treaties (including the Intermediate Range Nuclear Forces treaty), while simultaneously spiking rhetoric and policy around fears of a continued communist threat. Gorbachev, meanwhile, began ushering in a series of reforms known as *Glasnost* (openness) and *Perestroika* (restructuring) to imagine a new, more economical form of Soviet communism.[79] Against controversy surrounding nefarious aspects of rollback, the U.S. Congress passed new iterations of the existing Boland

Amendments to ban funding of Nicaraguan contras, as Reagan's CIA continued to funnel money to the guerrilla forces through illegal arms sales, later uncovered in the Iran Contra scandal.

Divided Berlin did not disappear entirely from Cold War consciousness in the United States, as the city continued its role as an integral military and cultural hub. Earlier in 1986, a West Berlin disco in the neighborhood of Schöneberg that was popular with American GIs was bombed at the behest of the Libyan government. The violent act killed two servicemen and one Turkish woman, and the United States responded by bombing Libya.[80] The following year, in June 1987, Reagan returned to Germany, this time to West Berlin as a speaker for the city's 750th anniversary celebration. On this trip he spoke in the British-occupied sector, within steps of the Brandenburg Gate. There, Reagan uttered some of the most memorable words of his presidency: "Mr. Gorbachev, tear down this wall." Reagan spoke on a stage within close proximity to the Berlin Wall, flanked by a backdrop of American and West German flags and a bulletproof, transparent window open to the Wall and Brandenburg Gate behind him. During Reagan's visit, thousands of West Germans also went to the streets to loudly protest his appearance, which occurred days after a series of homegrown May Day riots in Kreuzberg.[81] In addition to foreshadowing the ultimate thaw of the Cold War, the Reagan visit marked a "theatrical turn," as Ted Widmer suggests, in which "Reagan's inner actor proved shrewder than most who would have counseled realpolitik."[82] Cultural productions of the period continued to imagine ways to deal with the shifting geopolitical dynamics of Cold War Berlin.[83]

For Lorde, *Our Dead Behind Us* showcased for readers her approach to the ideas of diaspora and difference brought out through her travels to Europe, with an eye on related global sites of repression. Reviewers remarked on her geographic fluidity, though they varied in their views of the interrelatedness of her sites of poetry and the political approaches of her work. *TLS*'s Alice Phillips notes, "Lord [sic] travels instead to Grenada (at least in imagination), Berlin, Florida, Tashkent, reporting on old atrocities and new outbreaks of oppression, and returns to her racially unsettled neighborhoods in Staten Island, across the water from Manhattan, to write poems about them. . . . Lord [sic] is a mature poet in full command of her full craft; many of the poems here are classically austere, and even the more obviously message-ridden are tautly constructed."[84] An anonymous reviewer for *Booklist* writes of the ideological bent of the work, "She has been courageous in speaking her mind, in standing up as a witness. . . . The content is laudable; at least, if you agree with her."[85]

In either case, Lorde's movement across geography and history and her shifts in content and form work together. Similarly, Barbara Christian writes for the *San Francisco Chronicle* that as Lorde actually "moves through Germany, Grenada, Florida, New York, Lorde is irrevocably affected by events in South Africa, Chile, El Salvador, Russia—by women she meets as 'Sisters in Arms.'" Christian sees Lorde as outlining an approach to geography and history that is about reflection and transformation, and she shapes her review with inflections of Lorde's written discourse. She adds, "To change their pattern of life, those who 'left our dead behind us' must have rituals of healing, a 'lust for working tomorrow' . . . this ritual, this lust, this poetry is not a luxury. It is a necessity, Lorde says, if we are to survive."[86] Therefore poetry, like diaspora, is posited around its powers of connection and modes of healing that enable a mutually constitutive and communal form of survival.

Lorde's profound connection to divided Berlin continued to spawn possibilities for her and fellow writers. She stayed in regular contact with Schultz and with Afro-German women through letter writing. She applied for a DAAD fellowship for 1985, noting in a letter to the director that she would "like to develop my contacts with the Black German artistic community." In May 1988, on one of her return trips, Lorde addressed the Dream of Europe Conference organized in West Berlin, an event that was also significant to the early Afro-German movement. Again, for Lorde, poetry and diaspora are analogous concepts, and the time-space of the dream becomes a point of departure: "For most of my life I did not dream of Europe at all except as nightmare. . . . I was fifty years old before I came to Europe." Lorde's previous vision of Europe was transformed by her interactions and the connections she continued to cultivate after her first trip. Her fight for survival, and her Iscador treatments and self-care regimens, connected to her vision of what it meant to travel and change perspective at age 50. She adds, of her adjusted sense of place and purpose, "When I did, I found people there that now compose my dream of Europe. They are Afro-European and other Black Europeans, these hyphenated people who, in concert with other people of the African Diaspora are increasing forces for international change."[87] Berlin, the city she dwelled in and mapped in numerous ways, offered her a place to rethink and dream diaspora into existence.

In her remarks at the conference, she continued to weigh her status as an insider/outsider and riffing on dynamics of estrangement. She maintained distance despite the personal connections she forged for herself in Berlin. She noted, "I am an outsider, dreaming of Europe,"[88] while addressing a group she had cooperatively called into formation. Lorde's Berlin was a site of pilgrimage not only for joy or release but also to embody what she envisioned as "international change."

In the late 1980s, Lorde continued with her prolific period, as she continued to treat her terminal illness. Echoes of her earlier trips continued to mark her cultural productions. In *A Burst of Light*, her second volume of collected essays and a body of edited journal entries, as she had done with her previous *Cancer Journals* (1979) from her bout with breast cancer, she includes dozens of edited journal entries with embedded poetic and prose fragments to trace her processes of work, travel, and healing from cancer. The later entries span from 1984 to 1987. She reveals over time that though her living in West Berlin afforded her relief and a new form of homeopathic treatment, which inspired returns to Europe, she was in fact suffering from liver metastases. As in her earlier *Cancer Journals*, Lorde details conversations and thought experiments during her illness that more broadly pertain to her own creative process.

Though many of her poems dealt with similar issues of Cold War geopolitics and diaspora, her *A Burst of Light* prose and published journals indicated a commitment to poetics of diaspora by weaving together disparate written forms. In doing so, she emphasizes the poetic and travel methodologies that underwrote all of her work inspired by her time in Berlin. For example, her essay "Apartheid U.S.A." was written as a pamphlet in 1985 and reprinted in *A Burst of Light*. Lorde opens the essay with a similar approach, reading and intervening into divided urban spaces: "New York City, 1985. The high sign that rules this summer is increasing fragmentation." Lorde reads this "fragmentation" as a pitfall of the way violence is not only shaping the city but is mistreated in official narratives. She writes, "I am filled with a sense of urgency and dread: dread at the apparently random waves of assaults against people and institutions closet to me; urgency to unearth the connections between assaults. . . . You won't find that information in the *New York Times* or the *San Francisco Chronicle* or GQ."[89] Her writing aims to confront such disconnects and highlight violence and division as a part of geopolitics connecting home and abroad.

In "Apartheid U.S.A.," Lorde goes on to draw many connections: between South Africa's system of apartheid and "Nazi Germany's genocidal plan for European Jews"; violence perpetuated against black people across the United States and around the world; and the effects of the global market on people of color as affected by Cold War era policies, including the Star Wars missile system and the support of South Africa's apartheid regime. She ultimately calls for unity among people of the African diaspora in Europe, Asia, and the Americas: "The connections between Africans and African-Americans, African-Europeans, African-Asians, is real. . . . We need to join our differences and articulate our particular strengths in the service of our mutual survivals."[90] Lorde's vision of "Apartheid U.S.A." reckoned with historical and current practices of repression as well as pathways for connection and coalition.

Lorde's published journal in *A Burst of Light* includes eight entries located in West Berlin, drawn from a series that remain unedited in her archives. Alongside these Berlin entries are others from New York, Saint Croix, and Switzerland. Berlin again registers here within a global itinerary and imaginary, clearly mapping Germany into Lorde's work. The poet refers here to plans to return to the city for more mistletoe therapy and to work with Afro-German women.[91] In these entries, the words "Berlin Wall" do not appear. And yet, complex elements of German history and division play out in the entries through a mode that recalls and complements her poetry. The people, places, and modes of memory she melds into poetics of diaspora lend themselves to healing and political advocacy. In her final entry, listed as the epilogue and dated August 1987, she brings several of those threads together of writing, healing, and traveling. She notes, "I go to Germany this fall for further mistletoe treatment. I look forward to working again with the Afro-German Women's group." She closes with a vision of division and diaspora in that is both personal and collectively minded and that looks forward to her subsequent return to West Berlin: "My most deeply held convictions and beliefs can be equally expressed in how I deal with chemotherapy as well as how I scrutinize a poem. It's all about trying to know who I am wherever I am."[92]

Lorde advanced a poetics of diaspora through a creative discursive mapping of her identity in divided Berlin, connecting with the city as a significant and personal point of return. Whether for reasons of health, critical reflection, poetic inspiration, or advocacy, her commitment to the peoples of Berlin and to wrestling with the complexities of geopolitical division helped her further a concrete awareness based on location and the dreams of working across lines of difference.

CONCLUSION | **RETURNS**

1989 and Beyond

> In a divided culture, being undivided and synthesizing and
> connecting across broad areas can be an act of resistance. . . .
> And there's no firm dividing line between passionate political
> engagement and epiphany and pleasure. At the core of my
> writing is a desire to dissolve most of the cultural Berlin Walls
> running through our imaginations.
>
> —REBECCA SOLNIT

Like the construction of the city's first border divisions in the early hours of August 13, 1961, the demise of the formidable Berlin Wall on November 9, 1989, similarly left citizens of East and West Berlin, and others around the world, in disbelief. The infamous Wall's fate, at both its onset and eventual undoing, quickly drew the attention and involvement of American cultural figures and others who identified with the events in Berlin as sites of division and transformation. *A Wall of Our Own* reads these two flashpoints of history for the ways they prompted a wide range of American artists, writers, and activists toward new critical explorations of the Berlin Wall and its legacies, tapping alternative circuits of cultural diplomacy to approach and pivot toward understandings of division in U.S. culture. Neither of these landmark dates signals a simple start or end of Cold War antagonisms in divided Berlin. Each, however, offers a vantage point to map, examine, engage, and push beyond the borderlands of Cold War Berlin. Cultural producers such as Leonard Freed, Angela Davis, Shinkichi Tajiri, Audre Lorde, and many others sought divided Berlin as site and symbol, to grapple with boundaries of freedom and repression. Without coordination or state sanction, they practiced a collective choreography of encountering the Wall, moving in and out of Berlin during the time of its militarized border, and relaying their perspectives in artworks and publications that touched on matters of U.S. identity, history, and struggle. From 1961 onward, their books, artworks, poems, and other artifacts illustrated both the ideals and the contradictions of U.S. Cold War culture. Through alternate circuits of cultural diplomacies, they engaged divided Berlin as a matter of critical pilgrimage, continually asking questions of themselves and of the Wall's shifting contexts. After 1989, these artists powerfully adapted their approaches, embarking on new projects with a set of questions probing the redefining of the United States and Germany as each shifted away from Cold War dynamics. Without anticipation or telos, the American Berliners of this book also offered post-1989 reflections and works that focused on emergent forms of collective memory in Berlin, to gather additional histories and mark uneven flows of progress amid the spectacle of the border's dismantling.

———

In the spring and summer of 1989, due to public pressures from within, both at the party level and from grassroots activists, the ruling regimes of the Eastern bloc loosened expressive restrictions and select border controls. Each increment of change was spurred by a series of economic and social reforms in the wake of Soviet policies of *Glasnost* and *Perestroika*.[1] In East Germany, citizens in Leipzig protested the policies of one-party rule. Earlier that same year, on January 18, East German party leader Erich Honecker had promised a more advanced Berlin Wall that could stand for "fifty or a hundred years, if the reasons for its existence have not been removed."[2] But by July 1989, over 25,000 East Germans had fled through the recently opened Hungarian border. As the option to defect through Hungary emerged, the idea of change was also afoot for the large number of East Germans who intended to stay in the German Democratic Republic. Inspired and emboldened by the changing and increasingly public nature of dissidence, these citizens felt emboldened to reshape the government. The large and growing gatherings of protestors sought to reform the existing system, with demands including greater access to travel without danger of reprimand or retribution.[3] In the fall, a weekly Monday protest movement in Leipzig quickly swelled. The protest movement spread across East German cities. By October 30, approximately 300,000 citizens marched in Leipzig. That same night, 20,000 East Berliners also took to their streets. These public displays remained overwhelmingly peaceful and yet emphatically called for change, signaling the imminent demise of the regime. The ruling authorities of the GDR began planning reforms to quell the outrage but had to act fast due to the expanding public spectacle of the uprisings.[4]

On November 9, 1989, at six o' clock in the evening local time, a media spokesperson for the East German authorities, Günter Schabowski, read a report to television reporters of the regime's reform plans prompted as a rapid reaction to address the surging protests. "We want . . . through a number of changes, including the travel law, to [create] the chance, the sovereign decision of the citizens to travel wherever they want." He added with caution, "We are naturally concerned that the possibilities of this travel regulation — it is still not in effect, it's only a draft." Schabowski inadvertently revealed the GDR's plans to begin lifting travel restrictions and issuing more visas for permanent exit before procedures were secured. Though he noted the policy was being refined ahead of its implementation, Schabowski failed to notice instructions in his own papers that the announcement of any such plans was to be withheld until the following day, to allow the GDR to fully prepare and manage the new policy. However, when he was asked after his extended remarks at the press conference when this would all take effect, he quickly consulted his papers in front of him and responded, "right away."[5]

Mary Elise Sarotte documents the East German party's intentions in drafted language inadvertently shared by Schabowski. Their goal was to "[promote] freedom of travel" with "caveats — it was only temporary, still required multiple forms of permission" with the goal "to prevent the depopulation of East Germany."[6] But Schabowski's admission carried profound consequences. News of such a drastic and immediate amendment to concrete state policy did not break at once, but within several hours the consequences of this unplanned divulgence began to unfold at the city's internal border areas.[7] For the next several hours, as the East German authorities and unprepared border guards scrambled, crowds began to gather at several crossing points throughout the city. At approximately 11:30 P.M., East Berliners pushed down a security fence at the Bornholmer Strasse checkpoint. Then a flood began that the authorities did not stop.

The news traveled overseas to U.S. audiences, who continued to demonstrate great interest in the fate of divided Berlin. For example, that day newscaster Peter Jennings issued a special report for ABC News from his desk in New York City. In the first hours after the news broke, Jennings shared initial details, observing on-air, "What will happen now is hard to tell."[8] The following evening, on November 10, Tom Brokaw of NBC News, who was present at the Schabowski press conference, broadcast the evening news live from the west side of the Brandenburg Gate. Brokaw opened the program with a nod to the atmosphere: "The sound that you hear, and what you're seeing tonight, not hammers and sickles, but hammers and chisels, as young people take down this Wall, bit by bit. . . . Tonight, citizens from both Germanys are singing and dancing on the wall itself." Brokaw's on-scene reporting included elaborate references to the sounds and sights of the breached border, in which the politics and culture of the city mirrored each other. "Tonight, in this city, famous for its carefree nightlife," Brokaw added, "in this city where the song says, 'Life is a cabaret,' tonight in Berlin it's freedom night."[9] Noting that some celebrants were either too inebriated to participate in the collective gathering or had been escorted away by existing border control, Brokaw stated that as *Mauerpeckers* (wall peckers) began chiseling away chunks that night, East German border guards began clearing passages and new openings, thus participating in a new era that would render their own jobs obsolete.

That night and in the weeks that followed, the border was transformed into a stage for fantasies of political and cultural experimentation. The German term *Wende*, or turning point, refers to both the time period and the cultural shock of this historic change. (The Wende Museum, based in Los Angeles, was founded in 2002 by Justinan Jampol as a repository of historically relevant but discarded material culture from the former Eastern bloc.) The term also conjures the ambivalence of the moment for many Germans, torn between profound joy for outliving the border system and the unhinging, if not loss, of their respective ways of life. Freedom was one of the buzzwords of the moment, but the practice and follow-through of what the term "freedom" entailed would remain elusive among the newest of German ruins.[10]

———

From 1989 forward, returning and new cohorts of American Berliners — some of whom then resided in Berlin during the Cold War, while others were well versed in the American folklore of the city upon arrival — continued to treat the Berlin Wall as a central site and symbol of the U.S. cultural imagination, despite its disappearance as a formidable border and the subsequent reunification of Germany.[11] Over the next years, foreign visitors carried a wave of Wall fragments away from Berlin, with several larger concrete panels en route to new displays in American public spaces, national museums, presidential libraries, universities, and other sites of memory. Global politicians celebrated a new age of idealized borderlessness, on one hand, while building new walls of separation, on the other. As they had during the Cold War, artists and writers shaped the afterlife of the Berlin Wall in an extended critical exercise on newly cohering historical lessons and emergent forms and sites of division.[12]

As demonstrated throughout this book, American cultural producers and consumers had regularly turned to the Berlin Wall as a site where Cold War freedom and repression, history and identity, could be put to the test. Compellingly drawn to the divided city, the American Berliners of this book were profoundly moved by their encounters by the Wall and worked to consider the ways their American identity could be critically explored. Their works would fuel the discoveries of subsequent cohorts who, after 1989, continued to make pilgrimages to the city and the footprint of the former Wall. For those who had routinely visited the city before — Freed, Davis, Tajiri, and Lorde — the events of 1989 prompted returns and critical observations about what this former division signified. None of them had anticipated the dismantling of the Wall. But their eager returns to the city were marked by individual, deep connections with Berliners, as well as tempered reflections about the upheavals associated with historical change. Through new works or continued projects about Berlin, they tracked the Wall's transformation from geopolitical barricade to site of politicized memory and cultural commodity. Each person continued on paths they had already pursued, by returning to Berlin for critical and creative explorations and connecting new visions back to previous ideas about global freedoms and restraints near the Wall.

Just as he saw the Berlin Wall go up in August 1961, Leonard Freed returned on November 12, 1989, days after the border was breached, and documented scenes at the newly opened border. Freed took his time to reexplore the city and consider the evolution of military occupation and cultural connection on both sides of the former wall. In the days after the border was breached, he first captured images of an East German soldier standing outside the Neue Wache, the GDR war memorial on Unter den Linden (fig. 5.1). Experiencing an extreme moment of geopolitical flux, Freed recalled of that day, "Yesterday, if he had smiled while on guard duty this East German soldier would have been court-martialed. Today he can smile because he knows it will soon be over, the Wall has been breached."[13] Freed photographed the guard several times, from up close, waiting to get a frame in which he smiled back at the camera. Freed returned for Germany's official reunification ceremony in October 1990, viewing the events from Pariser Platz with the Brandenburg Gate illuminated behind the rejoined crowd, hovering as an icon and remainder.

After Freed's first trip to a reunified Berlin in 1989, he realized he wanted to follow up on his earlier Germany-focused projects, to weigh the unified "New Germany." He aimed to juxtapose contemporary images with others pulled from his own archive, many accompanied by diary-style annotations in which he pondered the past of Germany and of his career, in first-person prose through the window of his present. Freed faxed a letter to German

FIGURE 5.1 Leonard Freed, *Berlin, 1989/1990*.
(Estate of Leonard Freed/Magnum Photos)

curator Ute Eskildsen of the prestigious Folkwang Museum in 1990 at the
onset of this project, outlining his aims:

THE INTENTION IS TO FOLLOW UP ON MY 1970 BOOK WITH
A SECOND, TO DEVELOPE [*sic*] AND EXTEND MY EXPERIENCES AS
I HAVE BEEN DOING IN BOTH EAST AND WEST GERMANY OVER
THE YEARS SINCE ITS PUBLICATION. . . . I FEEL BEING BORN
IN THE UNITED STATES GIVES ME A FRESH OR EXTRA EYE TO
OBSERVE WHAT THE AVERAGE GERMAN WILL OVERLOOK. . . .
THE CENTER AND BASE OF THIS WORK WILL BE BERLIN, THE
UNIFIED BERLIN.[14]

He proposed several titles for the book — "The Children of Reich" and
"Die Neuen Deutschen" (The New Germans) — and worked with designers
to conceptualize the book's contours and look over the course of a decade.

Despite Freed's success as a renowned photographer, concurrently recognized with the planning of a major museum and book retrospective and regularly publishing with German magazines such as *Der Spiegel* and *Stern*, no publisher wanted to take on his post-Wall project. Freed was told it was too soon to look back across the newest dividing line of German history.

In 2005, Freed exhibited some of the prints of this unfinished book project at the Haus der Geschichte in Bonn, under the title *Ein Amerikaner in Deutschland*. Though his image of the trio of American GIs in a phalanx taken in August 1961 became the publicity image for the poster, other images addressed the layering of Freed's view of his career with the evolution of German history alongside American resonances. The exhibition's images complemented his broader cross-cultural connections made in landscapes of national history and memory. Indicative of such a posture is a vision of a reunified Berlin shot in 1990, also featured in this 2005 exhibition, featuring a statue of Otto Von Bismarck (fig. 5.2). Freed printed the photograph in a large, poster size for all the details to emerge. Here, a torso statue of the nineteenth-century unifier of Germany is sphinxed and delimbed, perched on a zigzagging steel beam, held directly above a bicycle and encircled by trolley tracks. Again, Freed approaches his subject at a middle distance. As a whole, the composition appears cubist, and the playful nature of the image contrasts with the serious historical moment. So much is up in the air, and public expressivity is having an impact on the moment, not just for Freed but for the people convening for Berlin's next chapter. Freed had imaged a bicycle in other post–*Wende* images as an emblem of progress, including one in a stationary position in the former death strip, not in the imagery of the American open road but in the potential for a shared fate of transformation and to convey momentary stillness amid enormous social upheaval. In that image, the absence of guards and the presence of the bicycle tell us that while the Wall's architecture remains for the time being, its very fact of openness means it has been neutralized. But in the Bismarck image, one can look past the foreground, as the steel beams construct a window to draw focus toward the signage of an infamous site of memory in Berlin: the Topography of Terror, a former Nazi-era Secret Police headquarters and notorious prison. The foundations of the site were rediscovered and excavated in 1987 during preparations for the 750th anniversary of Berlin. The area then reopened as an open-air museum. Since 1989, it also sits directly below one of the largest remaining continuous sections of the Berlin Wall, making it a site of layered historical archaeology and a marquee tourist attraction. Despite the location of this image along the former border, in this photograph, material remnants of the Berlin Wall are deliberately left

FIGURE 5.2 Leonard Freed, *Berlin, 1989/1990.*
(Estate of Leonard Freed/Magnum Photos)

out of Freed's field of vision. And though the sign for the Topography of Terror is nearly out of sight, it is nonetheless framed in the background of this image. Freed reminds us of the power of juxtaposing various layers of history and memory by using the Berlin Wall, to imagine the present around what traces remain and what new possibilities arise through this coexistence in post-Wall Berlin.

Following his exhibition, Freed wrote to the director of the Haus der Geschichte, Dr. Jürgen Reiche, in January 2006, describing the latest vision for this book. Before they could exchange dialogue about this proposal, Freed lapsed into illness from the effects of his nearly ten-year bout with cancer. He died near his home in Garrison, New York, in November 2006. The retrospective exhibition he prepared in his final years, *Worldview*, opened a year later and traveled posthumously to Berlin in the summer of 2008.

Freed never finished "Ein Amerikaner in Deutschland," though he intended to continue revising his writing and share unpublished post-1989 images. With his instructions found in a series of folders in his home archive in Garrison, those writings and images were packaged into a new critical edition of *Made in Germany*, which I edited with support from Freed's widow, Brigitte, and the Freed estate. The book was published in honor of a 2013 exhibition at Essen, Germany's Folkwang Museum, and included a supplementary pamphlet under the title *Re-Made: Reading Leonard Freed*. Freed's reflections include poignant observations about Germany that balance the changes and continuities of the nation over the fifty-year period throughout which he photographed there. For the cover of the booklet, I selected one of Freed's signature images from *Made in Germany*, a 1965 view of an Autobahn traffic jam. In the image, one of its central figures depicted is his widow, Brigitte, with a hand over her face to obscure her identity. She stands outside their parked car on the side of the highway, with hundreds of cars shown at a standstill. On a highway known for its speedy travel and cultural associations with national progress, Freed's posthumous book captures a halt in movement to remind viewers of the uneven flows of Germany's history, as well as Freed's own unfinished work.[15]

After the publication of her autobiography, Angela Davis turned to engaged academic and activist work. She returned to the University of California system as a professor and publishing several germinal books in the fields of cultural studies, including *Women, Class, and Race* (1983) and *Blues Legacies* (1999). Outside of life in the academy, she ran as the vice presidential candidate on the Communist Party USA's election ticket in 1980 and 1984. Her vision for communism continued to transcend U.S. and Soviet borders. After the dissolution of the USSR, Davis was among the early members of the Committees of Correspondence for Democracy and Socialism, an organization that sought to carry forward important political commitments of socialism.

Following the precedent of her autobiography, Davis continued to speak out on behalf of political prisoners and against the prison industrial complex. In 1997, she helped start the group Critical Resistance, with the goal of prison abolition. As their mission states, the organization "seeks to build an international movement to end the prison industrial complex (PIC) by challenging the belief that caging and controlling people makes us safe. We believe that basic necessities such as food, shelter, and freedom are what really make our communities secure." In books such as *Are Prisons Obsolete?* (2003) and *Abolition Democracy* (2005), Davis details how "a protracted engagement with the prison system has literally defined [her] life."[16] Davis joins her experience of her imprisonment with her critical work through highlighting the ramifications of mass incarceration, state violence, and criminalized dissent. The emphasis of her prison abolition work presents a political position that balances her experiences of her imprisonment with her role as a key leader in the emergence of the field. Davis's life work powerfully renders incarceration as a deeply foundational feature of life in the United States.

Davis continued to visit Berlin following its reunification, paying attention to grassroots perspectives on multiple forms of division. After appearances in solidarity with Occupy Wall Street camps in New York, Oakland, and Philadelphia, Davis also visited and gave a talk at the Occupy Berlin Camp in 2011. In each instance, she shared the links between previous eras of grassroots movements and ways to think through "occupation." In Berlin, speaking intermittently in German but addressing the crowd mostly with the help of a translator, she connected her own experiences in Germany with the contemporary activist movement located there. Greeted by a woman who had as a child written Davis a postcard for the Million Roses for Angela campaign, Davis shared, "I always say to people in the United States, that the schoolchildren in the GDR freed me," adding with a warm laugh, "And I should say that there were many people involved in West Germany as well."[17] In 2015, while in Berlin for a lecture, she attempted to visit the occupied Gerhard-Hauptmann school, where refugee activists demanding resources and fighting against deportation attempted to open an "International Refugee Center." Barred by Berlin authorities from entering the facility to host a lecture, Davis met instead with activists on the street next to a metal-fenced barrier, to discuss strategies and legacies of activism (fig. 5.3).[18]

In the thirty years since the dismantling of the Berlin Wall, Davis's theo-

Copyright Oliver Feldhaus

FIGURE 5.3 Oliver Feldhaus, Angela Davis talks to refugees in front of
the occupied Gerhard-Hauptmann School, 2015. (Oliver Feldhaus)

retical and literary recollections of divided Berlin have continued to echo
her autobiography's strategic disavowal of the Wall. In public discourse, one
would be hard pressed to hear or read Davis ever discuss the German border
as "the Berlin Wall." For example, in 2010, as she prepared to release a new
critical edition of *The Narrative of the Life of Frederick Douglass, an American
Slave, Written by Himself,* she joined Toni Morrison, the editor of her autobiography, in a public conversation at the New York Public Library. The two distinguished women discussed a range of topics and offered a rare glimpse into
the behind-the-scenes moments they shared in writing and publishing Davis's
autobiography. In also discussing the financial crises of the recent years, Morrison brought up the Berlin Wall and did most of the talking. Morrison said,

> Capitalism is not dead, obviously, but it's crumbling. Yes it is, they don't
> know it, I know it. . . . The Berlin Wall—interesting thing is when the
> Berlin Wall fell—this is how we talk all the time. . . . All sorts of other
> walls went up. The one between Israel and the West Bank and then the
> wall in the south, Mexico, it's the border. I mean, all these other walls
> jumped up, and then they're not physical walls, but there are other kinds
> of imprisonment walls, I mean we are just constantly separating—in
> some instances, the Berlin Wall was so people couldn't get out, now
> we're building walls so they can't get in. So you know it's a constant. This

shift looks to me long-range, like part and parcel of what I am certain, is, you know, it's the disconnect, you know, it's really crumbling.[19]

Davis nodded in agreement with Morrison but here again did not utter the words "Berlin Wall." Davis did, however, return to Morrison's mention of walls several minutes later, without mentioning Berlin, but by expanding the conversation to legacies and practices of division in the contemporary moment: "Toni, you were talking about the wall in Mexico, you talked about Palestinians, so how do we bring Palestinian freedom into our frame, how do we bring the freedom of immigrants into the way we imagine freedom today? How do we think about transgendered people? How do we think about gays, lesbians, bisexuals, within the frame of freedom? And what does that tell us about the extent to which our own framework of freedom is quite restricted?"[20]

Davis enacts her overture to communities of struggle through a series of identifications around walls. Regardless of her distancing or disavowals, she continues to be a vocal opponent of structures of repression, including political walls, without identifying the name of the infamous Berlin boundary.[21]

As a cultural trope and symbol, Davis still regularly draws on wall imagery and symbols within her work, as a matter of creative and critical linkage. The cover of one of her recent books, *The Meaning of Freedom and Other Difficult Dialogues* (2012), features Davis standing next to an unknown dividing wall topped with barbed wire. Davis wears a black leather jacket and stretches her hand to touch the metal wall painted with graffiti, looking upward. (fig. 5.4). A year later, in December 2013, in remarks to Great Britain's War on Want organization from London's School of Oriental and African Studies, Davis conjured language evocative of other writing projects to link prison abolition work and multiple sites of repressive division. She stated, "We're talking about prisons, and checkpoints, and the apartheid wall . . . from the wall in Israel to prison-like schools in the US and the wall along the US-Mexico border."[22] This speech, which was later included in her book *Freedom Is a Constant Struggle: Ferguson, Palestine, and the Foundations of a Movement* (2015), is a testament to the apartheid conditions in Palestine, which Davis describes in detail: "The wall, the concrete, the razor wire everywhere conveyed the impression that we were in prison. . . . We will have to expand and deepen our solidarity with the people of Palestine. People of all genders and sexualities. People inside and outside prison walls, inside and outside the apartheid wall."[23] Building solidarity through sites of injustice, in and out of Berlin,

FIGURE 5.4 Cover, Angela Davis, *The Meaning of Freedom and Other Difficult Dialogues*, 2012. (Keba Konte/City Lights)

Davis continues to remind us that if walls turned sideways can be bridges, freedom and repression can share the same resonant architecture.

Shinkichi Tajiri's multiple Berlin Wall projects continued to morph in the post-*Wende* years, as they had through the 1970s and 1980s. Berlin remained a space of conceptual and site-specific engagement for him, due to his established deep connections to the city. Tajiri retired from his post at the Hochschule der Künste in February 1989. To mark the occasion, several generations of students who made up the Klase Tajiri at the school produced an exhibition and catalog honoring him. Friend, former student, and fellow American expatriate Dorothy Iannone wrote in the catalog's accompanying essay, "The most wonderful thing about the class of Shinkichi Tajiri is that everyone feels free to do what they want. The way toward self-expression is not barred by the imposition of any aesthetic system or method." Iannone added, "The word, it seems has spread [internationally] that in Berlin there is a class which helps you on your way."[24] Tajiri remained close with students after his retirement

FIGURE 5.5 Shinkichi Tajiri, *Berlin Wall, 1989/1990*. (Shinkichi Tajiri Estate)

and was slated to return to Berlin in November 1989 for an exhibition of his paper knots at the Galerie Horst Dietrich. However, when attendance was reportedly low, he suspected the other opening in town, of the newly breached Wall, might have overshadowed his exhibition. (Tajiri was inadvertently featured in a local television broadcast about the demise of the border.) This unexpected conflict did not affect Tajiri, as he returned soon after to observe the dismantling of the Wall. Again fascinated by the Wall's materiality, he now observed its state of deconstruction and imposed decomposition. He recalled in his autobiography, "Immediately a new industry was born. Enterprising individuals and then whole families hacked away at the surface and sold fragments to tourists. An unequipped visitor could rent a hammer and a chisel for 5 marks an hour and carry off his own mementoes."[25] Tajiri made more photographic portraits by what remained of the Wall. In one, he lined up in front of an impromptu mirrored mosaic placed on its pockmarked surface and snapped a picture of himself. In another (fig. 5.5), he posed in front of a gaping hole in the Wall left by *Mauerpeckers*, as if he had emerged from the other side. His fascination after 1989 afforded him new opportunities. On January 9, 1990, he reported that he made his "last series of portraits," as "90 percent of it was still there, penetrated with large holes." He carried home pieces of the Wall, which he lined up along the windowsills of his studio in Baarlo.[26]

But Tajiri was not finished with the Wall and instead continually attempted to scale it through critical reflection. In 1990, he sent former student and then–art professor Nobuho Nagasawa a "digitized/colorized photo image of the Berlin Wall in a small picture frame, accompanied by a fragment of the real wall." (Nagasawa responded by creating a piece titled *Behind the Great Wall*, incorporating several of Tajiri's 1981 panoramas of the Wall with images from their class trip to China's Great Wall.) He traded similarly hybrid image-artifact versions of the Wall with family members and friends. He also produced an unnamed work, still hanging on a wall in his family's castle, of a large computer printout of a 1990 portrait of a hole in the Berlin Wall, with a side border with custom-made cubbyholes for Wall chunks. He continued to hold onto his own smaller artworks about the Wall, remaking the sprawling structural barrier into a critical keepsake.

Tajiri's critical and creative reflections on the Wall continued to evolve. Eventually, as he attempted to fully make sense of his original 1969–70 negatives, technological advances and his renewed interest helped drive an ultimate expression of his original survey. In 2003, with the help of a Macintosh G4 computer and a Nikon negative scanner, he digitized his images. He had not wanted to spend months in a darkroom, and this option allowed him to see the images at a pace and in a medium he preferred. In his first renewed attempt at this project, he randomly displayed one of every five images for an exhibition, creating a small catalog for a photography museum in The Hague. In 2005, he prepared the entire set of images in a book to be plainly titled *The Berlin Wall* (fig. 5.6). The publication would cover the entire survey project and feature an essay by Tajiri (and another by Künstlerhaus Bethanien founder Michael Haerdter). He aimed to give the book a sculptural quality by shaping it like an oversized brick. Tajiri's essay pulled together writings from various publications and newsletters and compiled his views from multiple moments in the life of the Wall:

> Seen from the air, the Wall looked like a gangrenous wound that wouldn't heal. On the East Side it appeared to be clinically clean. In an area of 100 meters along the Wall, the East had constructed concrete and iron obstacles against vehicles and had planted land mines to ward off pedestrians, who want to approach it. Soldiers with dogs patrolled regularly along its length. On the West side it was in a continuous state of

FIGURE 5.6 Shinkichi Tajiri, *The Berlin Wall*, 2005.
(Shinkichi Tajiri Estate/Tasha B.V.)

festering flux. Refuse and garbage was piled against the Wall along with wrecked and abandoned cars. After a while the trash would disappear only to be replaced by more. Graffiti covered the Wall; political slogans and declarations of love. Spray Can artists had left gigantic murals at choice tourist points, only to have them covered over by more recent arrivals.

Even as his project seemed to cohere in its own finished point of publication, his essay hinted at future iterations. In the published version, he gestured at the unfinished nature of the project: "I have tried to reconstruct the proper order but I am not 100% certain if I have succeeded. I would appreciate any corrections remedied in a later edition."[27]

After the book was completed, Tajiri experienced several unfortunate disruptions. He sued the printer because his negatives had been cropped and unapproved changes had been made to the individual images. Soon after, he became ill, and he made notes for his daughters Giotto and Ryu Tajiri to carry out the project to his intended specifications in any future exhibitions and versions. To this day, his former studio holds a small-scale model he envisioned for a panoramic pavilion of his 1981 project. Made with images from his archive, the model is located close to the chunks of the Berlin Wall by his windows. Tajiri passed away in his studio in Baarlo in March 2009 at age eighty-six.

Despite living outside the United States for over six decades, Tajiri retained his U.S. citizenship throughout his life. But at age eighty-five, a year before his death, Tajiri finally became a dual citizen with the Netherlands, his adopted home. Continuing to grapple with his American identity in self-exile, he remained a vocal critic of U.S. militarism, retaining a distrust dating back to his internment, as he voraciously followed American culture, sports, and news.

In 1999, after tossing aside what appeared to be an anonymous form letter sent from an American government agency, he nearly threw away a $20,000 reparation check from the government. This would not be the only time the federal government would reach out to Tajiri or his family about its repressive past. After his death, Tajiri's family accepted a posthumous distinction on his behalf. In 2011, he, along with the rest of the 442nd Regimental Combat Team of Nisei soldiers, who fought for the United States after being imprisoned in internment camps, were awarded the Congressional Medal of Freedom by President Barack Obama. Each medal was inscribed with the words of their commonly held slogan: "Nisei Soldiers of World War II — Go for Broke."

Poet Audre Lorde carried forward her reflections on border crossing and its poetic transformations through the historical brink of 1989. In a range of formats, including poetry, journals, letters, and opinion editorials, Lorde weighed the significance of a reunified Berlin, especially for Afro-Germans and others of the diaspora, including herself, around the dialectic of freedom of violence. The phrase "Berlin Wall" entered her lexicon most clearly after the Wall was breached in 1989. On the day after the border's initial dismantling began on November 10, 1989, Lorde wrote an unpublished journal entry evoking the words "Berlin Wall" as she reflected on the flood of East Germans visiting retail shops in West Berlin and noting her fear and skepticism on what the Wall coming down would mean for foreign workers.[28] Lorde spelled out more of her apprehension in another unpublished entry dated January 5, 1990, questioning challenges to freedom for Afro-Germans, as well as the balance of geopolitics and safety more broadly, including in the United States for people of color.[29]

In each case, Lorde called out the Berlin Wall more directly by name, as opposed to through poetic nomenclature or political allusions from *Our Dead Behind Us*, to recognize the concrete border's newfound symbolism and public feelings of historical estrangement in this *Wende* period. She treated the Wall as a gateway to a future of reunification that also risks spikes in xenophobic violence in Germany. She also wondered about Berlin's future as a site of precarious American geopolitics. In these journals, Lorde highlighted the

FIGURE 5.7 Dagmar Schultz, "Audre Lorde, Ika Hügel-Marshall, und Dagmar Schultz vor der zerstörten Berliner Mauer." (Audre Lorde Archive, John-F.-Kennedy-Institut für Nordamerikastudien, Freie Universität Berlin Archives)

Berlin Wall to bring into relief broader uncertainties and fears wrought in periods of seeming public revelry and progress.

Lorde's cautious and critical dispositions can also be explored in a pair of visual artifacts, in two photographs of Lorde taken by Schultz by the former Wall during the time of reunification in 1990 (fig. 5.7). They offer opposing stances on the newfound moments by the border, though together they can be read as part of Lorde's active engagement with new border politics. In the first, Lorde and Ika Hügel-Marshall, Schultz's partner, stand next to a series of foldable tables set up along a fenced barricade, with pieces of the chiseled Wall for sale. They are gathered at the edge of the city's Tiergarten in former West Berlin, steps away from tabled remnants of the Wall. Standing arm in arm with Lorde, Hügel-Marshall holds out a small bag with a piece of the Wall inside. The two widely smile, as if caught mid-laugh. A man on the other side of the table and a blonde woman with spiked hair leaning nearby on the fence by the Wall turn toward them with reserved smiles.

In another photo (fig. 5.8), a frontal portrait of Lorde taken by Schultz on a different day, Lorde makes eye contact with the photographer's lens, as she maintains an oblique stance, her torso and legs askew to the camera.

FIGURE 5.8 Dagmar Schultz, "Audre Lorde at the
Berlin Wall in 1990." (Dagmar Schultz)

Lorde wears an untucked, salmon-colored shirt and blue jeans and carries her own camera, which dangles from her hands. Behind her is a remnant of the Berlin Wall, apparently untouched by graffiti artists or *Mauerpeckers* but altered through the posted political signs dating to the first elections of a re-unified Germany. The question, rather than the promise, of a reunified German future seems to weigh on the scene. Through this image and Lorde's multidisciplinary writing in this period, we are reminded that even after its "fall," the Wall remained a site of projection and declaration as it was transformed into a ruin in Berlin.[30] As a result, Lorde's focus and skepticism in this period were centered on the waves of racially motivated violence erupting on Berlin and German streets.

Through her public writing, Lorde responded in numerous pieces to a series of racist attacks on people of color in Germany that coincided with the dismantling of the Wall and reunification. In 1990, along with her partner, Gloria Joseph, Lorde wrote an open letter to German chancellor Helmut Kohl to call attention to the early occurrences of these attacks. In this letter, published in German media outlets, the women outlined their concerns about street violence they learned about on their return trips. "Why has the dismantling of the Berlin Wall meant that we now feel less and less safe as Black Women visitors to ride the U-Bahn in Berlin? . . . Why must we become more and more afraid to walk the once safe streets around Alexanderplatz in East Berlin after dusk?" They use their intimate knowledge of Berlin, calibrated during their time in the city during its division, to offer a cautionary story about antiblack violence in the reunified city.[31]

In this letter, they presented the violence in Berlin to name the city as a vulnerable diasporic space, going beyond statistics and headlines to illuminate new and pervasive fears. They defended Afro-German women and deployed the grammatical "we" to identify with and remark on the dangers Lorde and Joseph faced as black women spending time in Germany. Lorde remained suspect of rapid geopolitical change without acknowledgment and discussion of the implications for people of color in Germany. She again turned to the symbolism of the Berlin Wall and the divided city for reflection and advocacy.[32]

Between 1987 and her death in 1992, Lorde composed more poems that addressed themes of travel and return. She prepared a manuscript of these poems in the years she fought her illness, but they were published posthumously in the collection *The Marvelous Arithmetics of Distance* (1993). The poet's habitual relationship with Berlin coincided with the continued rise in awareness of the Afro-German movement, for which she was, in part, responsible for cultivating. Her "Berlin years," as friend and filmmaker Dagmar

Schultz would term them, extended across a time of sweeping change in Germany, in particular the dismantling of the Berlin Wall in 1989 and Germany's reunification in 1990.

The Marvelous Arithmetics of Distance offers a poetic bridge across this historical divide. As demonstrated in chapter 4, Lorde's introduction to Berlin occurred in the years of its division. As the demise of the Wall was neither inevitable nor anticipated, Lorde's pre-1989 Berlin poems look for ways to undermine or connect across the lines of division. She would primarily consider the existence of the Berlin Wall amid other divisions. Alternately, her post-1989 poems and writing showcase Lorde's sense of wariness about how the *Wende* affected life in Berlin, especially for Afro-Germans and people of color, specifically employing the name "Berlin Wall" to make her critical insights more clear.

These interventions into the *Wende* period mark Lorde's poems in *The Marvelous Arithmetics of Distance*. Though her Berlin poems in *Our Dead Behind Us* also dealt with the division of the Wall, these later poems reflect the historical challenges of reunification after 1989. Several poems in *The Marvelous Arithmetics of Distance* explicitly deal with the Berlin Wall and the dynamics of Berlin's transformed border.[33] Despite the altered imperatives of the work, in each case Lorde's rendering of Berlin deals with its multiple intersections of division—and the city as a source of public and private reflection.

For example, the poem "East Berlin" opens with the declarative statement, "It feels dangerous now / to be Black in Berlin."[34] The subject of this poem is disembodied and impersonal. Yet her use of "it" makes her statement declarative and factual. Lorde's sense of the new geography of reunification is based on well-known urban landmarks but eschewed, as her narrator zigzags back and forth between the former West and East and through time, channeling a cosmopolitanism that incubates violent conditions ("sad suicides that never got reported / Neukölln Kreuzberg the neon Zoo / a new siege along Unter den Linden"). Her poetic mapping of "East Berlin" is as a geopolitical anachronism, as the notion of an "East Berlin" is defunct in the reunified Germany. Lorde's use of extra spatial pausing here separates her calling out of areas in former West Berlin (Neukölln, Kreuzberg, Zoologischer Garten) to suggest dislocation amid the post-Wall borderlines, with the separation furthered by the sequential references to East Berlin's Unter den Linden and Alexanderplatz. The concrete materiality and hard edges of the Wall are transferred to the sidewalk in a scene of violence plaguing reunified Berlin.

Though the Wall is already partially dismantled at the point of her writing,

Lorde repurposes the changes afoot around it as signs of the new dangers for people of color in Germany. She remains wary of the attempts to move forward from the past without reconciliation and proper attention for mourning. Lorde writes in the final paragraph, "Hand-held the candles wink / in Berlin's scant November light / hitting the Wall at 30 miles an hour." Here she uses the word "Wall," capitalized referring to the Berlin Wall as a proper noun. Lorde views Germany through rituals of commemoration and the time-space of a dream. She is wary of celebrations of triumph in light of the violence and uncertainty of the time. She comments on the nation's transformation through modes of cross-border travel, alluding to going back in space and time, to reexamine the sort of deep divisions that remain traceable in the city.

In another poem, "Peace on Earth: Christmas 1989," Lorde conjures the first holiday season after the Wall's destruction, considering the rapid shifts in history that occurred following November 1989. She imagines two simultaneous drives: to account for the continuities of conflict and to lay bare an aspiration for peace, healing, and regrowth. Lorde writes of a "six-pointed star/ in the eyes of a Polish child," as she is "lighting her first shabbas candle   fading / into a painted cross on the Berlin Wall."[35] The Star of David and shabbas lights convey a ghostly Jewish presence along the former border juxtaposed with a cross as a sign of commemorative loss. Together, they double as a call to heed lessons of the past, to slow the rhythms of historical time. Lorde uses spatial pausing in this instance again to slow the flow of the ideas and to double as an imagistic and physical reenactment of the act of "fading." The word "fading" functions as an enjambed "apo koinou" to share meaning and forge connection across two lines. The appearance of the Berlin Wall in the subsequent line reminds us that the Wall is a canvas for expression and a site of post-1989 projection.

Further into the poem, Lorde juxtaposes and alternates between symbols of war and peace to convey the liminal time and space of reunified Berlin. For example, there are references to World War II–era European suffering and images of American patriotism, including excerpted lines from "The Star-Spangled Banner" and a transposition of text sent on emergency relief materials ("THIS IS A GIFT FROM THE PEOPLE OF THE UNITED STATES OF AMERICA"), as well as a list of post–World War II and Cold War hot spots in Central America, South America, and Israel/Palestine ("Panama Nablus Gaza / tear gas clouding the Natal sun"). Moving between these places and historical references, her poem creates an invocation for diaspora and coexistence amid perpetual conflict.

Lorde continued to travel to Berlin, for sustenance and treatments. She opened her poem "Restoration: A Memorial—9/18/91" by writing, "Berlin again   after chemotherapy / I reach behind me once more / for days to come."[36] In September 1992, Lorde traveled to Berlin and gave a public reading once more in Schultz's apartment. For Lorde, a prolific and widely published poet, revision not only nourished her work toward refinement and revelation, but also allowed her to remain situated firmly within the creative process throughout her life. Documented and brought forward in a bonus clip from Schultz's film *Audre Lorde: The Berlin Years*, Lorde is shown seated by a table with a vase of sunflowers and an open notebook from which she reads her poem "1984," which also happens to be the year of her first visit to Berlin. She provides some historical context about the poem in which she imagines she becomes president of the United States, noting that she was inspired to revise U.S. power relations from George Orwell's vision of 1984. Moreover, this poem, like many of her others, began with a spark of a dream, inspired by thoughtful slumber during one April 4, the anniversary of the assassination of Dr. Martin Luther King Jr. But before she read she also reminded her listeners that this was a work-in-progress: "Now I really want some feedback about this poem. Because it's a dream and I feel different ways about it at different times."[37] Here and across Berlin's historical divides, open spaces, and hiding places, Lorde sought connection and a perch from which to reside within her creative process of writing poetry. Her call to revision was spurred on by her dreams of and in the city. Two months after this trip to Berlin, in November 1992, Lorde passed away in her home in Saint Croix after a prolonged fight with cancer.

For months and years after her death, friends, loved ones, and those inspired by her teachings held memorials—at the Haus der Kulturen der Welt (House of the Cultures of the World) in Berlin, at the Cathedral Church of Saint John the Divine in New York, and near her and Gloria Joseph's home in Saint Croix, among other locales. Lorde's biographer Alexis De Veaux captures the immediate forms of memorial Lorde had envisioned: "Lorde had spent a lifetime defying socially imposed boundaries and she wanted her ashes scattered in several places."[38] Lorde's final resting places include Buck Island in Saint Croix, a site in Hawaii from which she had seen an eclipse, her former yard in Staten Island, Washington Square Park in her hometown of New York City, and by Krumme Lanke, the lake she loved in the former West Berlin.

Lorde's impact lives on in Berlin through public and intimate expressions of her memory. In February 2012, Schultz premiered the film *Audre*

Lorde: The Berlin Years, 1984–1992 at the Berlin International Film Festival, and weeks later, in March, she held a U.S. premiere at the Brecht Forum in New York City. (Since July 2016, the film is shown in an unexpected monthly ritual in Berlin's Lichtblick Theatre located in Prenzlauer Berg.) The film features clips from Schultz's extensive personal archives covering Lorde's many trips to Berlin. Schultz later organized AudreLordeBerlin.com, a website that draws on the film's content and research for an "online journey" that includes sites of Lorde's poetry and wandering in the city. In packaging these traces of memory for public circulation, Schultz presents rare, poignant, and historically significant moments of cultural exchange shared among circles of new friends, including poetry readings, dance parties, and classroom visits. Schultz notes in a statement about the formation of the film, "Fortunately, during much of the decade this film covers, I photographed, audio- and video-recorded Audre with her consent, but without any plan whatsoever about what to do with this trove of material. In the ten plus years it has taken me to bring this film to fruition, it was clear to me that I definitely wanted to make this material available to as many people as possible."[39]

To complement the distribution, Schultz digitized much of the footage and prepared the previously personal materials for donation to the Free University in Berlin, joining Spelman College in Atlanta as the other major destination for Lorde archives.

The documentary and its associated materials place Lorde's Berlin years into the historical context of the emergence of the Afro-German movement and reminds her international audiences of the importance of Berlin in Lorde's life and work. The film also offers a window into Lorde's relationship with Berlin, in terms of her poetry and her health. In an interview, Lorde's partner, Gloria Joseph, states, "Berlin added years onto Audre's life." Indeed, in Berlin's open spaces and hiding places, Lorde flourished through connection by recognizing differences and working across lines of division, soothed and spurred on by dreams of the city.

American Berliners who returned to the reunified city in and after 1989 continued to find pathways to cultural understanding. Their resulting publications, continued dialogues, and private meditations highlight and extend a significant body of work that spanned the distinct periods of Germany's division and American history. Freed, Davis, Tajiri, and Lorde went to Berlin for different reasons but made the city a point of habitual return, after each found spaces of illumination and epiphany in varied corners of the divided city. They rendered their experiences in an array of creative productions that are distinguished by respective interdisciplinary formats, intended audiences, critical methodologies, and historical contexts of distribution. And yet they shared a profound sense of being both haunted and at home in Berlin, a balance they negotiated to present powerful works crucial to understandings of American culture. They coproduced a critical American tradition of engagement with the Berlin Wall and continue to evoke perspectives across multiple sites of U.S.-sponsored global freedom and repression. Four individuals set against an evolving history, they represent and stand in for a legion of others who also set foot in some of the most traumatized and divided spaces, whether in Berlin or elsewhere, as a means to remediate those places and transform themselves. Together, they remind us that the movement of history and the geographies of division cannot be scripted without space for intervention, reckoning, co-creation, and resistance.

We may never fully heed the lessons of previous generations of wall builders, whose historic constructions viciously divided societies, inhumanely practiced separation of families and neighbors, and left far-reaching destruction in their paths. Once these dividing walls are brought down, their ruins stand only as brutal, unintentional monuments to their own eventual demise. We can, however, continue to learn from artists, writers, and activists who have for generations approached dividing walls to pivot toward greater forms of interaction and acknowledgment and hasten the dismantling of repressive borders and social structures. This includes both the physical and social structures we encounter each day. As such, the mantle of the critical work on the Berlin Wall by Freed, Davis, Tajiri, Lorde, and others, carried out in response to physical and social boundaries in Berlin, the United States, and elsewhere, is brought forward by a new generation of cultural figures, who continue to approach sites of injustice and transform them into spaces of fuller freedoms, whether at the U.S. border, the walls of our criminal justice system, the institutional barriers made visible through intersectional feminist and queer organizing, transnational sites of apartheid and migration, or other spaces of repression. The American Berliners of the past and present map, create around and over, and seek to dismantle the walls of our own.

NOTES

Abbreviations

AACVR *The Civil Rights Struggle, African American GIs, and Germany*, German Historical Institute/Vassar College/Heidelberg Center for American Studies, digital archive

ADLDC Angela Y. Davis Legal Defense Collection, Schomburg Center for Research in Black Culture, New York Public Library, New York, N.Y.

ALA Audre Lorde Archive, John-F.-Kennedy-Institut für Nordamerikastudien, Freie Universität Berlin Archives, Berlin, Germany

ALP Audre Lorde Papers, Spelman College Archives, Atlanta, Ga.

CTEP Christopher Temple Emmet Papers, Hoover Institution Archives, Stanford University, Palo Alto, Calif.

DWP David Wojnarowicz Papers, Fales Library, New York University, New York, N.Y.

JEHP John Edward Heys Papers, Billy Rose Theatre Division, New York Public Library, New York, N.Y.

JP James E. Jackson and Esther Cooper Jackson Papers, Tamiment Library, New York University, New York, N.Y.

LFP Leonard Freed Papers, Garrison, N.Y.

LHP Langston Hughes Papers, Beinecke Rare Book and Manuscript Library, Yale University, New Haven, Conn.

PERP Paul and Eslanda Robeson Papers, Moorland-Spingarn Library, Howard University, Washington, D.C.

RHC Random House Records, 1925–1999, Columbia Rare Book & Manuscript Library, Butler Library, Columbia University, New York, N.Y.

STE Shinkichi Tajiri Estate, Baarlo, Netherlands

TMP Toni Morrison Papers, Rare Books and Special Collections, Firestone Library, Princeton University, Princeton, N.J.

Introduction

1. In this book, I use the terms "Cold War Berlin," "divided Berlin," or "Berlin" to refer to a vision of the city as symbolically or civically unified during the period of its division. Alternately, and when appropriate, I use "West Berlin" and "East Berlin" to refer to specific geopolitical sites, periods, and frameworks.

2. Kennedy, Kennedy, and Walther, *John F. Kennedy, Robert F. Kennedy*, 17.

3. Ibid., 19, 23.

4. For more on the interconnections between Cold War foreign policy and the domestic civil rights movement, see Dudziak, *Cold War Civil Rights*; Borstelmann, *Cold War and the Color Line*; Von Eschen, *Satchmo Blows Up the World*; and Singh, *Black Is a Country*.

5. "Berlin Salutes Robert Kennedy; He Vows Support," *New York Times*, February 23, 1962, 1.

6. Höhn and Klimke, *Breath of Freedom*, 6.

7. Said, "Traveling Theory," 196. For more on transnational travel and critical race perspectives, see Elam and Jackson, *Crossroads in Global Performance and Popular Culture*; Gaines, *American Africans in Ghana*; and Plummer, *Rising Wind*.

8. This includes Manghani, *Image Critique and the Fall of the Berlin Wall*; Pugh, *Architecture, Politics, and Identity in Divided Berlin*; and Sonnevend, *Stories without Borders*.

9. Boym, *Future of Nostalgia*, xviii.

10. Daum, *Kennedy in Berlin*, 36–37.

11. Daum, "America's Berlin," 51; Daum, *Kennedy in Berlin*, 39–41.

12. Ladd, *Ghosts of Berlin*, 4; see also Taylor, *Berlin Wall*.

13. U.S. Congress, *Congressional Record*, September 1961, vol. 107, pt. 14. For more on the expanding role of television in American life during the early 1960s, see Watson, *Expanding Vista*.

14. Von Eschen, *Satchmo Blows Up the World*, 11–12.

15. For more on regimes of border control in East Germany, see Funder, *Stasiland*.

16. William Tuohy, "Honecker Told of Need for Reforms: Gorbachev Urges Him to Accept Reality; Protests in Cities," *Los Angeles Times*, October 8, 1989. For other renditions of "We Shall Overcome" in East Berlin, see Dunaway, *How Can I Keep from Singing?*, 320, and Janik, *Recomposing German Music*, 286.

17. Kurin, *Smithsonian's History of America*, 500–505.

18. Clover, *1989*, 13.

19. For more on the pieces of the Berlin Wall installed around the United States and associations with Cold War memory, see Wiener, *How We Forgot the Cold War*.

20. Those included in the long list of American cultural producers mentioned here—as well as others not listed, those whose stories I did not discover during the course of my research or those who carry other transnational identifications with the city—also merit their own prolonged studies. For more on visual artists and their projects from this list, see Farber, *Wall in Our Heads*.

21. Mesch, *Modern Art at the Berlin Wall*, 5.

22. Anzaldúa, *Borderlands/La Frontera*, 25.

23. Braun, *City of Exiles*, 15.

24. Friedman, *Covert Capital*, 14.

25. Tillet, *Sites of Slavery*, 11.

Chapter 1

1. For more on the construction of the Berlin Wall, see Harrison, *Driving the Soviets Up the Wall*; Taylor, *Berlin Wall*; and Kempe, *Berlin 1961*. For more on the ex-

perience and impact of African American GIs in Germany, see Höhn and Klimke, *Breath of Freedom*.

2. Freed, *Made in Germany*, 88.

3. For more on Freed in Germany, see "Open Door: Leonard Freed in Germany," in Freed, Ebner, and Farber, *Re-Made*, 17–22.

4. Oltmans, *Memoires*, 252. I thank Frank Kelderman for his translation assistance. For more on U.S. military and Elvis Presley in Germany, see Wiener, *How We Forgot the Cold War*, 166–80; Höhn, *GIs and Fräuleins*, 55–59; and Schröer, *Private Elvis*, 68–69.

5. Neither Freed's private notes nor the photograph at its highest magnification bear any clear indication of the name on the soldier's uniform. Repeated attempts were made to identify the subject with U.S. veterans' groups and local historians in Berlin. Retired colonel Verner N. Pike of the Berlin U.S. Military Veterans' Association confirmed the soldier's battle group and infantry status via email, in Verner N. Pike, email message to research assistant, February 10, 2014.

6. Contact Sheets: 65-1-5-39, LFP. The date of this photograph has been previously listed in multiple publications and exhibitions as 1962 or 1965. According to my review of Freed's vintage contact sheets, the image was taken in 1961. Freed had changed his notation system in 1970 when he joined Magnum as an associate. All of his German images from 1958 to 1965 were relabeled as "1965." The original contact sheet bears an additional marking on its back denoting its original date. The timing of this photograph was further corroborated through Oltmans's journal and interviews with Leonard's widow, Brigitte Freed.

7. Freed, *Black in White America*, 10.

8. Ibid.

9. Freed, Ewing, and van Sinderen, *Worldview*, 14–15.

10. Brian Norman and Piper Kendrix Williams define segregation as "a diverse set of cultural practices, ethnic experiences, historical conditions, political ideologies, municipal planning schemes, and de facto social systems, though it is primarily associated with the Jim Crow South and the era between the Supreme Court cases *Plessy v. Ferguson* (1896) and *Brown v Board of Education* (1954), when segregation was no longer the law of the land but a persistent de facto condition" (Norman and Williams, *Representing Segregation*, 1).

11. For more on Freedom Rides and domestic civil rights protests of 1961, see Arsenault, *Freedom Riders*, and Niven, *Politics of Injustice*.

12. For more on Langston Hughes's 1964 visit to West Berlin, see Hughes, "Berlin Today," *Chicago Daily Defender*, April 3, 1965, 8, and LHP.

13. U.S. Congress, *Congressional Record*, September 1961, vol. 107, pt. 14; Gurnee, "Jack Paar at the Berlin Wall," 52.

14. The story of a divided Berlin was compelling for numerous cultural figures to consider the metaphor of a walled city. For example, Miss Toni Fisher's Top 40 hit "West of the Wall" premiered in 1962. This song features Fisher reinventing one of her own melodies from an earlier song, "Toot Toot Amore," but redeploying it here with lyrics about lovers separated by the new Berlin Wall. In the song, Fisher "waits"

for her lover in West Berlin: "That wall built of our sorrow / We know must have an end / Till then dream of tomorrow / When we meet again." The song reached no. 37 on the Billboard charts in a moment when the future status of the Wall was uncertain; the notion that the Wall would come down soon was a political possibility.

15. Taylor, *Berlin Wall*, 240.

16. By December 15, 1961, American filmgoers were provided with their most extended cultural glimpse of the Berlin Crisis with the release of Billy Wilder's comedy *One, Two, Three*. The fact that the movie was filmed in part on location in Berlin earlier in the summer of 1961 but released after the construction of the Wall made it historically significant and strange. Wilder presents a parodied depiction of Berlin as a crossroads of multiple divisions of national and historical nature, including those based on intertwined Cold War/civil rights discourses. For example, Wilder positions some of his film's humor through tropes of regional and racial strife in the United States. See Wilder, *One, Two, Three*.

17. "Rowan Urges Continued Fight on Bias; Warns 'Easing Up' Would Be Betrayal," *Chicago Daily Defender*, August 24, 1961, 9; "ICC Ruling Abolishes Bus Terminal Jim Crow," *Los Angeles Sentinel*, September 28, 1961, A1; "Troup Addresses Ft. Valley State Vespers Audience," *Atlanta Daily World*, October 6, 1961, 3. See also the editorial cartoon included in the *Chicago Daily Defender* on September 9, 1961, featuring a caricature of Jim Crow slamming down a newspaper with headlines that include "Dixie Schools Integrate Quietly," "Russia Tests A-Bomb," and "East-West German Wall."

18. "The Wall," *Pittsburgh Courier*, January 20, 1962, A9. Another *Pittsburgh Courier* staff editorial, published the week before on January 13, 1962, was titled, "The Walls Are Crumbling," without explicit reference to Berlin.

19. Kennedy, Kennedy, and Walther, *John F. Kennedy, Robert F. Kennedy*, 23.

20. "Tear Down 'Berlin Wall' of Race Hatred, Governor Kerner Urges," *Chicago Daily Defender*, July 2, 1963, 3; "Adlai Speaks Out," *Chicago Daily Defender*, July 2, 1963, 12; "Mrs. Tinglof Assails School District 'Walls,'" *Los Angeles Times*, August 13, 1963, 2.

21. This was unlike another localized, strategic American identification with the Wall, "Remember Berlin Day," organized in part by the CIA-funded Radio Free Europe, which commemorated the first anniversary of the Berlin Wall in over seventy American cities on August 13, 1962. For more on "Remember Berlin Day," the efforts by the Free Europe Committee (operators of Radio Free Europe) and the American Friends of Captive Nations to commemorate the first anniversary of the Berlin Wall in American cities, see box 49, CTEP.

22. Al Kuethner, "Atlanta's 'Berlin Wall' Divides Races," *Chicago Daily Defender*, December 24, 1962, 3.

23. "New Pressures Forcing Integration of Methodist Church," *Chicago Daily Defender*, March 2, 1963, 15.

24. Leonard, *Call to Selma*, 28. See also "Erect 'Berlin Wall' Block to Ease Tensions in Selma," *Chicago Daily Defender*, March 15, 1965, 1.

25. U.S. Commission on Civil Rights, *Time to Listen*, 65 (Boston); Foner, *Story of American Freedom*, 267 (Los Angeles); "'Chicago Wall': Dr. King Talks in Lansing,"

Chicago Daily Defender, March 12, 1966, 1 (Chicago); "Gregory Says, 'They Kick You Hard,'" *Pittsburgh Courier*, May 18, 1963, 29 (Birmingham); Clarence Mitchell, "From the Work Bench: Deerfield Stands for Hate," *Afro-American*, April 27, 1963, 4 (Deerfield); "Tension Grows in Greensboro, Barricade Separates Races," *Chicago Daily Defender*, July 28, 1965, 3 (Greensboro); "Dr. King Assails Policy at Girard: Likens Wall at Philadelphia School to Berlin Wall," *New York Times*, August 4, 1965, 19 (Philadelphia); "Small Towns Erect Negro Berlin Wall," *Chicago Daily Defender*, August 23, 1965, 7 (Rich Square); "Suburb Race-Wall Said to Outstrip Dixie Barriers," *Chicago Daily Defender*, October 25, 1965, 5 (St Louis); Leslie Cheek, "White Neighbors' Wall Stirs Negro Residents," *Washington Post*, June 5, 1966, B3 (Arlington); "Freedom News," *Crisis*, December 1966, 535 (Wheaton); Gertrude Wilson, "There's Only Isolation," *New York Amsterdam News*, August 12, 1967, 17 (Newark).

26. Langston Hughes, *Jericho-Jim Crow*, in Hughes, Rampersad, Hubbard, and Sanders, *Collected Works of Langston Hughes*; Miller, *Siege of Harlem*. For more on Hughes's 1964 visit to West Berlin, see Hughes, "Berlin Today," *Chicago Daily Defender*, April 3, 1965, 8, and LHP.

27. "Magnum, n.," *Oxford English Dictionary Online* (Oxford: Oxford University Press, 2000).

28. Ritchin and Frydman, *Magnum Photos*, 1.

29. Freed's focus on Germany also had much to do with his identity as a Jew of European descent and his being the husband of Brigitte, a German woman raised in the period of postwar reconstruction. Freed's parents escaped a hostile Europe (his father by way of Palestine) and settled in Brooklyn, only to realize years later that they became "survivors" of the Holocaust. According to Stefanie Rosenkrantz, Freed's friend and colleague, "[Freed] told me how he once came home from school in Brooklyn and found his father lying on the kitchen floor, hitting his head on the tiles, while holding a crumpled letter in his hands and crying. The letter said that most of his father's family had been murdered in Europe. A once large family of grandmothers, uncles, aunts, cousins, nieces, nephews and brothers and sisters had been killed by the Nazis. There were now only a handful of survivors" (Freed, *Leonard Freed*, 6).

30. Duganne, *Self in Black and White*, 21.

31. Freed, Ewing, and van Sinderen, *Worldview*, 15.

32. Ibid., 98.

33. Ibid., 104.

34. Freed interviews; 1963 Working Schedule (uncataloged), LFP.

35. Abbott, *Engaged Observers*, 18.

36. Freed, Ewing, and van Sinderen, *Worldview*, 204.

37. For more on Freed's images from the March on Washington, see Freed, Bond, Dyson, and Farber, *This Is the Day*.

38. While on this trip, King found out he would be the recipient of the Nobel Peace Prize. King traveled to Berlin from September 13 to 15, at the special invitation of Berlin mayor Willy Brandt. King participated as the prominent speaker for several West Berlin cultural events, including a memorial service to President Kennedy

and the opening of the Berlin Jazz Festival. In addition to being an esteemed guest of West Berlin, as further evidenced by his signature in the city's "Golden Book," King also crossed into East Berlin, where he preached at the St. Mary's and Sophia churches, with back-to-back evening speeches. He did not bring his passport with him to Checkpoint Charlie but was let through with his American Express card to East Berlin by guards aware of his intent to speak there. As Maria Höhn and Martin Klimke suggest, "King's visit to the front line of Cold War Europe gave him new perspectives to draw upon when he continued his civil rights struggle back at home" (Höhn and Klimke, *Breath of Freedom*, 105). The Berlin Wall would also soon become a part of King's lexicon to help picture segregation in the United States, including particular instances in Philadelphia and Chicago. In a 1965 editorial King writes of Philadelphia's then-segregated Girard College and its outer wall: "In this city known as the cradle of liberty . . . this wall is symbolic in the minds of many Negroes and freedom-minded whites — symbolic as the Berlin Wall is symbolic" (Martin Luther King Jr., "My Dream," *Chicago Daily Defender*, December 25, 1965, 10). In a 1966 article about housing protests in Chicago, the *Chicago Defender* cites him: "Housing developments along Chicago's S. State St. create a 'Berlin Wall situation like nothing I've ever seen before'" ("'Chicago Wall': Dr. King Talks in Lansing," *Chicago Daily Defender*, March 12, 1966, 1).

39. The image also serves as the cover of *Pillar of Fire*, the second volume of Pulitzer Prize–winner Taylor Branch's three-part biography of King.

40. While hospitalized in 1959, Freed studied August Sander's work of "young people with scarred faces" in the November issue of Swiss publication *DU*. See Freed, Ewing, and van Sinderen, *Worldview*, 305.

41. In 1967, Freed also was an officially credentialed photographer at the funeral for former West German chancellor Konrad Adenauer. The resulting images were later included in his *Made in Germany* portfolio.

42. Freed, Ewing, and van Sinderen, *Worldview*, 105.

43. U.S. Kerner Commission, *Report*.

44. For more on the protest movement contesting militarism in West Germany, see Klimke, *Other Alliance*.

45. Freed, *Black in White America*, 4.

46. Letter from Brother, April 1968 (uncataloged), LFP.

47. Mel Watkins, "Diversity of Experience," *New York Times Book Review*, April 27, 1969, 6.

48. In 2010, Getty Publications republished *Black in White America* after its forty years of being out of print and in conjunction with their *Engaged Observers* exhibition. Curator Brett Abbott writes in his foreword to the Getty reprinting of *Black in White America*, "More than forty years later the Berlin wall has come and gone, but the issue of race in America remains ingrained in the national conscience" (Freed and Getty Museum, *Black in White America*, 3).

49. Freed, *Made in Germany*, 4.

50. Gene Thornton, "Pictures You Won't See in a Travel Folder," *New York Times*, May 30, 1971, D14.

51. Freed, *Made in Germany*, 84.

52. Ibid., 80.

53. Ibid.

Chapter 2

1. Egon Bahr, West German chancellor Willy Brandt's press assistant, delivered the talk "Change through Convergence" in the summer of 1963, which Frederick Taylor claims "represented the beginning of a new era of relations between East and West Germany, and the beginning of what would become known as *Ostpolitik*" (Taylor, *Berlin Wall*, 326, 341–343). See also Daum, *Kennedy in Berlin*, and Fink and Schäfer, *Ostpolitik*. For more on the original coverage of Peter Fechter in Western media, see "The Wall of Shame," *Time*, August 31, 1962.

2. For more on Davis's time studying abroad in Paris, see Kaplan, *Dreaming in French*.

3. For more on German student movement organizing, see Klimke, *Other Alliance*; Davis, *Changing the World*; and Slobodian, *Foreign Front*.

4. Davis, *Angela Davis*, 139.

5. "Between Critical Theory and Civil Rights: A Sixties' Journey from Boston to Frankfurt to San Diego," October 2, 2009, Vassar College, Poughkeepsie, N.Y., http://www.aacvr-germany.org/index.php/movies-8/conference-talks.

6. Dates vary across accounts of Davis's first trip to Berlin. For this accounting of dating the trip to 1966, I checked against Esther Cooper's papers including a visa for travel into the German Democratic Republic dated from April 30 through May 5, 1966. The document includes a stamp from the Schönefeld Airport in East Berlin. See TAM 347, JP.

7. Margaret Burnham, email message to author, July 27, 2011.

8. "Between Critical Theory and Civil Rights: A Sixties' Journey from Boston to Frankfurt to San Diego," October 2, 2009, Vassar College, Poughkeepsie, N.Y., http://www.aacvr-germany.org/index.php/movies-8/conference-talks. For more on Davis's visit to East Berlin in 1966, see Steiniger, *Free Angela Davis*, 7.

9. Davis, *Angela Davis*, xvi.

10. "Angela Davis and Toni Morrison: Literacy, Libraries, Liberation," New York Public Library Video, October 27, 2010, http://www.nypl.org/events/programs/2010/10/27/angela-davis-toni-morrison.

11. Davis, *Angela Davis*, 347.

12. Ibid., 140.

13. Ibid., 143.

14. To further carry this out, the GDR practiced "border control"—itself a euphemistic term that reached far into the internal spaces and private lives of its citizens—by means of comprehensive state surveillance and armed violence against citizens. Davis's textual narrative highlights tactics similar to "border control" used in West Germany and the United States, bringing out paradoxes in Western democracy.

15. Davis, *Angela Davis*, 140.

16. Ladd, *Ghosts of Berlin*, 30.

17. Pugh, *Architecture, Politics, and Identity in Divided Berlin*, 3. Sunhil Manghani also writes of "a Berlin Imaginary" where "a complex, accumulative process whereby an internalized political and cultural discourse of East/West relations develops as the result of an external exchange of images and myths . . . richly fueled by the symbolic and real division of Berlin" (Manghani, *Image Critique and the Fall of the Berlin Wall*, 116). Brian Ladd refers to the Wall in one sense as "a zipper" that "signified both unity and division" by generating stories of geopolitical identification and alienation. See Ladd, *Ghosts of Berlin*, 30.

18. For production and postponement, see Val Adams, "N.B.C.-TV Plans Documentary on Berlin Tunnel It Helped Build," *New York Times*, October 12, 1962, and Richard F. Shepard, "N.B.C. Postpones Tunnel Telecast," *New York Times*, October 24, 1962.

A March 1964 episode of the hit *Twilight Zone* series, titled "I Am the Night—Color Me Black," featured an allegory of national mourning around the fallout from hate and violence, mapping the Berlin Wall with Dallas, Texas; a political prison in Budapest; Birmingham; Shanghai; North Vietnam; and Chicago.

19. Another statement about the Wall that echoes Davis's disavowed formulation can be found in the press conference recording from Louis Armstrong's visit to East Berlin to perform at the Friedrichstadtpalast in April 1965. When asked by reporters how he felt about the Wall, he responds, "Ain't worried about the Wall, worried about the audience I'm going to play to tomorrow night. I don't know nothing about no wall" ("Louis Armstrong in East Berlin," *rbb, The Berlin Wall: A Multimedia History*, http://www.the-berlin-wall.com/videos/louis-armstrong-in-east-berlin-739/).

20. For example, see Kelman, *Behind the Berlin Wall*. On p. 35, Kelman writes of seeing a poster in East Berlin that reads, "Free Angela Davis and the Other Political Patriots in Capitalist Countries."

21. For narratives of repression and resistance, see Funder, *Stasiland*.

22. Katherine Pence and Paul Betts identify "cold war Western logic, which often characterized state socialism as essentially a culture of surveillance, privation, economic mismanagement, and colorless lifestyles" (Pence and Betts, *Socialist Modern*, 7). For more on East German life and representations, see also Betts, *Within Walls*; Crew, *Consuming Germany in the Cold War*; and Stitziel, *Fashioning Socialism*.

23. Höhn and Klimke, *Breath of Freedom*, 125. For more on Bettina Aptheker attending a women's conference in Berlin in June 1969 at which she met Charlene Mitchell, see Aptheker, *Morning Breaks*, 58. For more on the Peace Council, see Daum, Gardner, and Mausbach, *America, the Vietnam War, and the World*; Grossman and Solomon, *Crossing the River*; McBride, Hopkins, and Blackshire-Belay, *Crosscurrents*; and Werner, "Convenient Partnerships?"

24. One counterexample can be found in African American comedian Dick Gregory's memoir *Up From Nigger*. Gregory had previously made comments comparing Birmingham and Berlin. In his memoir, he recalls a trip in 1964 to both West and East Berlin, where he attends a Peace Council meeting and writes, "I thought of a comedy line I would use back home to enlist support for world peace in the Black community: 'A lot of my friends say, "Greg, we weren't aware that you're interested

in bannin' the bomb," ' and I tell them, 'I wasn't at first, until I checked all the Black neighborhoods and found out we ain't got no fallout shelters. We got to ban the bomb — or learn how to catch it.' . . . From that moment on, I became an advocate of human rights, human dignity, and human survival." Later, in the same memoir, he recalls another peace meeting in East Berlin, this one in 1969, the World Assembly for Peace. On the way in London, Gregory reports he was given amateur footage from North Vietnam officials (he says "a home movie") of the My Lai Massacre and then details being tailed by U.S. government officials, who had listened to his phone conversations. See Gregory and McGraw, *Up from Nigger*, 191–92.

25. Siegfried Mews, "Spies Are Coming in from Cold War: The Berlin Wall in the Espionage Novel," in Schürer, Keune, and Jenkins, *Berlin Wall*, 51. Examples of spy dramas located in Cold War Berlin during this era include John le Carré's novel *The Spy Who Came in from the Cold* (1963) and film adaptation (1965), Len Deighton's *Funeral in Berlin* (1964), Adam Hall's *Quiller Memorandum* (1965), and Alfred Hitchcock's *Torn Curtain* (1966), which starred Paul Newman and Julie Andrews. Television episodes of *Kraft Suspense Theater* and Perry Mason's "Case of the Fugitive Fraulein" (1965) also featured such tales of intrigue in divided Berlin.

26. As much lore around Kennedy's speech suggests, grammarians have debated the president's declaration around its possible meanings. A "Berliner" refers to a citizen of the city of Berlin and, in some areas of Germany, a jelly-filled donut. Scholars such as Jürgen Eichhoff, however, have definitively demonstrated that Kennedy's usage referred to his urban identification with Berlin and not the pastry. See Eichhoff, " 'Ich bin ein Berliner.' "

27. For more on Kennedy's visit to Berlin, see Daum, *Kennedy in Berlin*, 147–56. See also Smyser, *Kennedy and the Berlin Wall*; Harrison, *Driving the Soviets up the Wall*; and Kempe, *Berlin 1961*.

28. Iton, *In Search of the Black Fantastic*, 35.

29. Robeson, *Here I Stand*, 1.

30. Given that the intended reason for Robeson's 1963 visit to East Berlin was related to his health care and recovery, connections to the widely held suspicion that he was poisoned by the CIA or by another government's counterintelligence agency remain pertinent. As biographers Martin Duberman and Paul Robeson Jr. have noted in their respective studies, there remain glaring omissions, redactions, and disappearances of health-related files within these law enforcement agencies' extensive surveillance records. For more on Robeson's health prior to East Berlin, see Duberman, *Paul Robeson*, 498–521, and Robeson, *Undiscovered Paul Robeson*, 308–30.

31. Eslanda Robeson, "Paul Robeson's Wife Tells Why He 'Sneaked' to East Germany," *Afro American*, November 2, 1963; Eslanda Robeson, "Wife Reveals How Robeson's Friends Helped, 'Escape' Reads Like Movie Thriller," *Afro American*, November 9, 1963; Eslanda Robeson, "Mrs. Robeson, in East Berlin, Says: 'Only Trying to Give Paul a Rest,' " *Afro American*, November 16, 1963.

32. In the Robeson archive at Howard University, a folder of unattributed photographs from the 1963 East Berlin trip includes one photo, taken on August 28, 1963.

The three are pictured within feet of the pillars of the gate, though no visible aspect of the border wall is in the frame. See NUCMC #DCLV96-A948, PERP.

33. Robeson was honored as an honorary citizen of East Germany and received accolades there related to his life's work. In 1965 the Paul Robeson Archive was founded at the Academy of Arts in East Berlin, and on April 8, 1968, the GDR held a cultural symposium honoring his seventieth birthday, featuring American singer Bernice Reagon and an exhibition on his resistance to fascism at Bahnhof Friedrichstrasse. Later, on April 13 and 14, 1971, a symposium assessing his legacy was held at the Deutschen Akademie der Künste. After Robeson's death in 1976, a street in East Berlin's Prenzlauer Berg was renamed Paul-Robeson-Strasse, and his face appeared on an East German stamp with the words, "For Peace against Racism, Paul Robeson, 1898–1976." Paul-Robeson-Strasse remains in reunified Berlin. See PERP; Höhn and Klimke, *Breath of Freedom*, 129–32; and Grossman and Solomon, *Crossing the River*, 173–88.

34. An added layer is that both of their respective German state hosts later extensively memorialized Kennedy and Robeson as American Berliner visitors, with posthumous street names and educational institutions and other cultural rites tied to their memory.

35. As Davis states in her autobiography, at least one of the writers was paid by the FBI to write the article. See Davis, *Angela Davis*, 216.

36. Jackson, *Soledad Brother*.

37. For more on Davis and prison abolition, see Davis, *Abolition Democracy*.

38. Smith, *Prison and the American Imagination*, 67. In 1927, American socialist and unionist Eugene Debs wrote *Walls and Bars: Prisons and Prison Life in The "Land of the Free"* about his time being incarcerated under the Espionage Act. Italian Marxist Antonio Gramsci published a series of epistolary exchanges between him and his sister-in-law in which he writes, "My practicality consists in this, in the knowledge that if you beat your head against the wall it is your head which breaks and not the wall—that is my strength, my only strength" (Gramsci, *Modern Prince*, 56).

39. Bernstein, *America Is the Prison*, 183–84.

40. Berger, *Captive Nation*, 114; "Statement of Principles: Prison Action Conference," Freedom Archives, http://www.freedomarchives.org/Documents/Finder /DOC510_scans/Prison_Conditions/510.tear.down.walls.1972.pdf. See also the poster in the collection of Oakland Museum of California titled, "Free all political prisoners: Angela: Bobby." Its description reads, "Poster has a red brick wall with a blue fist rising in front of it in the center. Over the fist is a small blue chain, and under the brick wall is a large blue chain. Above the poster reads, 'Free all political prisoners/ Angela/ Bobby.' Along the bottom is 'Young Workers Liberation League'" (All Of Us Or None Archive, Gift of the Rossman Family, 2010.54.1232).

41. Prominent visual representations of Davis, on materials ranging from an FBI Most Wanted poster to "Free Angela" paraphernalia to sprawling media coverage of her trial to the covers of her books and pamphlets, all fueled the extreme notoriety of her case. Davis writes of this in her oft-reprinted essay "Afro Images."

42. Additionally, popular musicians such as John Lennon and Yoko Ono

("Angela") (1972), the Rolling Stones ("Black Angel") (1972), Santana ("Free Angela") (1974), and Sun-Ra ("Music for Angela Davis") (1971) performed or released music about her life and case during her imprisonment, and state-sponsored solidarity campaigns from countries around the world and in particular in the Eastern bloc implored officials to consider the political nature of the case through massive public demonstrations and letter-writing campaigns.

43. Davis, "Lectures on Liberation."

44. This interview was printed in *Muhammed Speaks* packaged with text from New York editor Joe Walker. See "Exclusive: Angela Answers 13 Questions," Sc MG 410, ADLDC.

45. *Angela Davis Speaks* (Folkways Records), liner notes, 3.

46. Aptheker, *Morning Breaks*, 42; "The Legacy of George Jackson: A Eulogy by Angela Davis," http://www.usprisonculture.com/blog/2012/08/21/the-legacy-of -george-jackson-a-eulogy-by-angela-davis/.

47. National United Committee to Free Angela Davis, *A Political Biography of Angela Davis*, Sc MG 410, ADLDC.

48. James Baldwin, "An Open Letter to My Sister, Angela Y. Davis," in Davis and Aptheker, *If They Come in the Morning*, 19.

49. Ibid. For more on Baldwin's trip to Germany, see Leeming, *James Baldwin*.

50. Davis and Aptheker, *If They Come in the Morning*, xviii.

51. Ericka Huggins, "Poems from Prison," in ibid., 112.

53. "Prison Interviews with Angela Davis," in ibid., 190.

53. Angela Davis, "Prisoners in Rebellion," in ibid., 44–45.

54. Aptheker, *Morning Breaks*, 64.

55. For more on GDR efforts, see Steiniger, *Free Angela Davis*, and *Peace, Friendship, Solidarity*.

56. Davis and Aptheker, *If They Come in the Morning*, 190. Davis would also later capture the effectiveness of this campaign in her autobiography, quoting the presiding judge, Richard Arnason, when he ruled Davis was eligible for bail after months of detainment: Arnason mentioned "the mail I've received in the last two days and the telephone calls, none of which I have personally taken, but which my staff has taken, from . . . a tremendous number of states and telegrams from foreign countries. It is a case of amazing interest" (Davis, *Angela Davis*, 335).

57. Davis's vision of this shared destiny across lines of incarceration was further expressed in her eulogy for George Jackson, who was killed in San Quentin amidst a confrontation with prison guards in August 1971, after he was targeted for years for his political writing and organizing. Davis issued a statement to the press and then wrote a eulogy for Jackson, which Bettina Aptheker documents in her account as a legal team member and close friend/collaborator with Davis. A day and a half after hearing of his murder, with profound grief and sleepless, Aptheker writes, Davis sits "in front of the typewriter in her cell after George's death. . . . The place was littered with cigarettes, and dozens of pieces of paper, many of them containing half-completed sentences, random words and thoughts—drafts of the public statements she was now completing" (Aptheker, *Morning Breaks*, 42). In her eulogy, Davis men-

tions "walls" several times, which signify as a site to project Jackson's legacy in the face of extreme repression. For example, she honors him for a continued "source of inspiration to all our sisters and brothers inside prison walls and outside." She adds, "George, from behind seemingly impenetrable walls, has placed the issue of the prison struggle squarely on the agenda of the people's movement for revolutionary change. His book reveals the indivisible nature of the struggle on the outside of the prison system with the one inside." In this urgent, mournful missive, written from her cell to be shared at Jackson's funeral, Davis highlights Jackson's profound contribution to her life and to a worldwide community of others, as a visionary for connecting activism on both sides of prison walls, a feat that transcended the "seemingly impenetrable" nature of this manifestation of social division. See "The Legacy of George Jackson: A Eulogy by Angela Davis," http://www.usprisonculture.com /blog/2012/08/21/the-legacy-of-george-jackson-a-eulogy-by-angela-davis/.

58. National United Committee to Free Angela Davis, "Freed by the People," iv–v, Sc MG 410, ADLDC.

59. Branton interview.

60. Toni Morrison to Bettina Aptheker, June 27, 1972, MS#1048, box 1261, RHC.

61. Contract, Bantam Books, September 8, 1972, MS#1048, box 1261, RHC.

62. Agreement, Bantam Books and Random House, January 31, 1973, MS#1048, box 1261, RHC.

63. Toni Morrison to Bernard Geis, April 18, 1973, MS#1048, box 1261, RHC.

64. Silberman wrote Morrison on May 7, 1973, "I looked at some more of the Angela Davis manuscript and it seems to me generally good. It does, of course, need editing—particularly in those spots where the author lapses into vocabulary of the academic. But she does create scenes vividly and with your help they can be even more vivid." Morrison left detailed notes for revision. During this period, it seemed that the book took on new shape and gained a new title and new chapter structure. See James Silberman to Toni Morrison, May 7, 1973, MS#1048, box 1261, RHC.

65. "Angela Davis and Toni Morrison: Literacy, Libraries, Liberation," New York Public Library Video, October 27, 2010, http://www.nypl.org/events/programs /2010/10/27/angela-davis-toni-morrison.

66. Several rounds of incomplete editorial notes and line-edited pages can be found in RHC. The Toni Morrison Papers, held at Princeton University, contain a set of line-edited pages that include the section of the book "Waters" with the section on Davis's trip to Cold War Berlin. There is no cover page available in this folder to ascertain dates or details of these revisions. At this archive, some correspondence between Morrison and Davis will be made available at a later, undetermined date. Further, Harvard University has announced its procurement of Davis's own papers, and a preview image made available for press included line-edited sheets of the autobiography. At the time of this publication, the archive is closed for public access. See box 101, folder 8, TMP.

67. Morrison to Silberman, February 1, 1974, MS#1048, box 1261, RHC.

68. Ibid.

69. On March 13, Morrison wrote Aptheker with an update stating, "Angela's book

is now complete (more or less). We are still hoping to publish in June, but there may be some delay" (Morrison to Aptheker, March 13, 1974, MS#1048, box 1261, RHC).

70. Receipts, correspondence between Morrison and (Jan) Tigner, July 31, 1974, and letters from Morrison to Ellison and Angelou, MS#1048, box 1260, RHC.

71. Perkins, *Autobiography as Activism*, 7.

72. Davis, *Angela Davis*, 17.

73. Ibid., 36.

74. Ibid., 42–43.

75. Ibid., 78.

76. Ibid., 103.

77. Ibid., 117.

78. Ibid., 141.

79. Ibid., 138.

80. Ibid., 250–58.

81. Ibid., 269.

82. Ibid., 281.

83. Ibid., 305.

84. Ibid., 328.

85. Ibid., 396.

86. Ibid., 398.

87. For more on the Privacy Act, see Nelson, *Pursuing Privacy in Cold War America*.

88. Ogbar, *Black Power*, 199.

89. For more debates on continued domestic counterintelligence, see Medsger, *The Burglary*, and Rosenfeld, *Subversives*.

90. In 2013, Davis's life story continued to be a part of public debate and consideration. For example, Shola Lynch's 2013 documentary, *Free Angela and All Political Prisoners*, considers historical memory of her case.

91. *Publishers Weekly*, as quoted in a Random House ad for *Angela Davis: An Autobiography*, in *New York Times*, November 3, 1974.

92. Christopher Lehmann-Haupt, "Book of the Times: Not Quite Speaking Out," *New York Times*, October 23, 1974.

93. Gwendolyn Osborne, "Black Revolutionary," *Crisis*, April 1975.

94. Davis finished her doctoral work at Humboldt University in East Berlin. "It might be of some interest for you to know that she is getting her Ph.D., finally, in Germany. It will not require her to be in Germany—she can get it here and do the work here as well—but it is a very important matter to her" (Toni Morrison to Bernard Geis, August 2 1978, MS#1048, box 1157, RHC).

95. *Peace, Friendship, Solidarity*.

Chapter 3

1. Briese, "Different Aesthetics of the Berlin Wall," 44.

2. Ibid., 40.

3. Tajiri, *Autobiographical Notations*, 45.

4. Ibid., 32.

5. For more on the internment of Japanese Americans and the Tajiri family, see Robinson, *Tragedy of Democracy*.

6. Tajiri's brother Takeshige Vincent also served in this unit. He later became director of photography for *Playboy* magazine. His other brother Taneyoshi Larry was the editor and a columnist for the Japanese American *Pacific Citizen* newspaper. See Tajiri, Robinson, and Tajiri, *Pacific Citizens*.

7. Tajiri, *Autobiographical Notations*, 44.

8. Ibid., 69; Tajiri, *Berlin Wall*.

9. Schaden, "Berliner Mauer im Fotobuch," 14. See also Cox and Young, *Samurai in Space*, and Decke, "Shinkichi Tajiri erklärt die Berlin Mauer zur Land Art."

10. Westgeest, *Tajiri*, 23.

11. Els Barents, "Tajiri's Fotowerken," in Bavelaar, Barents, and Tajiri, *Shinkichi Tajiri*, 96.

12. Ibid., 98.

13. For more on the signing of the Four Powers Agreement, see Junker, Gassert, Mausbach, and Morris, *United States and Germany in the Era of the Cold War*; Richmond, *Practicing Public Diplomacy*; Smyser, *From Yalta to Berlin*; and Taylor, *Berlin Wall*.

14. Briese, "Different Aesthetics of the Berlin Wall," 50.

15. For more on Beuys and Germany, see Mesch, *Modern Art at the Berlin Wall*, and Michely, *Joseph Beuys*.

16. Klimke, *Other Alliance*, 6–7.

17. For more on the protests of 1968 and historical legacy, see Klimke and Scharloth, *1968 in Europe*; Gassert and Klimke, *1968*; and Gassert and Steinweis, *Coping with the Nazi Past*.

18. Mesch, *Modern Art at the Berlin Wall*, 49. In the United States, a different tenor around the cultural imagination of the Berlin Wall emerged. While the Wall continued to evoke cultural preoccupations with dangers of war and spy intrigue, a shift occurred during this time: the reemergence of cultural play and parody around the topic of Germany's division. In 1968, Hollywood director George Marshall released *The Wicked Dreams of Paula Schultz*, a slapstick comedy in which an East German track star, Schultz (played by Elke Sommer), pole vaults over the Berlin Wall to escape repressive control and the sexual advances of the party's leadership. When American huckster Bill Mason (played by Bob Crane) finds her, he aims to make a profit, even as he falls in love. He alternates between his contacts in East Germany's black market, the ruling party, and the American CIA to sell her for a reward. As Mason slips a contraband-filled briefcase over for unchecked access, the narration at the beginning of the film remarks on the shift in border relations: "To get into East Berlin it's not always necessary to go over the Wall, through it, or under it. You might just have something the fellow wants. And if he wants it bad enough, you get what you want." Mason eventually falls for Schultz, which complicates his attempted parlay. The film was panned by critics, not necessarily for its Wall depictions but for its crude portrayal of female sexuality as a form of currency to move back and forth

across the border. A *New York Times* reviewer noted, "It seems to view the cold war as a vast conspiracy to get people undressed, as clumsily and joylessly as possible." A year later, NBC's variety show *Laugh-In* made a joke at the Wall's expense. In a segment titled "News from the Future," comedian Dan Rowan reported, "Berlin, twenty years from now, 1989. There was dancing in the streets today, as East Germany finally tore down the Berlin Wall. The joy was short-lived, however, as the Wall was quickly replaced with a moat full of alligators." The underlying humor of the Wall's dismantling was paired with a notion that the division would nonetheless endure. In another program, the 1969 Emmy-nominated *Bob Hope Christmas Special: Around the World with the USO*, the celebrated entertainer shared scenes from his USO visit to West Berlin, in which he was presented by the mayor and U.S. Army command with "half a key to half a city." An audience of servicemen and women was shown erupting in laughter. The fact that the Wall could be leveraged for political humor marked a shift in its perception. The imagination for the Wall's demise remained, but most treated the boundary as ostensibly fixed in the geopolitical landscape.

19. Godfrey, *Conceptual Art*, 4.

20. Epigraph, pamphlet, Publikation der Berliner Festspiele, 2014, 3.

21. Kaprow, Block, and Deutscher Akademischer Austauschdienst, *Sweet Wall Testimonials*.

22. Mesch, *Modern Art at the Berlin Wall*, 185.

23. For more on Kaprow's other projects in Germany, see Kaprow, Herzog, Holtmann, and Kraft, *Allan Kaprow in Deutschland*.

24. Christo, Baal-Teshuva, Volz, Buddensieg, and Christo, *Christo*, 22.

25. Ibid., 23. See also O'Doherty et al., *Christo and Jeanne-Claude*.

26. In 1961, Christo and Jeanne-Claude also created a work in response to the Berlin Crisis, a blockade of oil barrels in Paris titled *Iron Curtain*.

27. Jennifer Mundy, "Lost Art: Christo and Jeanne-Claude," Tate.co.uk, http://www.tate.org.uk.

28. Christo, Baal-Teshuva, Volz, Buddensieg, and Christo, *Christo*, 11.

29. Several other American projects of note by the Berlin Wall immediately followed this period. Conceptual artist Lawrence Weiner is another figure of note in this history of artistic intervention. He began addressing the division of Germany in his work in 1971 when he adapted his *Broken Off* project to include a series of postcards that he sent from East Berlin. In 1975, Weiner was awarded a DAAD grant and directed the avant-garde film *A Second Quarter*. The film was shot on location in West Berlin and aimed to treat the city as a theoretical laboratory to explore themes of liberation, free expression, and aggression through language games. The scenes take place in a number of dramatized domestic vignettes and one iconic vista of the divided city—looking down along the perspective of the Wall from an observation deck at the bombed-out ruins of the abandoned Anhalter Bahnhof train station. In 1976, Gordon Matta-Clark intended to blow up a portion of the Wall for a show alternately titled *New York/Berlin* or *Soho in Berlin*. He was dissuaded from such a gesture and instead plastered advertising posters and stenciled the words "Made in America"

directly on the Wall. A film assemblage of his interventions and clashes with authorities is titled *The Wall*. See Weiner and Gregory, *Lawrence Weiner*, and Jenkins, *City Slivers and Fresh Kills*.

30. For more on German art perspectives/movements from both sides of Germany, see Barron, Eckmann, and Gillen, *Art of Two Germanys*.

31. Lou Reed's *Berlin* album begins with its title track, "Berlin," in somber discord, with the opening lines, "In Berlin, by the wall / you were five foot ten inches tall / It was very nice/ candlelight and Dubonnet on ice." Reed's conceptual album is about an American man, Jim, in Berlin who falls for a seemingly depraved German woman, Caroline. Much separates the lovers, not in terms of physical distance or in geopolitics in their shared apartment in West Berlin, but in terms of the alienation brought on by drugs, sex, and violence shared between them. Also for Jim, who sees himself as lacking in financial power, his laments include comparisons to "men of good fortune" against whom he cannot measure. The couple deals with the perilous nature of his failed power through acts of defiance and deviance. In turn, Jim ends up loathing Caroline. Berlin is the stage for stormy and sordid identities. Reed's character expresses sadness in embittered, angry, and desperate gestures. Reed sparingly uses the historical situation of occupied West Berlin to add texture to the story; however, he does include moments that place Jim's situation against those of U.S. military servicemen. On "The Kids," Reed sings, "The black Air-force sergeant was not her first one / and all the drugs she took every one . . . and I'm the water boy / the real game is not over here." Reed sings out of a wounded sense of masculinity, channeling his alienation through constructions of racial and gender otherness in Berlin. For more on Lou Reed's *Berlin*, see Anthony DeCurtis, "My Brilliant and Troubled Friend Lou Reed," *Guardian*, October 1, 2017.

32. "Shinkichi Tajiri: Interview MFZA mit Prof. Shinkichi Tajiri," 1988, rev. 2014, https://www.paranorm.de/paranorm_1986_2039/Tajiri_Interview_Biografie.htm.

33. Hillenius, Tajiri, and Marks, *Tajiri*.

34. Tajiri, *Autobiographical Notations*, 93; Hillenius, Tajiri, and Marks, *Tajiri*.

35. Tajiri, *Autobiographical Notations*, 74.

36. This echoed an earlier statue titled *Nagasaki* (1957), a figure with a classical form but with a headless and armless body and webbed skin. See ibid., 48.

37. Ibid., 69.

38. Tajiri and Tegenbosch, *Shinkichi Tajiri*, 4.

39. Hillenius, Tajiri, and Marks, *Tajiri*. In the rendering of this knot in his 1974 Boijmans-van Beuningen Museum and Bonnefantenmuseum exhibition catalog, he included a scraperboard rendering of this sculpture with his mother embedded in its scene.

40. All image readings draw from Tajiri, *Berlin Wall*. Giotta and Ryu Tajiri and Axel Klausmier also provided additional assistance in locating these images in Berlin.

41. Hildebrandt, *Divided Germany*. In historic documentation of this period of division, we often view the sign from the West. However, if we consider the mirrored signage of the GDR, other border imperatives emerge. The most common exit signs of the GDR, mostly viewed by foreign visitors rather than citizens, stated, "You Are

Now Leaving the Main City of the German Democratic Republic," a claim of ideological and urban authority.

42. Schaden, "Berliner Mauer im Fotobuch," 12.

43. Briese, "Different Aesthetics of the Berlin Wall," 42–43. Briese notes that East Germany continued making plans for additional renovations, at least through 1988.

44. In another image taken in Berlin, he portrayed friend and fellow American artist in Berlin Edward Kienzholz in a playful and nude position lying as a Manet *Olympia* in his workspace. See Tajiri, *Autobiographical Notations*, 130.

45. Mesch, *Modern Art at the Berlin Wall*, 87–90.

46. A selection of the Berlin panoramas can be seen in Tajiri, *Autobiographical Notations*, 138–39. Others are viewable at the Shinkichi Tajiri Estate in Baarlo, Netherlands (uncataloged). Helen Westgeest notes of one depicting the Bornholmer Strasse Bridge: "The open unfolding bridge, a border crossing between East and West Berlin, looks like an anthropomorphic sculpture and recalls association of form with Tajiri's polyester knots" (Westgeest, *Tajiri*, 25).

47. Dreyblatt, *Amerikanische Künstler in Berlin*.

Chapter 4

1. "Address to the Nation and Other Countries on United States-Soviet Relations, Ronald Regan Presidential Library," January 16, 1984, https://www.reaganlibrary .gov/research/speeches/11684a. For more on Reagan policies of rollback, see Brands, *Making the Unipolar Moment*; Gleijeses, *Visions of Freedom*; Grandin, *Empire's Workshop*; Mamdani, *Good Muslim, Bad Muslim*; and Von Eschen, "Di Eagle and di Bear."

2. Taylor, *Berlin Wall*, 374–76.

3. De Veaux, *Warrior Poet*, 337.

4. Lorde, *Burst of Light*, 54.

5. For more on Lorde's meetings with East German women, see unpublished journal entry [May 17, 1984], box 47, no. 17, and photographs, box 66A, ALP. Additionally, undated notes appear to document a meeting with East German women, including those identified as lesbian and of color. See undated notes, box 24, no. 2.3 106–8, ALP.

6. Lorde had been invited to West Berlin by Dagmar Schultz, an instructor at the Free University and editor of the Sub Rosa Orlanda Women's Press, which had first translated Lorde's work into German. Schultz was inspired by Lorde when she heard Lorde give talks at a pair of international women's conferences—in Copenhagen at the UN Women's World Conference in 1980 and in the Berkshires in 1981. In their correspondence surrounding the invitation, Schultz outlined her admiration of Lorde's work and the exciting potential she saw for Lorde's guest professorship. Among other reasons for teaching in Berlin, Schultz noted, there was a group of young women writers, some of whom were of African descent and would benefit from Lorde's tutelage: "One positive aspect is that you would certainly attract women from the German black community." See Dagmar Schultz invitation, box 5, 1.1.117, ALP, and Course Register 1983, 634–37, ALA).

7. Lorde, *Burst of Light*, 59, 65.

8. Unpublished journal entry [June 16, 1984], box 47, no. 17, ALP.

9. Lorde, *Burst of Light*, 62. See also Charly Wilder, "Audre Lorde's Berlin," *New York Times*, July 19, 2019.

10. This chapter refers to selected unpublished journal entries and poems, as read from and cited in her publicly available archives at Spelman College. Some of her unreleased work during her lifetime has been published in volumes, including Lorde, *I Am Your Sister*, and Bolacki and Broeck, *Audre Lorde's Transnational Legacies*.

11. By attending to Lorde's poetic mixed-genre approach, Linda Garber contends in her chapter on Lorde in *Identity Poetics* that "critics of all stripes exhibit a strange resistance to Lorde as a poet, however, preferring to discuss (and presumably read) her prose work" (105). Lexi Rudnitsky and Megan Obourn have raised similar arguments. My treatment of Lorde's work responds to a perceived lack of close formal readings of Lorde's poetry but also attempts to consider multiple and extra-literary forms of her work, as well as the historical context of her poems. The materials in her archive suggest the importance of revision and interdisciplinary genres of her own production process. See Rudnitsky, "'Power' and 'Sequelae' of Audre Lorde's Syntactical Strategies," and Obourn, "Audre Lorde."

12. Audre Lorde, "Poetry Is Not a Luxury," in Lorde, *Sister Outsider*.

13. "Lesung im Café Araquin in Berlin (Audio)," July 17, 1984, 3.1.68, ALA.

14. Lorde's published work on Germany includes poems in *Our Dead Behind Us* (1986) and *The Marvelous Arithmetics of Distance* (1992); the essay "Apartheid U.S.A." and journal entries from *A Burst of Light* (1988); and the preface to the foundational Afro-German text *Farbe Bekennen* (1987, 1992). Also relevant to this body of work are archival or collected works, such as several unpublished poems, her speech at the Dream of Europe Conference in Germany (1987), and interviews published in Lorde and Hall, *Conversations with Audre Lorde* (2004). There also remains a significant portion of her work translated into and published in German, pioneered by Schultz and the Sub Rosa Orlanda Women's Press. Other contemporary projects that continue to measure her impact on Afro-German and Afro-European cultural exchange from 1984 forward include Dagmar Schultz's 2012 documentary *Audre Lorde* and the scholarly volume edited by Bolaki and Broeck, *Audre Lorde's International Legacy*, to which I am a contributor.

15. Lester Olson, "Sisterhood as Performance in Audre Lorde's Public Advocacy," in Bolacki and Broeck, *Audre Lorde's Transnational Legacies*, 116; Audre Lorde, "Poetry Is Not a Luxury," in Lorde, *Sister Outsider*, 38.

16. As quoted in Hartman, *Bitburg in Moral and Political Perspective*, 94.

17. As quoted in ibid., 243.

18. Geoffrey Hartman notes, "Unfortunately, Mr. Reagan compounded his error by explanatory statements that made no distinction between the fallen German soldiers and the murdered Jews; indeed, he suggested that both were 'victims' of a Nazi oppression whose responsibility he limited by laying it upon the madness of 'one man'" (ibid., 65).

19. Ronald Reagan, "Remarks at a Joint German-American Military Ceremony

at Bitburg Air Base in the Federal Republic of Germany," http://www.reagan.utexas
.edu/archives/speeches/1985/50585b.htm.

20. Legs McNeil and John Holmstrom, "We're a Happy Family," *Spin*, August
1986, 78.

21. Harrington and Inge, *Dark Laughter*. For more on Harrington, see Harrington,
Why I Left America, 54–55. For more on Oliver Harrington in East Berlin, see Brown,
"'Bootise' in Berlin."

22. In the case of Berlin, the heightened rhetoric and military maneuvering of
this reanimated and further globalized Cold War shook but failed to undermine the
strange coexistence maintained between the two Germanys. Even remaining as foes,
they practiced diplomatic relations across their borders through a system of economic
credits and payments, and they permitted emigrations, trading of land borders, a
growing cross-border black market, and a lessening of sharp rhetoric about the Berlin
Wall. During this period the Wall was again updated with the Grenzmauer 75 panels.
And yet divisions within the respective Germanys would truly test the ideological
resolve of the structures of power; in the East, the call for expanded access to exit
visas gained public momentum. Soviet policies of *Perestroika* and *Glasnost* brought
about possibilities for reform across the Eastern bloc as well as tensions over political
change that reverberated through East Germany. In the West, the Euromissile Crisis
of 1983 sparked antinuclear protests and demonstrations in West Germany and across
Europe. Further, attention to the strained assimilation of racial and ethnic minori-
ties pitted Germans of color (in particular, Turkish and Afro-Germans) against the
ideologies of the *Volk*. Carmen Faymonville writes, "20th-century global migration
has fostered the creation and maintenance of transnational diasporas in all western
societies, including Germany. As a result . . . western nations can no longer maintain
their formerly territorialized, spatially-bounded, and culturally homogenous status."
In that sense both the global and internal divisions experienced through the two Germanys were a part of the larger emergence of globalization in the 1980s that brought
about increased cross-border economic and social relations, as well as tensions of
identity and economic self-determination within national borders. See Faymonville,
"Black Germans and Transnational Identification," and Taylor, *Berlin Wall*, 378, 395.

23. Nora, "Between Memory and History." In the United States, two signature
moments of the emergent memorial culture included debates about the legacy of
the Holocaust and Vietnam, as played out in the opening of Maya Lin's Vietnam War
Memorial in Washington, D.C., in 1982 and the release of Claude Lanzmann's Holocaust film *Shoah* in 1985. The impending AIDS epidemic would mark another moment the nation was confronting its own dynamics of memory and politics of death.
In each case, the question of how to appropriately memorialize was complicated by
the ongoing and unresolved legacies of these conflicts.

24. Sturken, *Tangled Memories*, 13. Identity served as a powerful and polemic organizing principle of this period of globalization, because, as Lauren Berlant suggests,
"the crisis of the national future . . . comes at a time when America feels unsure about
its value in a number of domains: in world military politics, in global economies, in

ecological practice, and in the claim that the nation has a commitment to sustaining justice, democracy, and the American Dream when there seems to be less money and reliable work to go around" (Berlant, *Queen of America Goes to Washington City*, 18). Such scholars suggest the ways the memory debates are interrelated — whether about the Holocaust or the Vietnam War — to continuing policies and attitudes about U.S. military policy and culture. For more on AIDS memory, see Cvetkovich, "AIDS Activism and the Oral History Archive."

25. Oates and Johnson, *Journal of Joyce Carol Oates*, 409.

26. Joyce Carol Oates, "Ich bin ein Berliner," in Oates, *Last Days*, 99–100.

27. Joyce Carol Oates, "Our Wall" in Oates, *Last Days*, 241. If Oates was drawn closer to the Berlin Wall only to ultimately affirm its looming endurance and cyclical patterns of violence, visual artist Keith Haring's October 1986 mural painted directly on the western side of the Wall near Checkpoint Charlie on Zimmerstrasse countered her method with an embodied gesture of expression that doubled as a call to action against the structure. At the invitation of the Haus am Checkpoint Charlie, Haring's site-specific intervention occurred at a high point for prominent American artists, including Jonathan Borofsky and David Wojnarowicz, expressing themselves with painted imagery directly on the Berlin Wall's western surface, as well as a moment of his own rise to international acclaim. In one day, Haring painted a 300-foot-long section of the Berlin Wall, featuring interlinked human figures rendered in black, red, and yellow, the colors of the German flags. Haring told a newspaper, "It's a humanistic gesture, more than anything else . . . a political and subversive act — an attempt to psychologically destroy the wall by painting it" ("Keith Haring Paints Mural on Berlin Wall," *New York Times*, October 24, 1986). His monumental artwork imagined the reunion of the two Germanys, as he coded a variety of subtle physical symbols of difference within the interlocked figures' abstract elements. Despite his monumental aim, Haring's gesture toward making a spectacle of aspirational German solidarity drew criticism for an overemphasis on symbols suggestive of universality rather than political recognition. Haring employed a complex semiotic system of Xs and Os on the bodies of the figures to conjure diversity and difference. But whereas many of his other contemporary public projects drew on site-specific political provocation, the mural lacked a direct, multilevel acknowledgment of German history beyond abstraction. While on the scene, however, Haring successfully drew attention to his own transnational project of grassroots public action in coverage surrounding the event. In a televised press conference at the Haus am Checkpoint Charlie, Haring drew attention to another region and crucible of political conflict: he wore a self-designed "Free South Africa" t-shirt, symbolically linking his mural on the Berlin Wall to his global antiapartheid advocacy. Within days of its creation, Haring's Berlin Wall mural was painted over by other artists, and audiences lost the opportunity to make connections between the Berlin Wall, scars of memory, and contemporary global conflicts. Haring also has a sculpture, *Boxer*, installed near West Berlin's Potsdamer Platz in 1987. For more on Haring, see Gruen, *Keith Haring*. For more on other Wall painters, see Gray, "Wall Painters." For more on Borofsky's painting on the Berlin Wall and public art/sculptures in Germany, see Rosenthal,

Borofsky, and Marshall, *Jonathan Borofsky*, and Farber, *Wall in Our Heads*. For more on Wojnarowicz's cow's head paintings on the Berlin Wall, images of the Berlin Zoo, and the adapted performance of his written monologues, *Sounds in the Distance*, in Berlin in 1984 (starring Allen Frame, John Edward Heys, and others, and accompanied by Nan Goldin), see DWP and JEHP.

28. Dhairyam, "'Artifacts for Survival,'" 249. For more on the historical strategies of *Our Dead Behind Us*, see also Gloria Hull, "Living on the Line: Audre Lorde and *Our Dead Behind Us*," in Wall, *Changing Our Own Words*.

29. Ilona Pache and Regina-Maria Dackweiler, "An Interview with Audre Lorde" (1987), in Lorde and Hall, *Conversations with Audre Lorde*, 166.

30. Lorde, *Our Dead Behind Us*, 3–5.

31. Lorde biographer Alexis De Veaux writes, "From the location as outsider Lorde criticized US hegemony in the Americas and its hypocrisy as a democracy" (De Veaux, *Warrior Poet*, 337).

32. Lorde, *Our Dead Behind Us*, 49.

33. Unpublished journal entry [April 27, 1984], box 46, no. 17, ALP.

34. For more on black women writers and "rituals of return," see Hardin, "Rituals of Return."

35. Lorde's poem evokes the Berlin photography of American artist Nan Goldin, whose *Ballad of Sexual Dependency* included an image taken of a friend, Suzanne, in East Berlin's Pergamon Museum bathroom. Goldin premiered a slide show version of *Ballad* in West Berlin in 1984. Bathrooms were important spaces for Goldin's intimate photographs, especially those taken in Berlin. She went on to take a self-portrait in a Berlin bathroom in 1991. See Goldin, *Ballad of Sexual Dependency*, and "The Berlin Ballad of Nan Goldin," *Economist*, January 6, 2011, http://www.economist.com /blogs/prospero/2011/01/contemporary_photography.

36. Lorde, "First Impressions," box 31.2.4.314, ALP.

37. Ibid.

38. Avi-Ram, "Apo Koinou in Audre Lorde and the Moderns."

39. Photographs, box 66A, ALP.

40. For more on workshops in West Germany and Europe, see ALA; Lorde, *Burst of Light*; De Veaux, *Warrior Poet*, 340–44; and Schultz, *Audre Lorde*. For more on Lorde's work with East German women's writers' groups, see unpublished journal entry [May 17, 1984], box 47, no. 17, ALP; photographs, box 66A, ALP; undated notes, box 24, no. 2.3 106–8, ALP; and Schultz interview, December 10, 2010.

41. Schultz interview, December 10, 2010.

42. Annotation, photograph, box 66A, ALP. For more on Lorde's reading at the Amerika Haus, see DVD extras on Schultz, *Audre Lorde*, and Melba Joyce Boyd, "Politics, Jazz and the Politics of Aesthetics," in Diedrich and Heinrichs, *From Black to Schwarz*, 359–61.

43. "Lesung im Amerika-Haus in Berlin-Charlottenburg (Audio)," June 13, 1984, 3.1.61, ALA.

44. Lorde, *Burst of Light*, 56–57. For more on the history of African American GIs and their German offspring, see Höhn, *GIs and Fräuleins*.

45. Wright, *Becoming Black*, 196.

46. Campt, *Other Germans*, 177.

47. Opitz, Oguntoye, and Schultz, *Showing Our Colors*. For more on the Afro-German movement, see Campt, *Other Germans*; Wright, *Becoming Black*; El-Tayeb, *European Others*; Tiffany N. Florvil, "Emotional Connections: Audre Lorde and Black German Women," and Katharina Gerund, "Transracial Feminist Alliances: Audre Lorde and West German Women," in Bolacki and Broeck, *Audre Lorde's Transnational Legacie*; Hügel-Marshall, *Invisible Woman*; and Lennox, *Remapping Black Germany*. Lorde was a key figure in women-of-color feminism, and her work forged connections with other diasporic work domestically and abroad. For more on Lorde's previous work as a prominent contributor to women-of-color feminism, see Moraga and Anzaldúa, *This Bridge Called My Back*, and Ferguson, *Aberrations in Black*.

48. Lorde, *Burst of Light*, 58.

49. For more on Lorde's wrestling with the terms of diaspora, see Lester Olson, "Sisterhood as Performance in Audre Lorde's Public Advocacy," in Bolacki and Broeck, *Audre Lorde's Transnational Legacies*.

50. Lorde, *Burst of Light*, 80.

51. Unpublished journal entry [June 6, 1984], box 46, no. 17, ALP.

52. Box 27, no. 2.4.132, ALP.

53. All citations of drafts of this poem refer to "Berlin Is Hard on Colored Girls," in box 31, no. 2.4.324, ALP.

54. Melba Joyce Boyd, "Politics, Jazz and the Politics of Aesthetics," in Diedrich and Heinrichs, *From Black to Schwarz*, 262.

55. Lorde's use of "colored" may also resonate with other such deployments in the post–civil rights era. See Ntozake Shange's 1975 choreopoem *For Colored Girls Who Have Considered Suicide When the Rainbow Is Enuf*.

56. For more on the dreamspaces of Lorde's poems, see Gloria Hull, "Living on the Line: Audre Lorde and *Our Dead Behind Us*," in Wall, *Changing Our Own Words*.

57. All citations of this poem refer to "Berlin Is Hard on Colored Girls," in Lorde, *Our Dead Behind Us*, 22–23.

58. Across her poetry, Lorde draws her poetic imagery from actual experiences and imaginative gestures. She uses the perspective of "I" for herself and to embody witnesses for others. This demands readers' close and open consideration of meaning and subjectivity.

59. The characterization of Berlin as a space of queer identifications and history, following the Weimar period, has been primarily studied through a gay male and critical masculinities focus. Renewed focus on the multiple and understudied overlaps between queer communities in Berlin may also yield new perspectives on the reputation of the city as a queer place. Important Western figures in this history include Christopher Isherwood and David Bowie. Lorde, as well as photographer Nan Goldin, writer Bill Van Parys, and others also represent intersections and significant narratives of queer life in Berlin through lesbian, feminist, and radical perspectives. See Stewart, *Greenwood Encyclopedia*, 193.

60. For more on the Berlin Opera, see "Music View; East Berlin Opera Nervously Awaits the Next Act," *New York Times*, June 24, 1990, and Pugh, "Berlin Wall and the Urban Space and Experience of East and West Berlin," 62.

61. De Veaux, *Warrior Poet*, 337.

62. Williams, *Interpreting Nightingales*.

63. Keats, *Complete Poems and Selected Letters*. Lorde addressed Keats, among other Romantic poets she critically read while at Hunter College. See Lorde and Hall, *Conversations with Audre Lorde*, 32.

64. Schultz interview, December 10, 2010.

65. Ladd, *Ghosts of Berlin*, 151–52, 162.

66. Box 43, ALP.

67. Unpublished journal entry [July 29, 1984], box 46, no. 17, ALP.

68. All citations of drafts of this poem refer to "This Urn Contains Earth from German Concentration Camps," in box 31, no. 2.4.322, ALP.

69. Claude Lanzmann, on *Shoah*: "Making a history was not what I wanted to do. I wanted to construct something more powerful than that. And, in fact, I think that the film, using only images of the present, evokes the past with far more force than any historical document" (Richard Bernstein, "An Epic Film about the Greatest Evil of Modern Times," *New York Times*, October 20, 1985, https://www.nytimes.com/1985/10/20/movies/an-epic-film-about-the-greatest-evil-of-modern-times.html).

70. Lorde does not use an umlaut in her published spelling of Plötzensee. In her earlier drafts, she also misspells the name as "Plotenzee" or "Plotensee," as she worked from a German-English transliteration.

71. All citations to this poem refer to "This Urn Contains Earth from German Concentration Camps: Plotzensee Memorial, West Berlin, 1984," in Lorde, *Our Dead Behind Us*, 24–25.

72. John Keats, "Ode on a Grecian Urn," in Keats, *Complete Poems and Selected Letters*, 193. I thank Lisa Moore, Meta DuEwa Jones, and the other fellow members of the critical poetry seminar at the Texas Institute for Literary and Textual Studies for pointing out this connection.

73. Box 31, no. 2.4.318, ALP.

74. Also titled "Either We March in Washington or We Blow It Up," as seen in box 31.2.4.306, ALP. All citations of drafts of this poem refer to this ALP listing.

75. Unpublished journal entry [January 30, 1984], box 46, no. 35, ALP.

76. For more on Afro-Germans and diaspora, see Wright, *Becoming Black*, 3; Campt, *Other Germans*, 171; and Weheliye, *Phonographies*, 147. See also Edwards, *Practice of Diaspora*.

77. All citations of this poem refer to "Diaspora," in Lorde, *Our Dead Behind Us*, 32.

78. Another reading of the poetic geography of the "Braceras Grande" can be seen in DeShazer, *Poetics of Resistance*, 24.

79. For more on Soviet policies of *Glasnost* and *Perestroika*, see Service, *History of Modern Russia*, 448–66, and Boym, *Future of Nostalgia*, 62–71.

80. For more on the Berlin bombing and the U.S. counterattack on Libya, see Nathalie Malinarich, "Flashback: The Berlin Bombing," on *BBC News.com*, http://news.bbc.co.uk/2/hi/europe/1653848.stm.

81. Taylor, *Berlin Wall*, 396; Serge Schmemann, "24,000 Demonstrate in Berlin against Reagan's Visit," *New York Times*, June 12, 1987.

82. Ted Widmer, "Reagan at the Wall," *New York Times*, June 12, 2012, A25.

83. Numerous other contemporary American cultural productions draw and reflect on Berlin's division. Some of these include texts such as Dr. Seuss's *The Butter Battle Book* (1984), Herbert Jay Stern's *Judgment in Berlin* (1984), and William Buckley Jr.'s *The Story of Henri Tod* (1984); popular music such as Elton John's "Nikita" (1986); television episodes of *MacGyver* (1986), *Alvin and the Chipmunks'* "The Wall" (1988), and the *Golden Girls* (1988); a comic book installment of *Spiderman vs. Wolverine*, no. 1 (1987); and film versions of *Judgment in Berlin* (1988). Several works also influenced American audiences by German cultural figures that closely considered the symbol and site of the Berlin Wall, including Peter Schneider's *Der Mauerspringer* (*The Wall Jumper*) (1983) and Wim Wenders's *Wings of Desire* (1987). The latter was released in West Germany in 1987; the film was predominantly in German but featured American actor Peter Falk, who spoke most of his lines in English. See Wim Wenders, *Wings of Desire* (New York: Criterion Collection, 1987).

84. Alice H. G. Phillips, "Calling for the Right Kind of Power," *TLS*, April 15–21, 1988.

85. Review, *Booklist*, October 1, 1986.

86. Barbara Christian, "Naming the Rage and the Courage," *San Francisco Chronicle*, review, July 20, 1986, 6.

87. Audre Lorde, "The Dream of Europe—Remarks," in Bolacki and Broeck, *Audre Lorde's Transnational Legacies*, 25–26. More on this speech can be found in box 17, 2.1.061, ALP. Box 31, no. 2.4.358, ALP, also includes drafts of an unpublished poem, "Berlin Second Time Around," dated October 12, 1988.

88. Bolacki and Broeck, *Audre Lorde's Transnational Legacies*, 26.

89. Audre Lorde, "Apartheid U.S.A.," in Lorde, *Burst of Light*, 27.

90. Ibid., 37–38.

91. Lorde, *Burst of Light*, 131.

92. Ibid., 131–34.

Conclusion

1. On May 2, Hungary began disassembling border fencing, opening up a crossing point into Austria. Protests across Poland and the Baltic republics of Estonia, Latvia, and Lithuania occurred with far less severe backlash from local authorities and the Soviet Union. See Service, *History of Modern Russia*, 448–66, and Boym, *Future of Nostalgia*, 62–71.

2. Taylor, *Berlin Wall*, 400.

3. Taylor writes, "On Monday 2 October, 10,000 citizens of Leipzig appeared on the streets. They chanted slogans about freedom, but above all they declared: 'We will stay here.' This message was, in its way, even more worrying for Honecker than

that conveyed by West Germany–bound hoards of refugees. The regime had gotten used to arresting its dissidents and dumping them in the West. Now they were determined to stay in the East, and there were too many to deport them all" (ibid., 409).

4. For more on Leipzig Movement, see Taylor, *Berlin Wall*, and Dale, *Popular Protest*.

5. Günter Schabowski, Press Conference in the GDR International Press Center, November 9, 1989, trans. Howard Sargeant, Cold War International History Project, Documents and Papers, Wilson Center, https://digitalarchive.wilsoncenter.org/document/113049.

6. Sarotte, *The Collapse*, xx.

7. Taylor adds, "The first reports from DPA [Deutsche Presse-Agentur] and Reuters, which came over the wires at a couple of minutes after seven p.m., simply said that any GDR citizen would be entitled, from now on, to leave the country via appropriate border crossing points. Low-key stuff. Then, at five past seven, Associated Press pulled ahead of the pack and spelled its interpretation out in a simple but sensational sentence: 'According to information provided by SED Politburo member Günter Schabowski, the GDR is opening its borders'" (Taylor, *Berlin Wall*, 425).

8. ABC News, November 9, 1989, http://www.youtube.com/watch?v=jnCPdLlUgvo.

9. NBC News, November 10, 1989, http://www.youtube.com/watch?v=fK1MwhEDjHg.

10. In the weeks following the initial breach of the Berlin Wall, after the wave of East German protests on the evening of November 9, Americans turned to popular culture to make meaning of this improvised historic moment. This was a process that built and revised previous patterns of cultural commentary and critique, including cautious reflection, sentimental attachments, and parody. For example, on November 18, *Saturday Night Live* comedian Mike Myers reprised his "Sprockets" skit, playing disaffected avant-garde West German TV host Dieter, as he had previously several times. In this installment, the first since the breach of the Wall, Dieter is finally able to interview fictional East German filmmaker Gregor Voss (played by guest star Woody Harrelson) days after the former "countercultural" and "suppressed visionary" is able to travel to the West for the first time. But on this segment, the spoils of capitalism have overcome Voss. He stumbles into the interview wearing a beer-can-holding helmet and proclaims, "Ich bin ein West Berliner." He has abandoned his harsh minimalist aesthetic in favor of the parodied spoils of capitalist culture, scarfing a hamburger and Mountain Dew and boasting of a rented American sedan. Even in this skit, jubilation provokes a sense of blurriness and a loss of identity. The linkages between Berlin's defunct Wall and Western consumer culture were not relegated to *Saturday Night Live*'s Sprockets but became embraced as a platform for celebratory consumerism. AT&T and Pepsi aired commercials during the subsequent Christmas season, with documentary-style footage from Berlin and sentimental soundtracks. Complementing the visuals, each commercial featured respective backing songs of Louis Armstrong's "What a Wonderful World" and Handel's *Messiah*, reinforcing the message of the Wall's dismantling as an event to be

celebrated—honoring the opening for movement of people and goods across the border—through products associated with the scene. For a critical reading of the news reporting and cultural imaginary of "the fall of the wall," see Manghani, *Image Critique and the Fall of the Berlin Wall.*

11. The soundtrack for the dismantling of the Berlin Wall would also include Leonard Bernstein's "Ode to Freedom," a take on Beethoven's Ninth Symphony performed in Berlin on Christmas Day 1989, altogether introducing grand and monumental sounds to visions of the scene. Burton et al., *Ode to Freedom*. For more on consumerism and the complexities of freedom in former East Germany, see Iyengar, *Art of Choosing.*

12. This collective of cultural producers includes a range of figures who spent substantive time in Berlin—perhaps before but definitely after the *Wende* period—and/or whose work drew from the cultural imaginary of a divided Berlin. A sampling of this group, beyond others mentioned in previous chapters, includes multidisciplinary musical theater producers John Cameron Mitchell (*Hedwig and the Angry Inch*) and Stew (*Passing Strange*); novelists Chloe Aridjis (*Book of Clouds*), Paul Beatty (*Slumberland*), Jeffrey Eugenides (*Middlesex*), Janet Fitch (*White Oleander*), Jonathan Franzen (*Freedom* and *Purity*), Andrew Sean Greer (*Less*), Ida Hattemer-Higgins (*The History of History*), Aleksandar Hemon (*Lazarus Project*), and Darryl Pinckney (*Black Deutschland*); musicians David Bowie ("Where Are We Now"), Leonard Cohen (*The Future*), Ani DiFranco ("Subdivision"), Michael Jackson (*Dancing the Dream* and *HIStory*), Prince ("Wall of Berlin"), Lou Reed (*Berlin*, "Brandenburg Gate"), Jake Shears of Scissor Sisters (*Nightwork*), and Michael Stipe of R.E.M. ("ÜBerlin"); filmmakers Tilda Swinton and Cynthia Beatt (*The Invisible Frame*); visual and performance artists Richard Avedon (*Brandenburg Gate*), Frank Hallam Day (*East Berlin*), Jenny Holzer (Reichstag entrance project), Adrian Piper (*Escape to Berlin: A Travel Memoir*, The Adrian Piper Research Archive Foundation Berlin), and Stephanie Syjuco (*The Berlin Wall*), among an extensive and growing list of others.

13. Unpublished German book folder (uncataloged), LFP, and Freed, Ebner, and Farber, *Re-Made*, 41.

14. Unpublished German book folder (uncataloged), LFP.

15. Freed, Ebner, and Farber, *Re-Made.*

16. Davis, *Are Prisons Obsolete?*

17. "Prof. Angela Davis at Occupy Berlin Camp, 18 November 2011," http://www.youtube.com/watch?v=4PrAL6BIfxE.

18. Johanna Heuveling, "Angela Davis speaks with refugees in Berlin," May 16, 2015, http://www.werkstatt-der-kulturen.de/download/Pressenza%20Angela%20Davis%20speaks%20with%20refugees%20in%20Berlin.pdf.

19. "Angela Davis and Toni Morrison: Literacy, Libraries, Liberation," New York Public Library Video, October 27, 2010, http://www.nypl.org/events/programs/2010/10/27/angela-davis-toni-morrison.

20. Ibid.

21 In Shola Lynch's film *Free Angela and All Political Prisoners* (2013), Davis notes

of her own development, "And then, of course, I ended up studying in Germany, when these new developments in the black movement happened. The emergence of the Black Panther Party. And my feeling was that, I want to be there. This is earth shaking, this is change. I want to be a part of that. . . . I saw the photograph of the Black Panther Party in some newspaper when I was studying in Germany. And again, I had this sense the world is changing, my world is changing, and I do want to be a part of this. And I decided that I would go back. I would go back, and I decided to go to San Diego, which is where Marcuse was."

22. Angela Y. Davis, "On Palestine, G4S and the Prison Industrial Complex," in *Freedom Is a Constant Struggle*, 55–56.

23. Davis, *Freedom Is a Constant Struggle*, 59–60.

24. *Klase Tajiri*, pamphlet (uncataloged), STE.

25. Tajiri, *Autobiographical Notations*, 72–73.

26. Ibid.

27. Tajiri, *Berlin Wall*, 4.

28. Unpublished journal entry [November 10, 1989], box 46, no. 35, ALP.

29. Unpublished journal entry [January 5, 1990], box 46, no. 35, ALP.

30. For the latter group, PDS (Party of Democratic Socialism), a poster that reads, "Für die Schwachen eine starke Opposition" (For the weak a strong opposition), attempts to leverage fears of swift change among East Germans by claiming strident opposition to the governing parties of the West even as they refer to their potential constituents as weak and in need of protection. Here, Lorde poses in front of ads for several political parties attempting to continue to reform the new government through socialism, including the Bündnis 90 and PDS. See Thompson, *Crisis of the German Left*, 116.

31. Audre Lorde and Gloria Joseph, "Black Women Find Racism Rampant in Germany," *Off Our Backs* 22, no. 10 (November 1992): 18. For more on racial violence during the period of reunification, see Panikos Panayi, "Racial Violence in the New Germany 1990–93," *Contemporary European History* 3, no. 3 (November 1994): 265–87.

32. Lorde also wrote an updated foreword for the release of *Farbe Bekennen*'s English translation, *Showing Our Colors*, in 1991. Writing from her home in St. Croix, with her updated foreword dated July 30, 1990, Lorde shares new perspectives on the reunification of Germany. She writes, "The material in *Farbe Bekennen* gains new importance now at this juncture in German history, when impending reunification raises critical questions about definitions of German identity." She adds, "The grim wall that once enclosed this city kept it at an equal distance from West Germany and Europe. . . . Now the wall is down." In addition to referring to the Berlin Wall, Lorde introduces the refrain "East and West" throughout the foreword to talk about both the coalitions of Afro-German organizations working together across the former divide and global conservative "white superpowers . . . deciding to come together despite their ideological differences because . . . even they can see the handwriting on the wall" (Opitz, Oguntoye, and Schultz, *Showing Our Colors*, x–xiv.

33. As Lorde described it to German publishers as she sat in Schultz's Berlin apartment in 1991, the project she realized had a lot to do with "the shifting of perspec-

tives" rather than fundamental or foundational change: "That is the kind of thing I'm talking about. It is not that you alter inside what you know to be so, it is that you see the shifting of differences. And that is why the magical and the marvelous arithmetics, the ways in which of what is, because arithmetics deals with basically what is" (private video, Dagmar Schultz, 1991; transcribed by the author).

34. All citations of this poem refer to Audre Lorde, "East Berlin," in Lorde, *Marvelous Arithmetics of Distance*, 50.

35. All citations of this poem refer to Audre Lorde, "Peace on Earth: Christmas, 1989," in Lorde, *Marvelous Arithmetics of Distance*, 39.

36. Audre Lorde, "Restoration: A Memorial—9/18/91," in Lorde, *Marvelous Arithmetics of Distance*, 40.

37. Audre Lorde "1984"—Last Reading in Berlin 1992, https://www.youtube.com /watch?v=ceXFKzO7gZQ.

38. De Veaux, *Warrior Poet*, 366.

39. Press kit, *Audre Lorde: The Berlin Years*, http://www.audrelordetheberlinyears .com/images/presskit/pressRelease.pdf. In July 2019, the *New York Times* published a travel feature by writer Charly Wilder, "A Berlin That Audre Lorde Would Appreciate," drawing on Schultz's archive and revisiting sites prominent to Lorde's history in Berlin.

BIBLIOGRAPHY

Special Collections

Ann Arbor, Mich.
    Labadie Collection, University of Michigan
Atlanta, Ga.
    Audre Lorde Papers, Spelman College Archives
Baarlo, Netherlands
    Shinkichi Tajiri Estate
Berlin, Germany
    Audre Lorde Archive, John-F.-Kennedy-Institut für Nordamerikastudien,
        Freie Universität Berlin Archives
    Mauer Documentation Center Archives
Garrison, N.Y.
    Leonard Freed Papers
Los Angeles, Calif.
    Allan Kaprow Papers, Getty Research Institute
    Wende Museum Archives
New Haven, Conn.
    Langston Hughes Papers, Beinecke Rare Book and Manuscript Library,
        Yale University
New York, N.Y.
    Keith Haring Foundation
    New York Public Library
        Angela Y. Davis Legal Defense Collection, Schomburg Center for
            Research in Black Culture
        John Edward Heys Papers, Billy Rose Theatre Division
    New York University
        James E. Jackson and Esther Cooper Jackson Papers, Tamiment Library
        David Wojnarowicz Papers, Fales Library
    Random House Records, 1925–1999, Columbia Rare Book & Manuscript
        Library, Butler Library, Columbia University
Oakland, Calif.
    Lisbet Tellefsen Collection
Palo Alto, Calif.
    Christopher Temple Emmet Papers, Hoover Institution Archives,
        Stanford University

Princeton, N.J.
   Toni Morrison Papers, Rare Books and Special Collections, Firestone Library,
      Princeton University
Washington, D.C.
   Paul and Eslanda Robeson Papers, Moorland-Spingarn Library, Howard
      University
Digital Archive
   The Civil Rights Struggle, African American GIs, and Germany, German Historical
      Institute/Vassar College/Heidelberg Center for American Studies

Newspapers and Periodicals

Afro-American

Art in America

Atlanta Daily World

Booklist

Chicago Defender

Crisis

Kunstzeitung

Los Angeles Sentinel

Los Angeles Times

New York Amsterdam News

New York Times

Pittsburgh Courier

Publishers Weekly

San Francisco Chronicle

Washington Post

Interviews Conducted by the Author

Audio recordings of all interviews are in the author's personal archives.

Aptheker, Bettina, telephone, October 21, 2011

Branton, Leo, telephone, January 17, 2012

Frame, Allen, telephone, March 23, 2011

Freed, Brigitte, Garrison, N.Y., June 15 and August 1–2, 2009

Grossman, Richard, telephone, October 5, 2010

Rodewald, Stew and Heidi, Ann Arbor, Mich., November 17, 2010

Schultz, Dagmar, New York, N.Y., December 10, 2010, and Berlin, August 5, 2011

Van Parys, Bill, Berlin, November 7, 2009

Books, Articles, Theses, Films, and Audio Recordings

Abbott, Brett. *Engaged Observers: Documentary Photography since the Sixties*. Los
   Angeles: J. Paul Getty Museum, 2010.

Adelson, Leslie A., and American Institute for Contemporary German Studies.
   "The Cultural After-Life of East Germany: New Transnational Perspectives."
   American Institute for Contemporary German Studies, 2002.

Alexander, Kirk, dir. *Square World of Jack Paar*. NBC Television Network, 1961.

Anzaldúa, Gloria. *Borderlands/La Frontera: The New Mestiza*. San Francisco:
   Spinsters/Aunt Lute, 1987.

Appy, Christian G. *Cold War Constructions: The Political Culture of United States
   Imperialism, 1945–1966*. Amherst: University of Massachusetts Press, 2000.

Aptheker, Bettina. *Intimate Politics: How I Grew Up Red, Fought for Free Speech,
   and Became a Feminist Rebel*. Emeryville, Calif.: Seal Press, 2006.

―――. *The Morning Breaks: The Trial of Angela Davis*. New York: International Publishers, 1975.

Arsenault, Raymond. *Freedom Riders: 1961 and the Struggle for Racial Justice*. Oxford: Oxford University Press, 2006.

Ashmore, Susan Youngblood. *Carry It On: The War on Poverty and the Civil Rights Movement in Alabama, 1964–1972*. Athens: University of Georgia Press, 2008.

Avedon, Richard, Michael J. Holm, and Helle Crenzien. *Richard Avedon Photographs, 1946–2004*. Humlebaek, Denmark: Louisiana Museum of Modern Art, 2007.

Avi-Ram, Amitai F. "Apo Koinou in Audre Lorde and the Moderns: Defining the Differences." *Callaloo* 26 (1986): 193–208.

Awkward, Michael. *Inspiriting Influences: Tradition, Revision, and Afro-American Women's Novels*. New York: Columbia University Press, 1989.

―――. *Negotiating Difference: Race, Gender, and the Politics of Positionality*. Chicago: University of Chicago Press, 1995.

―――. *Philadelphia Freedoms: Black American Trauma, Memory, and Culture After King*. Philadelphia: Temple University Press, 2013.

―――. *Soul Covers: Rhythm and Blues Remakes and the Struggle for Artistic Identity (Aretha Franklin, Al Green, Phoebe Snow)*. Durham, N.C.: Duke University Press, 2007.

Backman, Donald, Aida Sakalauskaite, and Interdisciplinary German Studies Conference. *Ossi Wessi*. Newcastle upon Tyne: Cambridge Scholars Publishing, 2008.

Balaji, Murali. *The Professor and the Pupil: The Politics of W.E.B. Du Bois and Paul Robeson*. New York: Nation Books, 2007.

Balbier, Uta A., Cristina Cuevas-Wolf, and Joes Segal. *East German Material Culture and the Power of Memory*. Washington, D.C.: German Historical Institute, 2011.

Barber, Stephen. *The Walls of Berlin: Urban Surfaces: Art: Film*. Los Angeles: Solar Books, 2011.

Barron, Stephanie, Sabine Eckmann, and Eckhart Gillen. *Art of Two Germanys: Cold War Cultures*. New York: Abrams, in association with the Los Angeles County Museum of Art, 2009.

Barthes, Roland. *Camera Lucida: Reflections on Photography*. New York: Hill and Wang, 1981.

Bavelaar, Hestia, Els Barents, and Shinkichi Tajiri. *Shinkichi Tajiri: Beeldhouwer–Sculptor*. Gravenhage: SDU, 1991.

Beatty, Paul. *Slumberland*. New York: Bloomsbury, 2009.

Beethoven, Ludwig van. *Ode to Freedom: The Berlin Celebration Concert, Beethoven Symphony No. 9*. Taipei: Universal Music, 1989. Audio recording.

"The Believer: Interview with Mike Davis." *The Believer*, February 2004. Internet resource.

Ben-Amos, Dan, and Liliane Weissberg. *Cultural Memory and the Construction of Identity*. Detroit: Wayne State University Press, 1999.

Bender, Thomas. *Rethinking American History in a Global Age*. Berkeley: University of California Press, 2002.

Benjamin, Walter, and Peter Demetz. *Reflections*. New York: Schocken Books, 1986.

Benjamin, Walter, Hannah Arendt, and Harry Zohn. *Illuminations*. New York: Harcourt, Brace & World, 1968.

Benjamin, Walter, Michael W. Jennings, Brigid Doherty, Thomas Y. Levin, and E. F. N. Jephcott. *The Work of Art in the Age of Its Technological Reproducibility, and Other Writings on Media*. Cambridge, Mass.: Belknap Press of Harvard University Press, 2008.

Benstock, Shari. *The Private Self: Theory and Practice of Women's Autobiographical Writings*. Chapel Hill: University of North Carolina Press, 1988.

Berg, Manfred, and Bernd Schäfer. *Historical Justice in International Perspective: How Societies Are Trying to Right the Wrongs of the Past*. Washington, D.C.: German Historical Institute, 2009.

Berger, Dan. *Captive Nation: Black Prison Organizing in the Civil Rights Era*. Chapel Hill: University of North Carolina Press, 2014.

Berlant, Lauren Gail. *The Anatomy of National Fantasy: Hawthorne, Utopia, and Everyday Life*. Chicago: University of Chicago Press, 1991.

———. *The Queen of America Goes to Washington City: Essays on Sex and Citizenship*. Durham, N.C.: Duke University Press, 1997.

Bernstein, Lee. *America Is the Prison: Arts and Politics in Prison in the 1970s*. Chapel Hill: University of North Carolina Press, 2010.

Betts, Paul. *Within Walls: Private Life in the German Democratic Republic*. Oxford: Oxford University Press, 2010.

Bhabha, Homi K. *The Location of Culture*. New York: Routledge, 2004.

Bial, Henry. *The Performance Studies Reader*. New York: Routledge, 2004.

Bieger, Laura, Ramón Saldívar, and Johannes Voelz. *The Imaginary and Its Worlds: American Studies after the Transnational Turn*. Hanover, N.H.: Dartmouth College Press, 2013.

Bischof, Werner, Fund for Concerned Photography, and New York Riverside Museum. *The Concerned Photographer: The Photographs of Werner Bischof, Robert Capa, David Seymour ("Chim"), André Kertész, Leonard Freed, Dan Weiner*. New York: Grossman, 1968.

Black, Monica. *Death in Berlin: From Weimar to Divided Germany*. Washington, D.C.: German Historical Institute, 2010.

Blair, Sara. *Harlem Crossroads: Black Writers and the Photograph in the Twentieth Century*. Princeton, N.J.: Princeton University Press, 2007.

Blair, Sara, and Jonathan Freedman. *Jewish in America*. Ann Arbor: University of Michigan Press, 2004.

Bolaki, Stella, and Sabine Broeck, eds. *Audre Lorde's Transnational Legacies*. Amherst: University of Massachusetts Press, 2015.

Borcila, Andaluna. *American Representations of Post-Communism: Television, Travel Sites, and Post–Cold War Narratives*. New York: Routledge, 2015.

Borneman, John. *After the Wall: East Meets West in the New Berlin*. New York: Basic Books, 1991.

Borstelmann, Thomas. *The Cold War and the Color Line: American Race Relations in the Global Arena*. Cambridge, Mass.: Harvard University Press, 2001.

Boyce Davies, Carole. *Black Women, Writing, and Identity: Migrations of the Subject*. New York: Routledge, 1994.

Boym, Svetlana. *Another Freedom: The Alternative History of an Idea*. Chicago: University of Chicago Press, 2010.

———. *Architecture of the Off-Modern*. New York: Buell Center/FORuM Project Princeton Architectural Press, 2008.

———. *The Future of Nostalgia*. New York: Basic Books, 2001.

Branch, Taylor. *Pillar of Fire: America in the King Years, 1963–65*. New York: Simon & Schuster, 1998.

Brands, Hal. *Making the Unipolar Moment*. Ithaca, N.Y.: Cornell University Press, 2016.

Braun, Joshua A. "The Imperatives of Narrative: Health Interest Groups and Morality in Network News." *American Journal of Bioethics* 7, no. 8 (2007): 6–14.

Braun, Stuart. *City of Exiles: Berlin from the Outside In*. Berlin: Noctua Press, 2015.

Briese, Olaf. "The Different Aesthetics of the Berlin Wall." In *The German Wall: Fallout in Europe*, edited by Marc Silberman, 37–58. New York: Palgrave Macmillan, 2011.

Broeck, Sabine. *Gender and the Abjection of Blackness*. Albany: State University of New York Press, 2018.

Brooks, Daphne. "'All That You Can't Leave Behind': Black Female Soul Singing and the Politics of Surrogation in the Age of Catastrophe." *Meridians: Feminism, Race, Transnationalism* 8, no. 1 (2008): 180–204.

———. *Bodies in Dissent: Spectacular Performances of Race and Freedom, 1850–1910*. Durham, N.C.: Duke University Press, 2006.

Brown, Lloyd L. *Iron City: A Novel*. New York: Masses & Mainstream, 1951.

Brown, Stephanie. "'Bootise' in Berlin: An Interview with Helma Harrington on Oliver Harrington's Life and Work in East Germany, 1961–1995." *African American Review* 44, no. 3 (Fall 2001): 353–72.

Brown, Wendy. *Walled States, Waning Sovereignty*. New York: Zone Books, 2010.

Buch, Esteban. *Beethoven's Ninth: A Political History*. Chicago: University of Chicago Press, 2003.

Buck-Morss, Susan. *Dreamworld and Catastrophe: The Passing of Mass Utopia in East and West*. Cambridge, Mass.: MIT Press, 2000.

———. *Hegel, Haiti, and Universal History*. Pittsburgh, Pa.: University of Pittsburgh Press, 2009.

Bullivant, Keith. *Beyond 1989: Re-reading German Literary History since 1945*. Providence, R.I.: Berghahn, 1997.

Burton, Humphrey, June Anderson, Sarah Walker, Klaus König, Jan-Hendrik Rootering, Leonard Bernstein, Friedrich Schiller, and Ludwig von Beethoven.

Ode to Freedom: Beethoven, Symphony no. 9. [Stuttgart, Germany]: EuroArts, 2009.

Butterfield, Stephen. *Black Autobiography in America*. Amherst: University of Massachusetts Press, 1974.

Calvino, Italo. *Invisible Cities*. New York: Harcourt Brace Jovanovich, 1974.

Campt, Tina. *Other Germans: Black Germans and the Politics of Race, Gender, and Memory in the Third Reich*. Ann Arbor: University of Michigan, 2004.

Carmichael, Stokely, and Charles V. Hamilton. *Black Power: The Politics of Liberation in America*. New York: Random House, 1967.

Carmody, Todd. "Missing Paul Robeson in East Berlin: The Spirituals and the Empty Archive." *Cultural Critique* 88 (Fall 2014), 1–27.

Carroll, Amy Sara. *REMEX: Toward an Art History of the NAFTA Era*. Austin : University of Texas Press, 2018.

———. *Secession*. San Diego, Calif.: Hyperbole Books, 2012.

Chambers, Colin. *Here We Stand: Politics, Performers and Performance: Paul Robeson, Isadora Duncan and Charlie Chaplin*. London: Nick Hern, 2006.

Chambers, Iain, and Lidia Curti. *The Post-Colonial Question: Common Skies, Divided Horizons*. New York: Routledge, 1996.

Christo, Jacob Baal-Teshuva, Wolfgang Volz, Tilmann Buddensieg, and Cyril Christo. *Christo: The Reichstag and Urban Projects*. Munich: Prestel, 1993.

Churchill, Ward, and Jim Vander Wall. *The COINTELPRO Papers: Documents from the FBI's Secret Wars against Domestic Dissent*. Boston: South End Press, 1990.

Clark, Kenneth Bancroft. *Dark Ghetto: Dilemmas of Social Power*. New York: Harper & Row, 1965.

Clifford, James. *Routes: Travel and Translation in the Late Twentieth Century*. Cambridge, Mass.: Harvard University Press, 1997.

Clover, Joshua. *1989: Bob Dylan Didn't Have This to Sing About*. Berkeley: University of California Press, 2009.

Conquergood, Dwight. "Performance Studies: Interventions and Radical Research." *TDR/The Drama Review* 46, no. 2 (2002): 145–56.

Cook, James W., Lawrence B. Glickman, and Michael O'Malley. *The Cultural Turn in U.S. History: Past, Present, and Future*. Chicago: University of Chicago Press, 2008.

Cooke, Paul, and Andrew Plowman. *German Writers and the Politics of Culture: Dealing with the Stasi*. Houndmills, U.K.: Palgrave Macmillan, 2003.

Cox, Paul, and Aden Young. *Samurai in Space*. South Melbourne, Victoria: Contemporary Arts Media, 2011.

Crew, David F. *Consuming Germany in the Cold War*. New York: Berg, 2003.

Cruse, Harold. *The Crisis of the Negro Intellectual*. New York: Morrow, 1967.

Cuordileone, K. A. *Manhood and American Political Culture in the Cold War*. New York: Routledge, 2005.

Cvetkovich, Ann. "AIDS Activism and the Oral History Archive." *Scholar and Feminist Online* 2, no. 1 (Summer 2003).

————. *An Archive of Feelings: Trauma, Sexuality, and Lesbian Public Cultures.* Durham, N.C.: Duke University Press, 2003.

Dale, Gareth. *Popular Protest in East Germany, 1945–1989.* London: Routledge, 2005.

Danticat, Edwidge. *Create Dangerously: The Immigrant Artist at Work.* Princeton, N.J.: Princeton University Press, 2010.

Daum, Andreas W. "America's Berlin, 1945–2000: Between Myths and Visions." In *Berlin: The New Capital in the East—A Transnational Appraisal,* edited by Frank Trommler, 49–73. Washington, D.C.: American Institute for Contemporary German Studies, 2000.

————. *Kennedy in Berlin.* Washington, D.C.: German Historical Institute; New York: Cambridge University Press, 2008.

Daum, Andreas W., and Christof Mauch. *Berlin, Washington, 1800–2000: Capital Cities, Cultural Representation, and National Identities.* Cambridge: Cambridge University Press, 2005.

Daum, Andreas W., Lloyd C. Gardner, and Wilfried Mausbach. *America, the Vietnam War, and the World: Comparative and International Perspectives.* Washington, D.C.: German Historical Institute; Cambridge University Press, 2003.

Davis, Angela Y. *Abolition Democracy: Beyond Empire, Prisons, and Torture.* New York: Seven Stories Press, 2005.

————. "Afro Images: Politics, Fashion, and Nostalgia." *Critical Inquiry* 21, no. 1 (1994): 37–39.

————. *Angela Davis: An Autobiography.* New York: Random House, 1974.

————. *Are Prisons Obsolete?* New York: Seven Stories Press, 2003.

————. *Freedom Is a Constant Struggle: Ferguson, Palestine, and the Foundations of a Movement.* Chicago: Haymarket, 2015.

————. "Lectures on Liberation." New York Committee to Free Angela Davis, 1970.

Davis, Angela Y., and Bettina Aptheker, eds. *If They Come in the Morning: Voices of Resistance.* New York: Third Press, 1971.

Davis, Angela Y., and Robin D. G. Kelley. *The Meaning of Freedom.* San Francisco: City Lights Books, 2012.

Davis, Belinda J. *Changing the World, Changing Oneself: Political Protest and Collective Identities in West Germany and the U.S. in the 1960s and 1970s.* New York: Berghahn, 2010.

Decke, Thomas. "Shinkichi Tajiri erklärt die Berlin Mauer zur Land Art." *Kunstzeitung,* September 2005.

DeShazer, Mary K. *A Poetics of Resistance: Women Writing in El Salvador, South Africa, and the United States.* Ann Arbor: University of Michigan Press, 1994.

De Veaux, Alexis. *Warrior Poet: A Biography of Audre Lorde.* New York: Norton, 2004.

Dhairyam, Sagri. "'Artifacts for Survival': Remapping the Contours of Poetry with Audre Lorde." *Feminist Studies* 18, no. 2 (1992): 229–56.

Diedrich, Maria, and Jürgen Heinrichs, eds. *From Black to Schwarz: Cultural Crossovers between African America and Germany*. East Lansing: Michigan State University Press; Lit Verlag, 2011.

Douglass, Frederick, and Angela Y. Davis. *Narrative of the Life of Frederick Douglass, an American Slave, Written by Himself*. San Francisco: City Lights Books, 2010.

Drechsel, B. "The Berlin Wall from a Visual Perspective: Comments on the Construction of a Political Media Icon." *Visual Communication* 9, no. 1 (2010): 3–24.

Dreyblatt, Arnold. *Amerikanische Künstler in Berlin: Arnold Dreyblatt, John Gerard, John Gossage, Karl Edward Johnson, Hal Meltzer, Raphael Pollack, Andrea Scrima, Shinkichi Tajiri*. Berlin: Amerika Haus Berlin, Initiative Berlin-USA, 1986.

Duberman, Martin B. *Paul Robeson*. New York: Knopf, 1988.

Du Bois, W. E. B. *The Souls of Black Folk*. Chicago: McClurg, 1903.

Dudziak, Mary L. *Cold War Civil Rights: Race and the Image of American Democracy*. Princeton, N.J.: Princeton University Press, 2000.

Duganne, Erina. *The Self in Black and White: Race and Subjectivity in Postwar American Photography*. Hanover, N.H.: Dartmouth College Press, 2010.

Dunaway, David King. *How Can I Keep from Singing? The Ballad of Pete Seeger*. New York: Villard Books, 2008.

Dyson, Michael Eric. *April 4, 1968: Martin Luther King, Jr.'s Death and How It Changed America*. New York: Basic Civitas Books, 2008.

———. *I May Not Get There with You: The True Martin Luther King, Jr.* New York: Free Press, 2000.

———. *Mercy, Mercy Me: The Art, Loves, and Demons of Marvin Gaye*. New York: Basic Civitas Books, 2004.

———. *Race Rules: Navigating the Color Line*. Reading, Mass.: Addison-Wesley, 1996.

Eckert, Astrid M. *The Struggle for the Files: The Western Allies and the Return of German Archives after the Second World War*. Washington, D.C.: German Historical Institute, 2012.

Edwards, Brent H. *The Practice of Diaspora: Literature, Translation, and the Rise of Black Internationalism*. Cambridge, Mass.: Harvard University Press, 2003.

Eichhoff, Jürgen. "'Ich bin ein Berliner': A History and a Linguistic Clarification." *Monatshefte* 85, no. 1 (1993): 71–80.

Elam, Harry Justin, and Kennell A. Jackson. *Crossroads in Global Performance and Popular Culture*. Ann Arbor : University of Michigan Press, 2006.

Ellin, Nan, and Edward J. Blakely. *Architecture of Fear*. New York: Princeton Architectural Press, 1997.

El-Tayeb, Fatima. *European Others: Queering Ethnicity in Postnational Europe*. Minneapolis: University of Minnesota Press, 2011.

Escaut-Marquet, Marie-Therese. *Die Mauer: Le Mur de Berlin, Vente aux Enchereres Exceptionnelle; the Berlin Wall Special Auction*. Berlin: Elefanten Press, 1990.

Eugenides, Jeffrey. *Middlesex*. New York: Farrar, Straus and Giroux, 2002.

Farber, Paul M. "The Last Rites of D'Angelo Barksdale: The Life and Afterlife of Photography in *The Wire*." *Criticism* 52, no. 3-4 (2010): 413-39.

──────. "National Museum of Crime & Punishment." *Museums and Social Issues* 6, no. 1 (2011): 91-98.

──────, ed. *The Wall in Our Heads: American Artists and the Berlin Wall*. Haverford, Pa.: Cantor Fitzgerald Gallery, 2015.

Faymonville, Carmen. "Black Germans and Transnational Identification." *Callaloo* 26, no. 2 (Spring 2003): 364-82.

Ferguson, Roderick A. *Aberrations in Black: Toward a Queer of Color Critique*. Minneapolis: University of Minnesota Press, 2004.

Fink, Carole, and Bernd Schäfer. *Ostpolitik, 1969-1974: European and Global Responses*. New York: Cambridge University Press, 2009.

Fink, Carole, Philipp Gassert, and Detlef Junker. *1968: The World Transformed*. Cambridge: Cambridge University Press, 1998.

Fishkin, Shelley Fisher. "Crossroads of Cultures: The Transnational Turn in American Studies — Presidential Address to the American Studies Association, November 12, 2004." *American Quarterly* 57, no. 1 (2005): 17-57.

Flanagan, Bill. *U2 at the End of the World*. New York: Delacorte Press, 1995.

Flatley, Jonathan. *Affective Mapping: Melancholia and the Politics of Modernism*. Cambridge, Mass.: Harvard University Press, 2008.

Fluck, Winfried. *Reframing the Transnational Turn in American Studies*. Hanover, N.H.: Dartmouth College Press, 2011.

Foner, Eric. *The Story of American Freedom*. New York: Norton, 1999.

Forché, Carolyn. *Against Forgetting: Twentieth-Century Poetry of Witness*. New York: Norton, 1993.

Forrester, Sibelan E. S., Magdalena J. Zaborowska, and Elena Gapova. *Over the Wall/After the Fall: Post-Communist Cultures through an East-West Gaze*. Bloomington: Indiana University Press, 2004.

Foucault, Michel. *Discipline and Punish: The Birth of the Prison*. New York: Vintage, 1995.

──────. *The History of Sexuality*. London: Penguin, 1990.

Freed, Leonard. *Black in White America*. New York: Grossman, 1968.

──────. *Leonard Freed: Photographs, 1954-1990*. New York: Norton, 1992.

──────. *Made in Germany*. New York: Grossman, 1970.

──────. *Police Work*. New York: Simon & Schuster, 1980.

Freed, Leonard, and J. Paul Getty Museum. *Black in White America*. Los Angeles: J. Paul Getty Museum, 2010.

Freed, Leonard, Florian Ebner, and Paul M. Farber, eds. *Re-Made: Reading Leonard Freed*. Göttingen: Steidl, 2013.

Freed, Leonard, William A. Ewing, and Wim van Sinderen. *Worldview*. Göttingen: Steidl; Musée de l'Elysée, 2007.

Freed, Leonard, Julian Bond, Michael Eric Dyson, and Paul M. Farber. *This Is the Day: The March on Washington*. Los Angeles: J. Paul Getty Museum, 2013.

Freeman, Mark. *Rewriting the Self: History, Memory, Narrative*. New York: Routledge, 1993.

Friedman, Andrew. *Covert Capital: Landscapes of Denial and the Making of U.S. Empire in the Suburbs of Northern Virginia*. Berkeley: University of California Press, 2013.

Funder, Anna. *Stasiland: Stories from Behind the Berlin Wall*. London: Granta, 2003.

Gaddis, John L. *The Cold War: A New History*. New York: Penguin, 2005.

———. *The United States and the Origins of the Cold War, 1941–1947*. New York: Columbia University Press, 1972.

———. *We Now Know: Rethinking Cold War History*. Oxford: Clarendon Press, 1997.

Gaines, Kevin K. *American Africans in Ghana: Black Expatriates and the Civil Rights Era*. Chapel Hill: University of North Carolina Press, 2006.

Garber, Linda. *Identity Poetics: Race, Class, and the Lesbian-Feminist Roots of Queer Theory*. New York: Columbia University Press, 2001.

Garrow, David J. *Bearing the Cross: Martin Luther King, Jr., and the Southern Christian Leadership Conference*. New York: Morrow, 1986.

Gassert, Philipp, and Martin Klimke. *1968: Memories and Legacies of a Global Revolt*. Washington, D.C.: German Historical Institute, 2009.

Gassert, Philipp, and Alan E. Steinweis. *Coping with the Nazi Past: West German Debates on Nazism and Generational Conflict, 1955–1975*. New York: Berghahn, 2006.

———. *Protest at Selma: Martin Luther King, Jr., and the Voting Rights Act of 1965*. New Haven: Yale University Press, 1978.

Genter, Robert. *Late Modernism: Art, Culture, and Politics in Cold War America*. Philadelphia: University of Pennsylvania Press, 2010.

Gerstenberger, Katharina. *Writing the New Berlin: The German Capital in Post-Wall Literature*. Rochester, N.Y.: Camden House, 2008.

Geyer, David C., and Bernd Schäfer. *American Détente and German Ostpolitik, 1969–1972*. Washington, D.C.: German Historical Institute, 2004.

Gilmore, Ruth W. *Golden Gulag: Prisons, Surplus, Crisis, and Opposition in Globalizing California*. Berkeley: University of California Press, 2007.

Gilroy, Paul. *Against Race: Imagining Political Culture beyond the Color Line*. Cambridge, Mass.: Belknap Press of Harvard University Press, 2000.

Gleijeses, Piero. *Visions of Freedom: Havana, Washington, Pretoria, and the Struggle for Southern Africa, 1976–1991*. Chapel Hill: University of North Carolina Press, 2013.

Godfrey, Tony. *Conceptual Art*. London: Phaidon, 1998.

Goldin, Nan. *The Ballad of Sexual Dependency*. New York: Aperture Foundation, 1986.

Gopinath, Gayatri. *Impossible Desires: Queer Diasporas and South Asian Public Cultures*. Durham, N.C.: Duke University Press, 2005.

Gordon, Avery. *Ghostly Matters: Haunting and the Sociological Imagination*. Minneapolis: University of Minnesota Press, 2008.

Gossage, John R., and Gerry Badger. *Berlin in the Time of the Wall: Photographs.* Bethesda, Md.: Loosestrife Editions, 2004.

Gramsci, Antonio. *The Modern Prince and Other Writings.* New York: International Publishers, 1967.

Grandin, Greg. *Empire's Workshop: Latin America, the United States, and the Rise of the New Imperialism.* New York: Henry Holt, 2013.

Gray, Cleve. "Wall Painters." *Art in America,* October 1985, 39–43.

Greene, Larry A., and Anke Ortlepp. *Germans and African Americans: Two Centuries of Exchange.* Jackson: University Press of Mississippi, 2011.

Gregory, Dick. *Dick Gregory's Political Primer.* New York: Harper & Row, 1972.

Gregory, Dick, and James R. McGraw. *Up from Nigger.* New York: Stein and Day, 1976.

Griffin, Ada Gay, Michelle Parkerson, and Newsreel. *A Litany for Survival: The Life and Work of Audre Lorde.* New York: Third World Newsreel, 1996.

Griffin, Farah Jasmine. *"Who Set You Flowin'?" The African-American Migration Narrative.* Oxford: Oxford University Press, 1995.

Grossman, Victor, and Mark Solomon. *Crossing the River: A Memoir of the American Left, the Cold War, and Life in East Germany.* Amherst: University of Massachusetts Press, 2003.

Gruen, John. *Keith Haring: The Authorized Biography.* New York: Prentice Hall, 1991.

Gurnee, Hal. "Jack Paar at the Berlin Wall: By Hal Gurnee, Who Directed the Late-Night Comedian's 1961 Program Filmed at This Historic Site." *Television Quarterly* 36, no. 3 (2006): 52.

Gusdorf, Georges. "Conditions and Limits of Autobiography." In *Autobiography, Essays Theoretical and Critical,* edited by James Olney, 28–48. Princeton, N.J.: Princeton University Press, 1980.

Halperin, David M. *How to Be Gay.* Cambridge, Mass.: Belknap Press of Harvard University Press, 2012.

Halperin, Ian. *Unmasked: The Final Years of Michael Jackson.* New York: Simon Spotlight Entertainment, 2009.

Hamburger, Michael. *East German Poetry: An Anthology.* New York: Dutton, 1973.

Hardin, Tayana L. "Rituals of Return in African American Women's Twentieth Century Literature and Performance." Ph.D. diss. 805802117. University of Michigan, Ann Arbor, 2012. ProQuest/UMI.

Hare, David. *Berlin/Wall: Two Readings.* London: Faber and Faber, 2009.

Harper, Donna Sullivan. *Not So Simple: The "Simple" Stories by Langston Hughes.* Columbia: University of Missouri Press, 1995.

Harrington, Oliver W. *Why I Left America and Other Essays.* Detroit: W. O. Evans, 1991.

Harrington, Oliver W., and M. Thomas Inge. *Dark Laughter: Satiric Art of Oliver W. Harrington. From the Walter O. Evans Collection of African-American Art.* Jackson: University Press of Mississippi, 1993.

Harrison, Hope Millard. *After the Berlin Wall: Memory and the Making of the New Germany, 1989 to the Present.* Cambridge: Cambridge University Press, 2019.

————. *Driving the Soviets up the Wall: Soviet–East German Relations, 1953–1961*. Princeton, N.J.: Princeton University Press, 2003.

Hartman, Geoffrey H. *Bitburg in Moral and Political Perspective*. Bloomington: Indiana University Press, 1986.

————. *The Longest Shadow: In the Aftermath of the Holocaust*. Bloomington: Indiana University Press, 1996.

Hattemer-Higgins, Ida. *The History of History: A Novel of Berlin*. New York: Knopf, 2011.

Hauck, Christopher. *(De)construction: Wall Art: Defining a Post Berlin Wall Culture*. Tucker, Ga.: C. Hauck, 2006.

Hedwig and the Angry Inch. Original Motion Picture Soundtrack. New York: Hybrid, 2001. Audio recording.

Hemon, Aleksandar. *The Lazarus Project*. New York: Riverhead Books, 2009.

Hepburn, Allan. *Intrigue: Espionage and Culture*. New Haven: Yale University Press, 2005.

Hildebrandt, Alexandra. *Divided Germany: Border Signs*. Berlin: Verlag Haus am Checkpoint Charlie, 2001.

Hill, Marc L. *Beats, Rhymes, and Classroom Life: Hip-hop Pedagogy and the Politics of Identity*. New York: Teachers College Press, 2009.

Hillenius, Dirk, Shinkichi Tajiri, and Leo Marks. *Tajiri: Sculptures, Drawings, Graphics, Books, Video Tapes, Films*. Rotterdam: Het Museum, 1974.

Hodgin, Nick. *The GDR Remembered: Representations of the East German State since 1989*. Rochester, N.Y.: Camden House, 2011.

Höhn, Maria. *GIs and Fräuleins: The German-American Encounter in 1950s West Germany*. Chapel Hill: University of North Carolina Press, 2002.

Höhn, Maria, and Martin Klimke. *A Breath of Freedom: The Civil Rights Struggle, African American GIs, and Germany*. New York: Palgrave Macmillan, 2010.

Hsu, Hua. "Three Songs from the End of History: Billy Joel, The Scorpions, and Jesus Jones." *The Believer*, June/July 2005. Internet resource.

Hubley, Emily, Christine Vachon, Katie Roumel, Pamela R. Koffler, John C. Mitchell, Andrea Martin, Michael Pitt, Alberta Watson, Rob Campbell, Theodore Liscinski, Michael Aronov, Miriam Shor, and Stephen Trask. *Hedwig and the Angry Inch*. New York: New Line Productions, 2001. Audio recording.

Hügel-Marshall, Ika. *Invisible Woman: Growing Up Black in Germany*. New York: Continuum, 2001.

Hughes, Langston. *I Wonder as I Wander: An Autobiographical Journey*. New York: Hill and Wang, 1964.

————. *Jericho-Jim Crow*. New York: Folkways Records, 1964. Audio recording.

Hughes, Langston, Arnold Rampersad, Dolan Hubbard, and Leslie C. Sanders. *The Collected Works of Langston Hughes*. Columbia: University of Missouri Press, 2001.

Huyssen, Andreas. *Present Pasts: Urban Palimpsests and the Politics of Memory*. Stanford, Calif.: Stanford University Press, 2003.

———. *Twilight Memories: Marking Time in a Culture of Amnesia*. New York: Routledge, 1995.

Iton, Richard. *In Search of the Black Fantastic: Politics and Popular Culture in the Post–Civil Rights Era*. New York: Oxford University Press, 2008.

Iyengar, Sheena. *The Art of Choosing*. New York: Twelve Books, 2010.

Jacir, Emily, and Susan Buck-Morss. *Emily Jacir & Susan Buck-Morss: 100 Notes—100 Thoughts 004*. Ostfildern, Germany: Hatje Cantz, 2011.

Jackson, George. *Soledad Brother: The Prison Letters of George Jackson*. New York: Coward-McCann, 1970.

Jackson, Michael. *Dancing the Dream*. New York: Doubleday, 1992.

Jacobs, Jane. *The Death and Life of Great American Cities*. New York: Random House, 1961.

Jacobson, Matthew Frye, and Gaspar González. *What Have They Built You to Do? "The Manchurian Candidate" and Cold War America*. Minneapolis: University of Minnesota Press, 2006.

Janik, Elizabeth. *Recomposing German Music: Politics and Musical Tradition in Cold War Berlin*. Boston: Brill, 2005.

Janssen, David A., and Edward J. Whitelock. *Apocalypse Jukebox: The End of the World in American Popular Music*. Brooklyn: Soft Skull Press, 2009.

Jarausch, Konrad Hugo. *After Unity: Reconfiguring German Identities*. Providence, R.I.: Berghahn, 1997.

Jay, Paul. *Global Matters: The Transnational Turn in Literary Studies*. Ithaca, N.Y.: Cornell University Press, 2010.

Jenkins, Steven, ed. *City Slivers and Fresh Kills: The Films of Gordon Matta-Clark*. San Francisco: Cinematheque, 2004.

Johnson, E. Patrick. *Appropriating Blackness: Performance and the Politics of Authenticity*. Durham, N.C.: Duke University Press, 2003.

Johnson, E. Patrick, and Mae Henderson. *Black Queer Studies: A Critical Anthology*. Durham, N.C.: Duke University Press, 2005.

Joseph, Peniel E. *The Black Power Movement: Rethinking the Civil Rights–Black Power Era*. New York: Routledge, 2006.

Junker, Detlef, Philipp Gassert, Wilfried Mausbach, and David B. Morris, eds. *The United States and Germany in the Era of the Cold War, 1945–1990: A Handbook*. New York: Cambridge University Press, 2004.

Kackman, Michael. *Citizen Spy: Television, Espionage, and Cold War Culture*. Minneapolis: University of Minnesota Press, 2005.

Kaplan, Alice Yaeger. *Dreaming in French: The Paris Years of Jacqueline Bouvier Kennedy, Susan Sontag, and Angela Davis*. Chicago: University of Chicago Press, 2012.

Kaplan, Amy. *The Anarchy of Empire in the Making of U.S. Culture*. Cambridge, Mass.: Harvard University Press, 2002.

———. "Where Is Guantanamo?" *American Quarterly* 57, no. 3 (2005): 831–58.

Kaplan, Amy, and Donald E. Pease. *Cultures of United States Imperialism*. Durham, N.C.: Duke University Press, 1993.

Kaprow, Allan, Galerie René Block, and Deutscher Akademischer Austauschdienst. Berliner Künstlerprogramm. *Sweet Wall Testimonials*. Berlin: Edition René Block, in Zusammenarbeit mit dem Berliner Künstlerprogramm des DAAD, 1976.

Kaprow, Allan, Günter Herzog, Heinz Holtmann, and Charlotte Kraft. *Allan Kaprow in Deutschland: Wärme-und Kälteeinheiten*. Nürnberg: Verlag für Moderne Kunst, 2011.

Kayden, Jerold S., New York (NY) Dept. of City Planning, and Municipal Art Society of New York. *Privately Owned Public Space: The New York City Experience*. New York: John Wiley, 2000.

Keats, John. *Complete Poems and Selected Letters of John Keats*. Edited by Edward Hirsch. New York: Modern Library, 2001.

Kelman, Steven. *Behind the Berlin Wall: An Encounter in East Germany*. Boston: Houghton Mifflin, 1972.

Kempe, Frederick. *Berlin 1961: Kennedy, Khrushchev, and the Most Dangerous Place on Earth*. New York: G. P. Putnam's Sons, 2011.

Kennedy, John F., Robert F. Kennedy, and Christian Walther. *John F. Kennedy, Robert F. Kennedy: Reden an Der Freien Universität en Universitat*. Berlin: Freie Universität Berlin, 1996.

Kermode, Frank. *The Sense of an Ending: Studies in the Theory of Fiction*. New York: Oxford University Press, 1967.

Klausmeier, Axel, and Leo Schmidt. *Wall Remnants, Wall Traces: The Comprehensive Guide to the Berlin Wall*. Berlin: Westkreuz-Verlag, 2004.

Kleihues, Josef Paul, and Christina Rathgeber. *Berlin/New York: Like and Unlike: Essays on Architecture and Art from 1870 to the Present*. New York: Rizzoli, 1993.

Klein, Christina. *Cold War Orientalism: Asia in the Middlebrow Imagination, 1945–1961*. Berkeley: University of California Press, 2003.

Klimke, Martin. *The Other Alliance: Student Protest in West Germany and the United States in the Global Sixties*. Princeton, N.J.: Princeton University Press, 2010.

Klimke, Martin, and Joachim Scharloth. *1968 in Europe: A History of Protest and Activism, 1956–1977*. New York: Palgrave Macmillan, 2008.

Knapp, Raymond. *The American Musical and the Formation of National Identity*. Princeton, N.J.: Princeton University Press, 2005.

——— . *The American Musical and the Performance of Personal Identity*. Princeton, N.J.: Princeton University Press, 2006.

Kolossa, Alexandra, and Keith Haring. *Keith Haring, 1958–1990: A Life for Art*. Köln: Taschen, 2004.

Kun, Josh. *Audiotopia: Music, Race, and America*. Berkeley: University of California Press, 2005.

Kurin, Richard. *The Smithsonian's History of America in 101 Objects*. New York: Penguin, 2013.

Ladd, Brian. *The Ghosts of Berlin: Confronting German History in the Urban Landscape*. Chicago: University of Chicago Press, 1997.

Lanzmann, Claude, dir. *Shoah*. [Paris]: Les Films Aleph, 2003.

————. *Shoah: An Oral History of the Holocaust. The Complete Text of the Film.* New York: Pantheon, 1985.

Lee, Spike, Steve Klein, Stew, Annie Dorsen, de'Adre Aziza, Eisa Davis, Colman Domingo, Chad Goodridge, Rebecca N. Jones, Daniel Breaker, Heidi Rodewald, and Matthew Libatique. *Passing Strange.* New York: IFC Films, 2010.

Leeming, David A. *James Baldwin: A Biography.* New York: Knopf, 1994.

Leffler, Melvyn P. *For the Soul of Mankind: The United States, the Soviet Union, and the Cold War.* New York: Hill and Wang, 2007.

Leffler, Melvyn P., and Jeffrey Legro. *In Uncertain Times: American Foreign Policy after the Berlin Wall and 9/11.* Ithaca, N.Y.: Cornell University Press, 2011.

Leffler, Melvyn P., and David S. Painter. *Origins of the Cold War: An International History.* London: Routledge, 2002.

Léger, Marc James. "A Fragment of the Berlin Wall in the Centre de commerce mondial de Montréal: Notes toward a Theory of the Public Artefact at the 'End of History.'" M.A. thesis, 1997.

Lennox, Sara. *Remapping Black Germany: New Perspectives on Afro-German History, Politics, and Culture.* Boston: University of Massachusetts Press, 2016.

Leonard, Richard D. *Call to Selma: Eighteen Days of Witness.* Boston: Skinner House Books, 2002.

Lessig, Lawrence. *Remix: Making Art and Commerce Thrive in the Hybrid Economy.* New York: Penguin, 2008.

Light, Alan. *The Holy or the Broken: Leonard Cohen, Jeff Buckley, and the Unlikely Ascent of "Hallelujah."* New York: Atria Books, 2012.

Loeb, Carolyn. "The City as Subject." *Journal of Urban History* 35, no. 6 (2009): 853–78.

Lorde, Audre. *A Burst of Light: Essays.* Ithaca, N.Y.: Firebrand Books, 1988.

————. *The Collected Poems of Audre Lorde.* New York: Norton, 1997.

————. *I Am Your Sister: Collected and Unpublished Writings of Audre Lorde.* Edited by Rudolph P. Byrd, Johnnetta B. Cole, and Beverly Guy-Sheftall. Oxford: Oxford University Press, 2009.

————. *The Marvelous Arithmetics of Distance: Poems, 1987–1992.* New York: Norton, 1993.

————. *Our Dead Behind Us: Poems.* New York: Norton, 1986.

————. *Sister Outsider: Essays and Speeches.* Trumansburg, N.Y.: Crossing Press, 1984.

————. *Undersong: Chosen Poems, Old and New.* New York: Norton, 1992.

————. *Zami: A New Spelling of My Name.* Trumansburg, N.Y.: Crossing Press, 1982.

Lorde, Audre, and Joan Wylie Hall. *Conversations with Audre Lorde.* Jackson: University Press of Mississippi, 2004.

Love, Heather. *Feeling Backward: Loss and the Politics of Queer History.* Cambridge, Mass.: Harvard University Press, 2007.

Mamdani, Mahmood. *Good Muslim, Bad Muslim: The Cold War and the Roots of Terror.* New York: Pantheon, 2004.

Manghani, Sunil. *Image Critique and the Fall of the Berlin Wall*. Chicago: Intellect, 2008.

Marshall, George, dir. *The Wicked Dreams of Paula Schultz*. United Artists, 1968.

Martens, Lorna. *The Promised Land? Feminist Writing in the German Democratic Republic*. Albany: State University of New York Press, 2001.

Mazón, Patricia M., and Reinhild Steingröver. *Not So Plain as Black and White: Afro-German Culture and History, 1890–2000*. Rochester, N.Y.: University of Rochester Press, 2005.

McBride, David, Leroy Hopkins, and Carol Blackshire-Belay, eds. *Crosscurrents: African Americans, Africa, and Germany in the Modern World*. Columbia, S.C.: Camden House, 1998.

Medsger, Betty. *The Burglary: The Discovery of J. Edgar Hoover's Secret FBI*. New York: Knopf, 2014.

Menne, Lothar, and Klaus Vack. *Am Beispiel Angela Davis*. Offenbach: Sozialistisches Büro + Verlag 2000, 1971.

Mesch, Claudia. *Modern Art at the Berlin Wall: Demarcating Culture in the Cold War Germanys*. New York: Tauris Academic Studies, 2008.

Michely, Viola M. *Joseph Beuys: The Reader*. Cambridge, Mass.: MIT Press, 2007.

Miller, Oliver, Daniel Schwaag, and Ian Warner. *Slab: The New Death Strip*. Nürnberg: AdBK, 2011.

Miller, Warren. *The Siege of Harlem*. New York: McGraw-Hill, 1964.

Mitchell, W. J. T. *Picture Theory: Essays on Verbal and Visual Representation*. Chicago: University of Chicago Press, 1994.

Moraga, Cherríe, and Gloria Anzaldúa, eds. *This Bridge Called My Back: Writings by Radical Women of Color*. New York: Kitchen Table Press, 1983.

Morrison, Toni. *Playing in the Dark: Whiteness and the Literary Imagination*. Cambridge, Mass.: Harvard University Press, 1992.

———. "Site of Memory." In *Out There: Marginalization and Contemporary Cultures*, edited by Russell Ferguson, 299–326. New York: New Museum of Contemporary Art, 1990.

Morson, Gary Saul, and Caryl Emerson. *Mikhail Bakhtin: Creation of a Prosaics*. Stanford, Calif.: Stanford University Press, 1990.

Nadelson, Regina. *Who Is Angela Davis? The Biography of a Revolutionary*. New York: P. H. Wyden, 1972.

National United Committee to Free Angela Davis. *A Political Biography of Angela Davis*. Los Angeles: Committee, 1970.

Neal, Mark A. *Looking for Leroy: Illegible Black Masculinities*. New York: New York University Press, 2013.

———. *Soul Babies: Black Popular Culture and the Post-Soul Aesthetic*. New York: Routledge, 2002.

Nelson, Deborah. *Pursuing Privacy in Cold War America*. New York: Columbia University Press, 2001.

Nightingale, Carl H. *Segregation: A Global History of Divided Cities*. Chicago: University of Chicago Press, 2012.

Niven, David. *The Politics of Injustice: The Kennedys, the Freedom Rides, and the Electoral Consequences of a Moral Compromise.* Knoxville: University of Tennessee Press, 2003.

Nora, Pierre. "Between Memory and History: Les Lieux de Mémoire." *Representations* 26 (1989): 7–24.

Norman, Brian, and Piper Kendrix Williams. *Representing Segregation: Toward an Aesthetics of Living Jim Crow, and Other Forms of Racial Division.* Albany: State University of New York Press, 2010.

Oates, Joyce Carol. *Last Days: Stories.* New York: Dutton, 1984.

Oates, Joyce Carol, and Greg Johnson. *The Journal of Joyce Carol Oates, 1973–1982.* New York: Ecco, 2007.

Obourn, Megan. "Audre Lorde: Trauma Theory and Liberal Multiculturalism." *MELUS: Society for the Study of the Multi-Ethnic Literature of the United States* 30, no. 3 (2005): 219–45.

O'Doherty, Brian, Christo, Jeanne-Claude, G. W. Clough, Edwin C. Anderson, Elizabeth Broun, and George Gurney. *Christo and Jeanne-Claude: Remembering the Running Fence.* Washington, D.C.: Smithsonian American Art Museum, 2010.

Ogbar, Jeffrey Ogbonna Green. *Black Power: Radical Politics and African American Identity.* Baltimore: Johns Hopkins University Press, 2004.

Olden, Marc. *Angela Davis.* New York: Lancer Books, 1973.

Oltmans, Willem. *Memoires [5] 1961.* Baarn: In den Toren, 1989.

Omi, Michael, and Howard Winant. *Racial Formation in the United States: From the 1960s to the 1990s.* New York: Routledge, 1994.

Opitz, May, Katharina Oguntoye, and Dagmar Schultz. *Showing Our Colors: Afro-German Women Speak Out.* Amherst: University of Massachusetts Press, 1991.

Page, Norman. *Auden and Isherwood: The Berlin Years.* New York: St. Martin's Press, 1998.

Parker, J. A. *Angela Davis: The Making of a Revolutionary.* New Rochelle, N.Y.: Arlington House, 1973.

Pascal, Roy. *Design and Truth in Autobiography.* Cambridge, Mass.: Harvard University Press, 1960.

Passing Strange: Original Broadway Recording. New York: Ghostlight, 2008. Audio recording.

Patterson, Anita H. *Race, American Literature and Transnational Modernisms.* Cambridge: Cambridge University Press, 2008.

Peace, Friendship, Solidarity: Angela Davis in the GDR. Dresden: Verlag Zeit im Bild, 1969.

Pease, Donald E., and Robyn Wiegman. *The Futures of American Studies.* Durham, N.C.: Duke University Press, 2002.

Peele, Thomas. *Queer Popular Culture: Literature, Media, Film, and Television.* New York: Palgrave Macmillan, 2007.

Pence, Katherine, and Paul Betts. *Socialist Modern: East German Everyday Culture and Politics.* Ann Arbor: University of Michigan Press, 2007.

Perkins, Margo V. *Autobiography as Activism: Three Black Women of the Sixties.* Jackson: University Press of Mississippi, 2000.

Perry, Imani. *Looking for Lorraine: The Radiant and Radical Life of Lorraine Hansberry.* Boston: Beacon Press, 2018.

———. *More Beautiful and More Terrible: The Embrace and Transcendence of Racial Inequality in the United States.* New York: New York University Press, 2011.

Peterson, James Braxton. "'Dead Prezence': Money and Mortal Themes in Hip Hop Culture." *Callaloo* 29, no. 3 (2006): 895–909.

———. *The Hip Hop Underground and African American Culture: Beneath the Surface.* New York: Palgrave Macmillan, 2014.

Petry, Ann L. *The Street.* Boston: Houghton Mifflin, 1946.

Phoenix Art Museum, Brady M. Roberts, and Bass Museum of Art. *Constructing New Berlin: Contemporary Art Made in Berlin.* New York: Prestel, 2006.

Piper, Adrian. *Escape to Berlin: A Travel Memoir.* Berlin: The Adrian Piper Research Archive Foundation Berlin, 2018.

———. *Out of Order, Out of Sight.* Vol. 1, *Selected Writings in Meta-Art, 1968–1992.* Cambridge, Mass.: MIT Press, 1996.

———. *Out of Order, Out of Sight.* Vol. 2, *Selected Writings in Art Criticism, 1967–1992.* Cambridge, Mass.: MIT Press, 1996.

Plummer, Brenda. *Rising Wind: Black Americans and U.S. Foreign Affairs, 1935–1960.* Chapel Hill: University of North Carolina Press, 1996.

Poiger, Uta G. *Jazz, Rock, and Rebels: Cold War Politics and American Culture in a Divided Germany.* Berkeley: University of California Press, 2000.

Pommerin, Reiner. *The American Impact on Postwar Germany.* Providence, R.I.: Berghahn, 1997.

Pugh, Emily. *Architecture, Politics, Identity in Divided Berlin.* Pittsburgh: University of Pittsburgh Press, 2014.

———. "The Berlin Wall and the Urban Space and Experience of East and West Berlin, 1961–1989." Ph.D. diss. 3311209. University of Michigan, Ann Arbor, 2008. ProQuest/UMI.

Rainwater, Lee. *Behind Ghetto Walls: Black Families in a Federal Slum.* London: Allen Lane, 1971.

Raphael-Hernandez, Heike. *Blackening Europe: The African American Presence.* New York: Routledge, 2004.

Ratnesar, Romesh. *Tear Down This Wall: A City, a President, and the Speech That Ended the Cold War.* New York: Simon & Schuster, 2009.

Reed, Lou. *Berlin.* Santa Monica, Calif.: Weinstein Co. Home Entertainment, 2008.

Reed, Lou, and Julian Schnabel. *Berlin.* New York: Rizzoli, 2009.

Richmond, Yale. *Practicing Public Diplomacy: A Cold War Odyssey.* New York: Berghahn, 2008.

Ritchin, Fred, and Julien Frydman. *Magnum Photos.* London: Thames & Hudson, 2008.

Roach, Joseph R. *Cities of the Dead: Circum-Atlantic Performance.* New York: Columbia University Press, 1996.

Robeson, Paul. *Here I Stand*. New York: Othello Associates, 1958.

Robeson, Paul, Jr. *The Undiscovered Paul Robeson: Quest for Freedom, 1939–1976*. Hoboken, N.J.: Wiley, 2010.

Robinson, Greg. *A Tragedy of Democracy: Japanese Confinement in North America*. New York: Columbia University Press, 2009.

Rose, Kenneth D. *One Nation Underground: The Fallout Shelter in American Culture*. New York: New York University Press, 2001.

Rosenfeld, Seth. *Subversives: The FBI's War on Student Radicals, and Reagan's Rise to Power*. New York: Farrar, Straus and Giroux, 2012.

Rosenthal, Mark, Jonathan Borofsky, and Richard Marshall. *Jonathan Borofsky*. New York: Abrams, 1984.

Rowe, John C. *Post-Nationalist American Studies*. Berkeley: University of California Press, 2000.

Rudnitsky, Lexi. "The 'Power' and 'Sequelae' of Audre Lorde's Syntactical Strategies." *Callaloo* 26, no. 2 (2003): 473–85.

Ryback, Timothy W. *Rock around the Bloc: A History of Rock Music in Eastern Europe and the Soviet Union*. New York: Oxford University Press, 1990.

Said, Edward W. *Reflections on Exile and Other Essays*. Cambridge, Mass.: Harvard University Press, 2000.

———. "Traveling Theory." In *The Edward Said Reader*, edited by Moustafa Bayoumi and Andrew Rubin, 195–217. New York: Vintage, 2000.

Sarotte, Mary E. *The Collapse: The Accidental Opening of the Berlin Wall*. New York: Perseus Books, 2014.

———. *Dealing with the Devil: East Germany, Détente, and Ostpolitik, 1969–1973*. Chapel Hill: University of North Carolina Press, 2001.

———. *1989: The Struggle to Create Post-Cold War Europe*. Princeton, N.J.: Princeton University Press, 2009.

Savage, Kirk. *Monument Wars: Washington, DC, the National Mall, and the Transformation of the Memorial Landscape*. Berkeley: University of California Press, 2009.

———. *Standing Soldiers, Kneeling Slaves: Race, War, and Monument in Nineteenth-Century America*. Princeton, N.J.: Princeton University Press, 1997.

Schaden, Christoph. "Berliner Mauer im Fotobuch." In *Photo Researcher: European Society for the History of Photography*, 8–15. Croydon, Surrey, England: The Society, 2009.

Scheffler, Judith A. *Wall Tappings: An Anthology of Writings by Women Prisoners*. Boston: Northeastern University Press, 1986.

Schildt, Axel, and Detlef Siegfried. *Between Marx and Coca-Cola: Youth Cultures in Changing European Societies, 1960–1980*. New York: Berghahn, 2007.

Schneider, Peter. *The Wall Jumper*. London: Penguin, 2005.

Schneider, Rebecca. *Performing Remains: Art and War in Times of Theatrical Reenactment*. London: Routledge, 2011.

Schreiber, Rebecca Mina. *Cold War Exiles in Mexico: US Dissidents and the Culture of Critical Resistance*. Minneapolis: University of Minnesota Press, 2008.

Schröer, Andreas. *Private Elvis: Elvis in Germany, the Missing Years*. London: Boxtree, 1993.

Schultz, Dagmar, dir. *Audre Lorde: The Berlin Years, 1984 to 1992*. New York: Third World Newsreel, 2012.

Schürer, Ernst, Manfred Erwin Keune, and Philip Jenkins, eds. *The Berlin Wall: Representations and Perspectives*. New York: P. Lang, 1996.

Schwartz, Richard A. *Cold War Culture: Media and the Arts, 1945–1990*. New York: Facts on File, 1998.

Seabrook, Thomas Jerome. *Bowie in Berlin: A New Career in a New Town*. London: Jawbone Press, 2008.

Selma Freedom Songs. New York: Folkways Records, 1965. Audio recording.

Service, Robert. *A History of Modern Russia: From Nicholas II to Putin*. London: Penguin, 2003.

Shaw, Tony. *Hollywood's Cold War*. Amherst: University of Massachusetts Press, 2007.

Sheen, Martin. *Judgment in Berlin*. Los Angeles: Twentieth Century Fox Home Entertainment, 2003.

Singh, Nikhil Pal. "The Afterlife of Fascism." *South Atlantic Quarterly* 105, no. 1 (2006): 71–94.

———. *Black Is a Country: Race and the Unfinished Struggle for Democracy*. Cambridge, Mass.: Harvard University Press, 2004.

Slobodian, Quinn. *Foreign Front: Third World Politics in Sixties West Germany*. Durham, N.C.: Duke University Press, 2012.

———, ed. *Comrades of Color: East Germany in the Cold War World*. New York: Berghahn, 2017.

Smith, Caleb. *The Prison and the American Imagination*. New Haven: Yale University Press, 2009.

Smith, Sidonie, and Julia Watson. *De/Colonizing the Subject: The Politics of Gender in Women's Autobiography*. Minneapolis: University of Minnesota Press, 1992.

Smyser, W. R. *From Yalta to Berlin: The Cold War Struggle over Germany*. New York: St. Martin's Press, 1999.

———. *Kennedy and the Berlin Wall: "A Hell of a Lot Better Than a War."* Lanham, Md.: Rowman & Littlefield, 2009.

Solnit, Rebecca. *A Field Guide to Getting Lost*. New York: Viking, 2005.

Solzhenitsyn, Alexander. *Warning to the West*. New York: Farrar, Straus and Giroux, 1976.

Sonnevend, Julia. *Stories without Borders: The Berlin Wall and the Making of a Global Iconic Event*. Oxford: Oxford University Press, 2016.

Sontag, Susan. *On Photography*. New York: Farrar, Straus and Giroux, 1977.

Soyinka, Wole. *The Blackman and the Veil: A Century On; and, Beyond the Berlin Wall: Lectures Delivered by Wole Soyinka on 31st August and 1st September 1990*. Accra, Ghana: SEDCO: W. E. B. Du Bois Memorial Centre for Pan-African Culture, 1993.

Stahl, Geoff. "Cowboy Capitalism." *Space and Culture* 11, no. 4 (2008): 300–324.

Steele, Cassie P. *We Heal from Memory: Sexton, Lorde, Anzaldúa, and the Poetry of Witness*. Houndmills, U.K.: Palgrave, 2000.

Steiniger, Klaus, *Free Angela Davis: Hero of the Other America*. [Germany]: National Council of the National Front of the German Democratic Republic, Peace Council of the German Democratic Republic, and GDR Committee for Human Rights, 1971.

Stew, Heidi Rodewald, and Annie Dorsen. *Passing Strange: The Complete Book and Lyrics of the Broadway Musical*. New York: Applause Theatre & Cinema Books, 2009.

Stewart, Chuck. *The Greenwood Encyclopedia of LGBT Issues Worldwide*. Vol. 2. Santa Barbara: ABC Clio, 2010.

Stewart, Jeffrey C. *Paul Robeson: Artist and Citizen*. New Brunswick, N.J.: Rutgers University Press, 1998.

Stitziel, Judd. *Fashioning Socialism: Clothing, Politics, and Consumer Culture in East Germany*. Oxford: Berg, 2005.

Stockton, Kathryn B. *Beautiful Bottom, Beautiful Shame: Where "Black" Meets "Queer."* Durham, N.C.: Duke University Press, 2006.

Sturken, Marita. *Tangled Memories*. Berkeley: University of California Press, 1997.

———. *Tourists of History: Memory, Kitsch, and Consumerism from Oklahoma City to Ground Zero*. Durham, N.C.: Duke University Press, 2007.

Sussman, Elisabeth. *Nan Goldin: I'll Be Your Mirror*. New York: Whitney Museum of American Art; Scalo, 1996.

Tadiar, Neferti Xina M., and Angela Y. Davis. *Beyond the Frame: Women of Color and Visual Representations*. New York: Palgrave Macmillan, 2005.

Tajiri, Larry, Greg Robinson, and Guyo Tajiri. *Pacific Citizens: Larry and Guyo Tajiri and Japanese American Journalism in the World War II Era*. Urbana: University of Illinois Press, 2012.

Tajiri, Shinkichi. *Autobiographical Notations: Autobiography, Words and Images, Paintings, Sculptures, Printed Matter, Photography, Paperworks, Computergraphics*. Eindhoven: Kempen, 1992.

———. *The Berlin Wall*. Baarlo: Tasha B.V., 2005.

Tajiri, Shinkichi, and Lambert Tegenbosch. *Shinkichi Tajiri: Knots for Meditation*. Berlin: Galerie Horst Dietrich, 1989.

Tajiri, Shinkichi, Helen Westgeest, Giotta Tajiri, and Ryu Tajiri. *Shinkichi Tajiri: Universal Paradoxes*. Chicago: University of Chicago Press, 2015.

Tate, Dennis. *Shifting Perspectives: East German Autobiographical Narratives before and after the End of the GDR*. Rochester, N.Y.: Camden House, 2007.

Taussig, Michael T. *Mimesis and Alterity: A Particular History of the Senses*. New York: Routledge, 1993.

Taylor, Diana. *The Archive and the Repertoire: Performing Cultural Memory in the Americas*. Durham, N.C.: Duke University Press, 2003.

Taylor, Frederick. *The Berlin Wall: A World Divided, 1961–1989*. New York: HarperCollins, 2006.

Thompson, Peter. *The Crisis of the German Left: The PDS, Stalinism, and the Global Economy*. New York: Berghahn, 2005.

Throgmorton, James. "Where Was the Wall Then? Where Is It Now?" *Planning Theory & Practice* 5, no. 3 (2004): 349–65.

Till, Karen E. *The New Berlin: Memory, Politics, Place*. Minneapolis: University of Minnesota Press, 2005.

Tillet, Salamishah. *Sites of Slavery: Citizenship and Racial Democracy in the Post–Civil Rights Imagination*. Durham, N.C.: Duke University Press, 2012.

Timothy, Mary. *Jury Woman*. Palo Alto, Calif.: Empty Press, 1974.

Trachtenberg, Alan. *Brooklyn Bridge: Fact and Symbol*. New York: Oxford University Press, 1965.

————. *Reading American Photographs: Images as History, Mathew Brady to Walker Evans*. New York: Hill and Wang, 1989.

Trask, Stephen, and John Cameron Mitchell. *Hedwig and the Angry Inch*. Woodstock, N.Y.: Overlook Press, 2000.

Trommler, Frank, and American Institute for Contemporary German Studies. *Berlin — The New Capital in the East: A Transatlantic Appraisal*. Washington, D.C.: American Institute for Contemporary German Studies, the Johns Hopkins University, 2000.

Trouillot, Michel-Rolph. *Silencing the Past: Power and the Production of History*. Boston: Beacon Press, 1995.

U2 and Neil McCormick. *U2 by U2*. New York: HarperCollins, 2006.

United States. Commission on Civil Rights. *A Time to Listen . . . A Time to Act; Voices from the Ghettos of the Nation's Cities; [a Report]*. Washington, D.C.: U.S. Government Printing Office, 1967.

United States. House Un-American Activities Committee, and Eric Bentley. *Thirty Years of Treason: Excerpts from Hearings Before the House Committee on Un-American Activities, 1938–1968*. New York: Viking Press, 1971.

United States. Kerner Commission. *Report*. Washington, D.C.: U.S. Government Printing Office, 1968.

"Vom Regenwald der Guerilla in den Mediendschungel: Ein Gespräch mit Lothar Menne über die Anfänge der 68er-Bewegung." *Mittelweg 36*. Hamburg: Hamburger Institut für Sozialforschung (April 2008).

Von Eschen, Penny M. "Di Eagle and di Bear: Who Gets to Tell the Story of the Cold War?" In *Audible Empire: Music, Global Politics, Critique*, edited by Ronald Radano and Teju Olaniyan, 189–208. Durham: Duke University Press, 2016.

————. "Memory and the Study of U.S. Foreign Relations." In *Explaining U.S. Foreign Relations*, edited by Fran Costigliola and Michael Hogan, 304–16. Cambridge: Cambridge University Press, 2016.

————. *Race against Empire: Black Americans and Anticolonialism, 1937–1957*. Ithaca, N.Y.: Cornell University Press, 1997.

————. *Satchmo Blows Up the World: Jazz Ambassadors Play the Cold War*. Cambridge, Mass.: Harvard University Press, 2004.

Wall, Cheryl A. *Changing Our Own Words: Essays on Criticism, Theory, and Writing by Black Women*. New Brunswick, N.J.: Rutgers University Press, 1989.

The Wall in My Head: Words and Images from the Fall of the Iron Curtain. Rochester, N.Y.: Open Letter, 2009.

Warner, Michael. *Publics and Counterpublics*. New York: Zone Books, 2002.

Waters, Roger. *The Wall: Berlin 1990*. [United Kingdom]: Universal Music, 2008.

Watson, Mary Ann. *The Expanding Vista: American Television in the Kennedy Years*. New York: Oxford University Press, 1991.

Weheliye, Alexander G. *Phonographies: Grooves in Sonic Afro-Modernity*. Durham, N.C.: Duke University Press, 2005.

Weiner, Lawrence, and Jarrett Gregory. *Lawrence Weiner: As Far As the Eye Can See, 1960–2007*. New York: Whitney Museum of American Art, 2007.

Weiss, George. *Zoo TV: Live from Sydney*. Universal City, Calif.: Island, 2006.

Wenders, Wim, dir. *Wings of Desire*. New York: Criterion Collection, 1987; Santa Monica, Calif.: Distributed by MGM Home Entertainment, 2003.

Werner, Anja. "Convenient Partnerships? African American Civil Rights Leaders and the East German Dictatorship." In *Anywhere but Here: Black Intellectuals in the Atlantic World and Beyond*, edited by Kendahl Radcliffe, Jennifer Scott, and Anja Werner, 139–64. Minneapolis: University of Minnesota Press, 2015).

Westgeest, Helen. *Tajiri: Silent Dynamism and Oneness in Multiformity*. Zwolle: Waanders, 1997.

Whitfield, Stephen J. *The Culture of the Cold War*. Baltimore: Johns Hopkins University Press, 1991.

Wiener, Jon. *How We Forgot the Cold War: A Historical Journey across America*. Berkeley: University of California Press, 2012.

Wilder, Billy, dir. *One, Two, Three*. Santa Monica, Calif.: Metro-Goldwyn-Mayer, 1961, 2003.

Williams, Jeni. *Interpreting Nightingales: Gender, Class, and Histories*. Sheffield: Academic Press, 1997.

Winant, Howard. *The New Politics of Race: Globalism, Difference, Justice*. Minneapolis: University of Minnesota Press, 2004.

———. *The World Is a Ghetto: Race and Democracy since World War II*. New York: Basic Books, 2001.

Wise, Michael Z. *Capital Dilemma: Germany's Search for a New Architecture of Democracy*. New York: Princeton Architectural Press, 1998.

Wojnarowicz, David. *Close to the Knives: A Memoir of Disintegration*. New York: Vintage, 1991.

———. *Sounds in the Distance*. London: Aloes Books, 1982.

———. *The Waterfront Journals*. New York: Grove Press, 1996.

Wojnarowicz, David, and Amy Scholder. *In the Shadow of the American Dream: The Diaries of David Wojnarowicz*. New York: Grove Press, 1999.

Wojnarowicz, David, Barry Blinderman, and Illinois State University. *David Wojnarowicz: Tongues of Flame*. Normal: University Galleries, Illinois State University, 1990.

Wollman, Elizabeth L., Galt MacDermot, and Stephen Trask. *The Theater Will Rock: A History of the Rock Musical, from Hair to Hedwig*. Ann Arbor: University of Michigan Press, 2006.

Wright, Michelle M. *Becoming Black: Creating Identity in the African Diaspora*. Durham, N.C.: Duke University Press, 2004.

Wright, Richard. *Black Boy*. New York: Harper & Brother, 1945.

Young, James Edward. *The Texture of Memory: Holocaust Memorials and Meaning*. New Haven: Yale University Press, 1993.

Yúdice, George. *The Expediency of Culture: Uses of Culture in the Global Era*. Durham, N.C.: Duke University Press, 2003.

Zaborowska, Magdalena J. *James Baldwin's Turkish Decade: Erotics of Exile*. Durham, N.C.: Duke University Press, 2009.

Zatlin, Jonathan R. *The Currency of Socialism: Money and Political Culture in East Germany*. Washington, D.C.: German Historical Institute, 2007.

Zukin, Sharon. *The Cultures of Cities*. Cambridge, Mass.: Blackwell, 1995.

———. *Naked City: The Death and Life of Authentic Urban Places*. New York: Oxford University Press, 2010.

INDEX